CROSSING THE TIBER

CROSSING THE TIBER

Evangelical Protestants Discover the Historical Church

STEPHEN K. RAY

ABRIDGED

SPECIAL LIGHTHOUSE CATHOLIC MEDIA EDITION

IGNATIUS PRESS SAN FRANCISCO

Nihil Obstat: Reverend Robert Lunsford

Imprimatur: ✠ Carl F. Mengeling
Bishop of Lansing

Cover art: *Saint Peter Receives the Keys*,
by Orazio de Ferrari
From the second altar to the right,
Chiesa di S. Giovanni, Chiavari, Italy.
Alinari/SEAT/Art Resource, NY

Background illustration: Detail of
the view of Rome showing the Vatican,
painted by Antonio Danti between 1580 and 1583,
Gallery of Maps, the Vatican
Cover design: Riz Boncan Marsella

ISBN 978-0-89870-577-5
Library of Congress catalogue number 95–79951
Printed in the United States of America

DEDICATION

To my parents, Charles and Frances Ray, who raised me in a godly Evangelical home, who taught me to love the Lord, who spent untold hours praying for me, and who gave me a passion for truth and learning (see 2 Timothy 3:15).

To Al and Sally Kresta, who with great love and patience helped us find our way through the parched desert to a magnificent oasis. With their courage, excitement, and example they gently led the way home to the Catholic Church.

To Dennis Walters, who spent many hours working on our behalf, offering religious instruction, answering questions, and clearing the way for us to enter Christ the King parish and the Roman Catholic Church.

And most of all to my wife, Janet, and my children, Cindy, Jesse, Charlotte, and Emily, who were all received into the Church with me and who have patiently endured this project and encouraged me as I worked. I love them more than words can tell.

CONTENTS

PREFACE

There are times in one's life when an overwhelming urge arises somewhere deep in the soul, and one has to write. Our discovery of the world's best-kept secret inspired such a passion. This story had to be written. We would have burst with pent-up joy had it not found its way onto paper. My wife, Janet, and I discovered a treasure, and we pursued it. The result was a major decision that affected not only us but all those around us. Because of them, we felt it was necessary to attempt an explanation.

This book was put together quickly, with the little spare time I have available. It started out as a letter to my distressed Baptist parents, trying to explain our momentous decision and excitement. Many different sorts of people may eventually read this book, from sympathizers to critics, from Christians to agnostics, from Catholics to Protestants. I have tried to be honest and fair, as best I could, without intending to hurt anyone or cause discomfort. In this book, I am thinking out loud and have simply invited you into our "smoke-filled room."

If I seem at times to be critical of Protestant theologies, the criticism is directed first at myself, because I myself was a Protestant and subscribed to those theologies. I am arguing with no one but myself, with my past views, with my past convictions. Janet continues to remind me: "This book needs to be 'pastoral' in tone—not combative or harsh." I hope I have explained well and argued persuasively, and I hope I have maintained my equilibrium in response to Janet's reminders.

The main reason I am writing this book is to put our many thoughts into a simple story. There have been many things going through our minds, and Janet and I have spent many delightful hours discussing them. It is a great joy to have a wife, a marriage, and a family such as I have. I am fortunate beyond words. I hope this book will help you, the reader, understand us and the Catholic Church. I also want to explain this amazing turn of events to our children and our future progeny, for they deserve an explanation—our choice will profoundly impact their lives.

For those who do read this book of adventure and discovery—

this impassioned discussion—we hope you will be free enough, and honest enough, to share with us, to confront us, and to discuss these matters with us.

I finished the first section of this book on Pentecost Sunday, May 22, 1994. Early that morning, with Fr. Ed Fride, smiling in his red vestments, with our friends and family seated nearby—some with joy and some with utter disbelief—we were received into the Roman Catholic Church as a family. My remarkable father, a good Baptist since 1953, was courageous enough to witness the event and open his arms in love and guarded approval. I can never thank him enough for honoring us with his presence.[1]

Words can never express the emotions, the intellectual sense of having arrived, and our awareness of continuity with the apostles and the early Church. We stood shoulder to shoulder in historical, liturgical, and theological continuity with the apostles, the martyrs, the saints, the Fathers, and the billions of common folks who have entered and loved the Catholic Church for twenty centuries. We were home, our ship had arrived in port, and the human soul cannot contain the joy that overflowed, expressed with tears by all of us. I want to thank my wife, Janet, my daughter Cindy, Al Kresta (my sponsor), Rob Corzine (received with us into the Catholic Church), and Dennis Walters, for proofreading and making helpful suggestions. I appreciate their help and friendship.

1 It was through the dedicated love and godliness of my father that I first learned to appreciate the love and mercy of our Heavenly Father. I never had the problem of seeing God as an angry old man in heaven waiting to strike me down for the least offense. Instead, I viewed God through the eyes of a small child, looking up at a loving dad who was always there and always kind—an example of God's love.

PART ONE
CROSSING THE TIBER

Our Conversion

Janet and I, along with our four children, have converted to the Roman Catholic Church, which claims to be the fullness of the "one, holy, catholic,[1] and apostolic Church".[2] *How could we have done such a thing?* This book is an attempt to give a brief and reasoned defense—an explanation of our decision. It is brief and inadequate, but it is better than silence, and better than the short snips of discussion that arise in casual conversation.

Scientists tell us that no two snowflakes are alike; which is a peculiar thing to say, since no one can examine each and every one. Stars number in the billions, each different and unique. Conversions are just as dissimilar, being reached from many roads and paths, for many reasons and impulses. They are just as dissimilar as snowflakes, but they can be more closely analyzed. The word *conversion* comes from two Latin words: *vertere*, meaning to turn, and *con*, a prefix of emphasis; therefore, an emphatic or strong turning.

Our conversion was a turning from one thing to something dif-

1 The word *catholic* (Καθολικην) has its origin in the Greek language and means "universal" or "general." It was used as early as the time of Ignatius of Antioch (a.d. *c.* 35–*c.* 107), a contemporary of the Apostle John, and was later used in 325 as a binding term within the Nicene Creed, which has been recognized by all Christian Churches throughout the world and throughout history.

2 A brief perusal of early Christian writings shows that the tradition and succession left by the apostles were the source of unity and theological orthodoxy centuries before the canon of the New Testament was established. This is what the early Church meant by "apostolic." This was one of the central tenets spelled out in 325 at the Council of Nicaea as essential to the Christian faith. This phrase had been used as a creedal statement from the earliest times and is found in both the Apostles' Creed and the New Testament itself.

ferent—though not so different as some would think. As the story develops, we will explain a few of the reasons why we left our Protestant heritage. A strong turning was required, and though such a turning would have seemed impossible only a short time before, our research and study of the primitive Church were compelling, and, as Chesterton said of the Catholic faith,

> He has come too near to the truth, and has forgotten that truth is a magnet, with the powers of attraction and repulsion. . . . The moment men cease to pull against it [the Catholic Church] they feel a tug towards it. The moment they cease to shout it down they begin to listen to it with pleasure. The moment they try to be fair to it they begin to be fond of it. But when that affection has passed a certain point it begins to take on the tragic and menacing grandeur of a great love affair. . . . When he has entered the Church, he finds that the Church is much larger inside than it is outside.[3]

We had opposed this Catholic Church, in no uncertain terms. So our conversion was no insignificant event. The "something" we had once militantly resisted, the Catholic Church, was found to be glorious, beautiful, and splendid—like a massive creature, too grand and colossal to comprehend fully, yet modest and personal enough to put affectionately in your pocket. It was a fullness. Why the term *fullness*? Because the Catholic Church encompasses so much more than we had ever known in our Protestant past—the fullness of the faith carefully preserved and nurtured through endless centuries. We are not going from Christian to Catholic, as though we're leaving the "Christian" part behind. We are developing and experiencing the Christian faith more fully by becoming Catholic Christians. Catholicism is ancient, yet forever young; it is constant and firm, yet forever lively and robust; it is old, yet always new and vital. It is simple enough for a mouse to wade in, yet deep enough for an elephant to swim in.

Our Inherited Protestant Roots

The Protestant view of life and the Church was my home; it was the womb from which I was born. In fact, my very arrival on this planet was tied intimately with the Americanized version of Protes-

3 G. K. Chesterton, *The Catholic Church and Conversion* (1927), in vol. 3 of *The Collected Works of G. K. Chesterton* (San Francisco: Ignatius Press, 1990), 92, 94.

tant Christianity. I was raised with Billy Graham on TV, anti-Catholic books on the shelf, and Sunday School every week without fail. I was born after my mother had experienced twelve years of miscarriages. My parents (under the influence of Billy Graham for my mother, and of a close friend at work for my father) turned from a life of fear and complacency to a new life in Christ. Theirs is another example of two strong conversions, and it has imprinted an indelible and blessed mark upon my life. At Joy Road Baptist Church in Detroit, I was, like Samuel of old,[4] ceremoniously presented to God by my parents, to be his servant—a dedication I have always cherished and always strived to be worthy of.

My wife, Janet, comes from a long line of Protestant Christians. One side of her family sailed to Plymouth Rock on the Mayflower in 1620 as religious immigrants, seeking a land in which to worship freely.[5] On her paternal side, her family is traced back to 1611, to Moravia, greatly influenced by the Reformation. We know from family records that in the first generation the males became ardent followers of Jan Hus' Reformation teaching, while the women remained loyal to the Catholic Church. Other ancestral lines flowed from Presbyterian Scotland. In Janet's family, many roads lead back to the Protestant Reformation.

Why We Chose Christianity

Every person eventually questions the beliefs he was raised with. Why did each of us continue in the Christian faith? Janet and I, independently of each other and before we met, became ardent followers of Jesus Christ in the Evangelical tradition—not out of familial loyalty or cultural pressures, as some would like to allege. In fact, just the opposite was true for me. I hated going to church as a child because I would rather have been catching frogs or playing baseball. I saw Christianity as restrictive as I grew older and certainly didn't want to be what my parents were. Most teenagers seem to have similar sentiments at seventeen years of age, when the teenage reality of dissolving ties with parental authority coexists with a desire for con-

4 1 Sam 1:1–28.

5 Her family lineage derives from four of the original Mayflower passengers: Alden, Rogers, Bradford, and Smith.

formity to peer groups and friends. My choosing to be a Christian was in direct conflict with *both* of these adolescent impulses. First, I was becoming what my parents were, and, second, I was going against the tide of teenage liberation in the late sixties and early seventies.

Knowledge and truth have a particular attraction for some. I have always had a strong desire to know truth and to do the right thing. That may be why I am an incurable bibliophile to this day. I want to challenge reality, ask questions, and find answers; I want to know and understand. Irrational emotion, blind faith, insecurity, or sociological pressures had nothing to do with my decision to be a Christian. I recall none of these as residing in my psyche. Truth was the issue. As one grows older, the thought process deepens. Philosophical and religious concepts developed in my late teens and expanded during my early twenties. The choice for Christ was made, and later solidified, as I desired to understand the universe with its beauty, awesomeness, and mathematical order, and the human race with its paradoxical nobility and cruelty.

Modern materialism[6] in its many forms offers very unacceptable answers, and it runs contrary to all the desires for fulfillment and meaning that mankind has always experienced. In their painful existential struggles, Sartre and Camus searched blindly and despairingly for any ultimate meaning to life and existence.[7] Our generation is their progeny. The music that permeated the decades of my youth longed for answers to the "big questions"[8] but finally, in the eighties, gave up

---

6 Modern secularism and materialism are not logical developments based on modern discoveries or philosophical necessities. Denying God and ultimate truth was a choice. It was a denial of a higher power and the acceptance of man as the center of all things. Most modern people have not, however, chosen this view as a result of rational processes; they have instead caught it from the surrounding society, much as one catches the measles. Wisdom demands that we choose our worldview carefully and not absorb it subconsciously through our pores from the society around us.

7 The impressionists, postimpressionists, expressionists, and cubist painters, along with most modern artists, expressed the same philosophy in their paintings.

8 The popular rock group Kansas was representative of the quest and the ultimate despair. Their ubiquitous and haunting song "Dust in the Wind" tells us that ultimately life is meaningless, that we are on a journey to nowhere on a revolving planet spinning around and around and around. They remind us

the quest, accepting the ultimate meaninglessness of existence. Our society now plays out the game, acting as though existence has meaning when we really think it doesn't; but our bold culture continues on, courageously, in the face of ultimate meaninglessness. The basic tenets of historical Christianity (as opposed to secularism, humanism, pantheism, atheism, Marxism, existentialism,[9] the New Age, and so on) gave answers to the realities I faced as I looked at the universe, which objectively existed around me, and the humanness and personality within me and others. Reality demands an explanation. The truths of the Christian faith provided the missing pieces of the puzzle. The detective must find the answers that best correspond to the questions, and with these he solves the case. The solution must be consistent throughout and fill every corner with light, not with further confusion. Christianity is the only philosophy that does this, and Janet and I are most fortunate to be part of the glorious and splendid heritage we share with others through history, a heritage that has stood tall and beaming through twenty centuries.[10] It is an intelligent answer, a philosophically satisfying answer, comprehensive, consistent, and rich. It answers Gauguin's existential longings. It addresses the *full* spectrum of existence and is accompanied by an inner joy that only those who know the joy can understand. Former atheist C. S. Lewis wrote a book entitled *Surprised by Joy*, which recounts his discovery of true Christianity.

The Foundations of Our Evangelicalism

Ours was a fertile strain of Protestantism called Evangelicalism, which was much influenced by Fundamentalism.[11] Evangelicalism

---

of the fleeting nature of time, that we are just a "drop of water in an endless sea," and that all that we are or do is just "dust in the wind, . . . everything is dust in the wind" (produced by Jeff Glixman; CBS, 1977).

9 A philosophy that admits the plight of the individual, the ultimate absurdity of the universe, and the meaninglessness of life, but in which, by an act of the will, one tries to validate oneself and create a temporary meaning to existence—fleeting and illusory though it may be.

10 It actually exceeds forty centuries, inasmuch as Christianity (two millennia) is the continuation and fulfillment of Judaism, which existed two thousand years before the Incarnation of Christ.

11 Fundamentalism as a movement was born at the turn of the century; it

draws some of the brightest and most fervent followers within the Christian faith. It emphasizes a literal interpretation of the Bible and belief in the Virgin Birth of Christ and the physical Resurrection. One of its unifying elements is its resistance to, and condemnation of, the Roman Catholic Church. It believes in the sole sufficiency of the Bible, the imminent rapture, eternal security, blood atonement, the invisible unity of the Church, denominationalism, and so on. These beliefs were ours, and we defended them avidly.

Evangelicalism finds its roots in the sixteenth-century Protestant Reformation. Martin Luther (1483–1546) had developed two "*sola*" doctrines that advanced new ideas. They were developed as a result of his scrupulosity and out of his reaction to the Catholic Church, thus the name Protestant ("*protest*-ant", or "one who protests"). The first of these new ideas was *sola Scriptura*, stating that the Scriptures alone were sufficient to provide all knowledge that God wanted Christians to have for salvation, the Church, and the Christian life. According to this view, the Bible interprets itself, and anyone can come to a full knowledge of God's word by the help of the Holy Spirit, in other words, through individual interpretation and private judgment. It denies that any ecclesiastical authority can be binding upon the conscience. It was a reductionist reaction to the Catholic view of Scripture and sacred tradition.

The second of Luther's new ideas was *sola fide*, which meant that salvation was attained by faith alone.[12] In other words, Christ com-

---

derived its name from a twelve-volume work entitled *The Fundamentals* (Grand Rapids, Mich.: Kregels, 1990), which was edited by R. A. Torrey. This book was a reaction against the evolutionary theory and the "Modernists" with their liberal criticism in the early 1900s. The contributors were influential Protestant theologians who became known as Fundamentalists.

12 Martin Luther, in translating the Book of Romans into the German language, inserted the word "alone" to explain the word "faith" (e.g., Rom 3:28; 5:1) where the Greek original did not call for it. The pivotal text was Romans 3:28. The inclusion of the word "alone" radically altered the meaning of the text and Paul's thought. Calvin said the whole of the Reformation would stand or fall on that verse and the newly devised interpretation. This has become part of the Protestant tradition, an example of how Protestants have added to the word of God "Protestant traditions" that conflict with other truths that the Bible teaches and that the Church had held sacred for fifteen centuries. This *faith alone* concept is a new concept, one not taught prior

pleted the work of atonement, and the Judge of the universe makes a legal declaration that those who simply believe and "accept Christ as their personal Lord and Savior" will be eternally justified. All sins, past, present, and future, are automatically removed, and one has eternal security, no matter how he lives his life subsequent to the act of "believing," or "mental assent." Once accomplished, there is nothing that can reverse the one time act that will be culminated some day in heaven.[13] Faith *alone*, uninfluenced by subsequent choices—immorality, sin, disbelief, apostasy, or a profligate lifestyle—assures the Evangelical a full and overflowing cup of eternal life and everlasting bliss.[14] This is contrary to the teaching of Paul, who speaks of "faith

---

to Wycliffe and Luther's time. Interestingly, the only time the phrase "faith alone" is used in the New Testament is in James 2:24: "You see that a man is justified by works and not by faith alone."

13 When push comes to shove, it can be demonstrated that the Catholic position has been made a big bogeyman. The Catholic Church has always taught that faith and grace alone are the necessary means for obtaining eternal life. The *Catechism of the Catholic Church* (Vatican City: Libreria Editrice Vaticana, 1994; hereafter cited as CCC) says, "Believing in Jesus Christ and in the One who sent him for our salvation is necessary for obtaining that salvation. 'Since without faith it is impossible to please [God]' and to attain to the fellowship of his sons, therefore without faith no one has ever attained justification, nor will anyone obtain eternal life, 'but he who endures to the end' " (CCC 161). The Catholic teaching is biblically consistent throughout. Having held to both positions in my life at one time or another, I find the Catholic position is much more biblical, historical, consistent, and satisfactory. On top of that, it is the teaching faithfully proclaimed since the first centuries.

14 I want to question the way 1 John 5:13 is often promoted as a proof text for "eternal security." It is frequently used by people to prove they can "know" for sure they have eternal life. Catholics are often asked, "Do you know you are going to heaven? Are you positive of eternal life?" The Catholic usually stumbles around and looks foolish as the great proof text is read to him. I would make two points. First, the thirteenth verse (1 John 5:13) begins the conclusion to John's epistle, and the intent of John's letter was primarily to defend the true faith against the heresies of the Gnostics, who said one needed special knowledge (implying a knowledge the Christians did not have) to obtain eternal life. John is refuting the Gnostics and comforting the Christians with the fact that they *do* have the true knowledge, which John has seen, heard, and handled (1 Jn 1:1–3), and that true knowledge through Jesus Christ is the true and only way to eternal life. *It was not meant as a proof text between those who hold eternal security and those who deny it.* John's words had a higher

working [itself out] in love" (Gal 5:6). As a Fundamentalist I was quick to accuse the Catholic Church of teaching what I perceived as a "gospel of works" and not the true gospel of "faith alone".[15] Luther's two new doctrines (*sola Scriptura* and *sola fide*) eventually ruptured the unity of the Church.

The great sacraments of the Church, instituted by Christ and cel-

---

purpose that had little to do with the question of eternal security or absolute knowledge and confidence of eternal life. His argument was between the Christian and the Gnostic, between the physical incarnation of God and the illusory phantom god of the Gnostics.

This is borne out in my second point, that the verse, which begins the epistle's conclusion, summarizes the preceding text. It should be noted that the conditional word "if " is used twenty times in the epistle and seems to be saying, "If you understand and abide by the conditions of this letter, if you love one another, if you avoid sin, if you believe in the Son, etc., you may know that you have eternal life." Eternal life, then, is meant to be a moral certainty if one measures up to the conditions given in the preceding pages. Evangelical John Stott comments, "They [the recipients of John's letter] had been unsettled by the false teachers and become unsure of their spiritual state. Throughout the epistle John has been giving them criteria (doctrinal, moral, social) by which to test themselves and others. His purpose was to establish their assurance" (*The Epistles of John* in the *Tyndale New Testament Commentary* series [Grand Rapids, Mich.: Eerdmans, 1964], 184–85). But, could these believers securely "rest in their absolute assurance of salvation" if they were not living up to the "criteria" John gave them? One should be cautious about reading too much into a text without understanding its literary and historical context and the rest of Christian teaching.

15 In a roundabout way, J. I. Packer admits that Luther's views were new and not part of the teachings of the early Church. He says, in his chapter in *God's Inerrant Word*, ed. J. W. Montgomery (Minneapolis, Minn.: Bethany Fellowship, 1974): "Apart from Augustine none of them [the Fathers] seemed to be quite clear enough on the principle of salvation by grace and not even Augustine had fully grasped imputed righteousness" (45). Stott then elaborates in an endnote, "Misled by the meaning of '*justificare*' in Latin, he [Augustine] understood justification as God's work of making sinners subjectively righteous by pardoning their sins and infusing into them the grace of love" (61). What is being said is that no one prior to Luther properly understood justification, not even those who knew and succeeded the apostles. Alister McGrath also acknowledges that Luther's "faith alone" was an innovation. He writes, "A fundamental discontinuity was introduced into the western theological tradition where none had ever existed, or ever been contemplated, before. The Reformation understanding of the *nature* of justification—as opposed to its *mode*—must therefore be regarded as a genuine theological *novum*" (Alister E. McGrath, *Justitia Dei* [New York: Cambridge Univ. Press, 1986], 186–87).

ebrated from the time of the apostles, were also radically redefined by some of the Reformers.[16] They are no longer called sacraments[17] by the Fundamentalists and Evangelicals but are now renamed "ordinances" and therefore performed out of obedience, reduced to mere outward symbols of inward things. They are performed somewhat perfunctorily, not for any substantive reasons or effective impartations of grace, but simply out of obedience. Again, the result has been a great negation. The sacraments of the Church have been stripped of the fullness intended and left barren, as we will see.

Our Thinking Begins to Shift

Janet and I were happy in this Evangelical Christian environment, both as teenagers and after our marriage on December 4, 1976. It was our Protestant faith that drew us together initially. It was the root of our lives, our marriage, our family, and our business. It led us twice to Europe to research and bask in our Reformation heritage and to study with Presbyterian theologian and philosopher Francis Schaeffer at L'Abri Fellowship in Switzerland.[18] Evangelical Protestantism was an empowering force for our independence; it was the impetus for starting my own business and teaching our children at home; it was the philosophy that awoke my strong curiosity and drove me to read, to learn, and to teach; in short, it was the core of our lives. But

16 The second and third sections of this book deal extensively with the sacraments of baptism and the Eucharist. We will examine the Scriptures and the teaching of the Church in the first five centuries.

17 According to St. Augustine, a sacrament is the "visible form of invisible grace" (*Ep.* 105, 3, 12, quoted in the *Catholic Encyclopedia*, ed. Peter M. J. Stravinskas [Huntington, Ind.: Our Sunday Visitor, 1991], 849). It is "an outward sign of an inward grace, that causes what it signifies," according to Dennis Walters, who was our instructor as we prepared to enter the Catholic Church. Sacraments are intimately linked to the Incarnation, the Spirit working in and through matter.

18 *Time* magazine called Francis Schaeffer the missionary to the intellectuals in that he presented Christianity in a historical, philosophical, and intelligent manner. Young people from around the world flocked to the Swiss Alps to hear him lecture at his L'Abri community. He was a consummate Evangelical Protestant whose theology was firmly rooted in the Reformation teaching of Martin Luther, John Calvin, and Guillaume Farel. Schaeffer's foundational principles were Luther's *sola Scriptura* and *sola fide*.

in time we grew to see the internal contradictions inherent in the Protestant theology. The petty disputes and rival interpretations of Scripture that caused the proliferation of competing denominations had always grieved us and indicated something was very wrong. Without continuity with the early Church and the intervening centuries, Protestantism was like a branch without the tree, a wing without a bird. A friend described it as a large pool of water never exceeding a depth of two inches. Janet and I attended many different Evangelical churches during the first eighteen years of our marriage and taught classes most of the time, both at home and in adult Bible classes in the churches, but we always sensed the shallowness and deficiency of Evangelicalism, especially, for me, when it came to theological and historical continuity with the early Church and, for Janet, when it came to worship. She often said, "I can't sit and listen to a simple sermon for an hour and call it worship." We occasionally thought of starting a "church" in our home, at the request of other likeminded friends.

Our Evangelical Foundations Begin to Crumble

The very bedrock upon which Protestant theology is founded became the fulcrum that eventually pried me out of my lifelong tradition. I discovered that *sola Scriptura* was weak, unbiblical, unhistorical, and untenable. *Sola Scriptura* left the entire structure unsound and flawed at the very base, like a house built on sand, and yet it was the bedrock of Protestant theologies. Being a fraction of a degree off when calculating a rocket trajectory will put you far off your course, and the rocket will pass through a sector of the universe you did not intend. A house built on sand will eventually show signs of serious structural problems (Mt 7:24–25). So it is with Protestantism. *Sola Scriptura* is nowhere taught in Scripture, nowhere even *implied*! The very foundational principle of Protestantism, the doctrine upon which all others are built, is not found in the very book it supposedly builds a bulwark to support. As an honest Protestant, I found it to be the Achilles' heel for me. The closest I came to establishing a biblical case for *sola Scriptura* was 2 Timothy 3:16,[19] which was certainly not intended by St.

19 2 Tim 3:16–17: "All scripture is inspired by God and profitable for teaching, for reproof, for correction, for training in righteousness; that the man of God may be adequate, equipped for every good work." Interestingly enough,

Paul as a proof text for the sole sufficiency of Scripture. In fact, if it were used in that way, the text would prove *too* much, since the term "Scripture" in this passage is referring to the Old Testament (there was no New Testament canon yet) and would thereby exclude the New Testament from the proof.

Where does Scripture tell us that "God's word" can and must be only in written form, typed on paper or parchment?[20] Jesus Christ himself never wrote anything down (other than unknown words on the ground), and it was not recorded that he ever commissioned his followers to write everything down. Had it been as important to him as it was to me as an Evangelical, shouldn't he have made it clear for all time that only what was written down could be considered God's word? But Jesus never promised us an authoritative book, nor did his apostles; rather, he promised us an authoritative Church.[21] Jesus' "word" was orally transmitted to the twelve apostles.[22] We know from

---

we find St. Paul writing to the Ephesians (Eph 4:11–14), using the same language, informing his readers that the equipping and perfecting of saints is accomplished through the leaders of the Church: apostles, prophets, evangelists, pastors, and teachers.

20 A study of the phrases "word of God" and "word of the Lord" as used in the New Testament is very enlightening. As an Evangelical, when I read the phrase "word of God" I would automatically plug in the word "Bible"; this, however, is not at all the meaning usually intended in the Bible itself. Roughly nine out of ten times, "word of God" is referring to the spoken word, not the written word (e.g., 1 Th 2:13). The *spoken* words, the oral tradition, were *also* the very "words of God." When did Paul's spoken words cease being the word of God? After the sound-wave vibrations fell from the air? Is God's spoken word self-retiring after it hits the human ear? Or does it continue to be God's word the following day, and the following century, even if not written on parchment? How would God preserve his spoken word? Through tradition in the heart of the Church.

21 See Mt 16:18–19; 18:17; 1 Tim 3:15; 5:17.

22 A perfect example of this is Acts 20:35, "In all things I have shown you that by so toiling one must help the weak, remembering the words of the Lord Jesus, how he said, 'It is more blessed to give than to receive.' " Do you remember these latter words related anywhere in the Gospels? They aren't. How did Paul know Jesus said them, and why did he assume his listeners were well acquainted with these words? Because of the oral tradition. In fact, the Gospels hadn't even been written yet. The early Church would wait another fifty years to receive the Gospel of John. See also Jude 14, 17; and 2 Tim 3:8.

the Old Covenant that oral tradition was established side by side with the Torah.[23] Jesus was Jewish, and his teachings and his Church were built upon the Old Testament and the Jewish experience—traditions he laid out during his three years of traversing Israel. He passed this word and teaching on to the Twelve in the form of oral tradition. He promised that when the Holy Spirit came, he would teach them all things and bring to their remembrance "all that I said to you" (Jn 14:26).[24] The Apostle John tells us that if everything Jesus accomplished were written down, all the world could not contain the books. Since Jesus spent three intimate years with his disciples, we know for a fact that the content of the Gospels is only a small fraction of what Jesus taught them. Few realize that Jesus spent forty days after the Resurrection instructing the twelve apostles through the Holy Spirit,[25]

---

23 For example, even though there is no seat of Moses mentioned in the Old Testament, Jesus recognizes the Jewish tradition as binding upon the people of Israel and commands them to respect the authority of that tradition. "Then said Jesus to the crowds and to his disciples, 'The scribes and the Pharisees sit on Moses' seat; so practice and observe whatever they tell you, but not what they do; for they preach, but do not practice' " (Mt 23:1-2).

24 Many, unfortunately, arrogate this promise to themselves even though the recipients of this promise are clearly defined. This is a promise Jesus gave to his apostles and one that would be realized in the apostolic tradition—which included the New Testament writings—and the teaching authority of the Church. Just as the Founding Fathers of the United States did not leave a "book alone" but also a Supreme Court to interpret and protect it, so the Lord Jesus did not give a book alone, but also a Church to establish, interpret, and defend it. Just as the Founding Fathers did not leave the interpretation of the nation's legal documents up to each citizen's private judgment, so the Bible was not left solely in the hands of individuals for their own private interpretation of how to live the Christian life. As in all his previous covenants, God had established visible and divinely protected leaders. If this had not been so, the result would have been anarchy and chaos. This, however, is not to diminish the need for individual Christians to read and understand the Bible; quite the contrary. It is not an *either/or* statement (*either* the Church *or* the Holy Spirit); it is a *both/and* statement (*both* the Church *and* the Holy Spirit; in fact the Holy Spirit *in* the Church).

25 Acts 1:2–3 : "Until the day when he was taken up, after he had given commandment through the Holy Spirit to the apostles whom he had chosen. To them he presented himself alive after his passion by many proofs, appearing to them during forty days, and speaking of the kingdom of God." This is also made clear in the last chapters of the Gospels of John, Luke, and Matthew.

giving them special commands concerning the Kingdom of God and the Church. The early Church depended upon the apostolic tradition. The Apostle Paul referred to the Church, not the Bible, as the pillar and foundation of the truth.[26] This is hard for a Protestant to grasp but makes perfect sense to a Catholic. It was clearly understood and taught for fifteen centuries and is still faithfully held within the sacred tradition of the Catholic Church.[27]

Did Jesus ever promise to give us an authoritative book? No. Why didn't the apostles, namely, St. John, who was the last to die, give us a final list of infallible books? Did the apostles promise or hand us an authoritative book? Again, the answer is No. Did Jesus promise us an authoritative Church? Yes.[28] He instituted a Church, his Body,

---

26 1 Tim 3:15: "If I am delayed, you may know how one ought to behave in the household of God, which is the church of the living God, the pillar and bulwark of the truth."

27 The fullness of the apostles' teaching, written and unwritten, was not contained in the Bible alone but was deposited in the Church. Fr. John Hardon, S.J., writes: "Tradition first means all of divine revelation, from the dawn of human history to the end of the apostolic age, as passed on from one generation of believers to the next, and as preserved under divine guidance by the Church established by Christ. Sacred Tradition also means, within this transmitted revelation, that part of God's revealed word which is not contained in Sacred Scripture" (*Pocket Catholic Dictionary* [New York: Doubleday, 1980], 510). "Catholicism believes that the whole content of God's revealed word is not limited to the biblical page. But it also sees that the Bible and tradition are intimately related, in fact are interdependent. . . . The two may not be separated. . . . Moreover, both have been left with the Church and in the Church as a 'sacred deposit', which may not be profaned either by adulteration or competition with mere human wisdom" (*The Catholic Catechism* [New York: Doubleday, 1981], 47).

28 Mt 16:18–19; 18:15–20. Jesus clearly explains that he will build a single visible Church that will have clearly defined leaders with judicial authority to bind and loose and to discipline the members. Believers must "listen to the Church." The Church will have the power to make decisions that are binding upon the individual consciences of the believers. It seems obvious from the context and the need that this is an authority that is to carry on until the end of time.

"Rabbinic terms used in Mt 16:19 of Peter's doctrinal authority to declare things forbidden or permitted; and in Mt 18:18 of the disciples' disciplinary authority to condemn and absolve" (J. D. Douglas, ed., *The Illustrated Bible Dictionary* [Downers Grove, Ill.: InterVarsity Press and Tyndale House, 1980],

that would pass on the truth, always carefully preserving the tradition entrusted to her. Where was the truth of Christ first deposited? In a book? We read in Jude 3 that the first Christians were challenged to "contend earnestly for the faith which was once for all delivered to the saints." The Church was viewed as the bank into which Christ and the apostles deposited the fullness of the faith. As a Protestant I saw the deposit as being placed solely in the Bible. Yet, there was no established New Testament canon, nor would there be one for several centuries. The truth had been delivered from Christ to the apostles, and the apostles deposited the truth into the Church.

Why did the Holy Spirit wait for almost four centuries before finally collecting and forming the apostolic writings into a collection called the New Testament? Why didn't the apostles collect all the inspired writings and authoritatively announce to Christians that "this is now the sole rule of faith for your individual interpretations"? The early Church seemed to be in no hurry, for the truth was not to be deposited exclusively into a book, as the Protestant doctrine of *sola Scriptura* teaches, but the truth, the fullness of the faith, was deposited in the Church—to the saints once and for all.[29] And the Church is

---

1:199).

"No other terms were in more constant use in Rabbinic canon-law than those of binding and loosing. They represented the legislative and judicial powers of the Rabbinic office. These powers Christ now transferred . . . in their reality, to his apostles; the first, here to Peter" (M. Vincent, *Word Studies in the New Testament* [1887; Grand Rapids, Mich.: Eerdmans, 1980], 1:96). This Petrine authority can be seen exercised in the Council of Jerusalem in Acts 15 and in all subsequent ecumenical councils of the Catholic Church.

29 St. Epiphanius (*c.* 315–403) wrote, "It is needful also to make use of Tradition; for not everything can be gotten from Sacred Scripture. The holy Apostles handed down some things in the Scriptures, other things in Tradition" (*Panarion* or *Haereses*, 61, 6, in Jurgens, *Faith of the Early Fathers*, 2:73).

St. John Chrysostom (*c.* 347–407) wrote, "It is manifest, that they did not deliver all things by epistle, but many things also unwritten, and in like manner both the one and the other are worthy of credit. Therefore let us think the tradition of the Church also worthy of credit. It is a tradition, seek no farther" (*Hom. 6 in 2 Thess.*, in Philip Schaff, ed., *Nicene and Post-Nicene Fathers*, 1st series [Grand Rapids, Mich.: Eerdmans, 1983], 13:390).

St. Augustine (354–430) wrote, "I believe that this practice comes from apostolic tradition, just as so many other practices not found in their writings

the pillar and foundation of the truth, the defender and custodian of the faith that God has put in her care. The twelve apostles, spoken of as the foundation of the Church,[30] fulfilled their office in Jerusalem, Samaria, and then throughout the world. Thomas went to India; Peter and Paul were martyred in Rome; John traveled to Asia and ended up in Ephesus; and the others spread throughout the known world. They were the vehicles for divine revelation. They spoke the "words of the Lord." Paul was a latecomer but was accepted by the Twelve as an apostle to the Gentiles. He said his spoken word was accepted "for what it was, the word of God."[31] The apostles left to the Church not only their writings but also their oral traditions and practices. Paul tells the Thessalonians to hold fast to the traditions he gave them, whether in spoken word or in epistle. He commends those in Corinth for holding to the traditions he had left them.[32] Paul seems unaware that his letters will someday be collected, printed on a press with gold-leafed pages, and bound with leather. His principal means of transmitting the gospel and training new believers was oral instruction, which was to be preserved in the Church and handed down[33] through the tradition of the Church. This tradition was to be the means of preserving the "spoken" word of God. In short, it was a tradition he was bequeathing to the churches, and the letters he wrote were only a small, crystallized portion of that larger tradition. In some ways the New Testament documents were incidental: sent to correct a problem, remind the readers of the oral tradition, or to supplement the preaching of the gospel.

The apostles spent months and years in various localities relaying

---

nor in the councils of their successors, but which, because they are kept by the whole Church everywhere, are believed to have been commended and handed down by the Apostles themselves" (*De Baptis. Contra Donat.* 1, v. 23, in Jurgens, *Faith of the Early Fathers*, 3:66).

30 Eph 2:20; Rev 21:14.

31 1 Th 2:13.

32 2 Th 2:15:

33 Notice 1 Corinthians 15:3. That which Paul had received was not in written form, and his original "delivering" was oral and *not* written. The writing was secondary, almost an afterthought. Paul's primary means of promulgating the faith was by passing it down through apostolic tradition. Another example of this is 2 Timothy 2:2.

the truth and teaching the people (for example, Acts 18:11). They taught them how to live, how to start a local *ecclesia*, and how to function within it. Then, before moving on, they chose and ordained bishops to succeed them and rule the Church in that diocese. The new church was left with the apostolic tradition and apostolic succession as the basis for their faith and the means for the transmission of the tradition to the next generation. The New Testament, as a corpus, did not yet exist. Eusebius writes, "Thus they proclaimed the knowledge of the kingdom of heaven through the whole world, giving very little thought to the business of writing books."[34] As a Protestant I had never considered the important question of what came first, the apostolic tradition or the New Testament canon. It was a shock for me to discover that the term "canon" was being used for the oral tradition and confessions of faith long before it was used to describe the list of accepted books. In fact, this canon, or tradition, was an important criterion for determining which books would eventually become part of the New Testament. This was oral tradition, passed from one to another—no one even *thought* of writing it all down. Many of the first believers could not read, writing material was scarce and expensive, and printing presses had not yet been invented.

Did the New Testament give birth to the Church, or did the Church give birth to the New Testament? This is an important question, one that I had failed to consider as a Protestant. The New Testament is the "child" or product of the Church.[35] It is the collected and

---

34 Eusebius, *History of the Church*, 3, 24. Notice that "proclaim" is essentially an act of oral proclamation, not writing, and what they proclaimed was the "knowledge of the kingdom of God" and not just the "simple gospel."

35 The Catholic Church teaches that the primary author of the New Testament writings is the Holy Spirit—God is the author. Our current argument in no way minimizes this fact. The writers were a part of the Church, and the Church had the authority to recognize the inspired books and the authority to close the canon. Without the authority of the Catholic Church, how does a Protestant know which books belong in the New Testament? Reformed theologian R. C. Sproul honestly admits that the Protestant position can at best claim "a fallible collection of infallible books" (*Essential Truths of the Christian Faith* [Wheaton, Ill.: Tyndale House, 1992], 22). That is not very reassuring. How do we know that a *fallible* book didn't slip into the collection by mistake? How do we know that we are not missing an essential book? If Christ wanted us to have an infallible collection of writings, he needed to do

inspired writings of the apostles and their immediate followers. It is not, however, the sum total of all their teachings and traditions.[36]

We know from one of the earliest followers of the apostles, Papias (*c.* 60–130), Bishop of Hierapolis in Asia Minor,[37] that the oral tradition was held in very high esteem, even more so than written material. Papias, a disciple of the Apostle John, said, "I used to inquire what had been said by Andrew, or by Peter, or by Philip, or by Thomas or James, or by John or Matthew or any other of the Lord's disciples, and what Aristion and the Elder John, the disciples of the Lord, were saying. For books to read do not profit me so much as the living voice clearly sounding up to the present day in [the persons of] their authors."[38] Papias was referring to the living and oral tradition that was the mainstay and message of the early Christians.

Had you been alive at the time of the Resurrection and believed in the Jewish Messiah, chances are you'd have never seen or read the Gospel of John, his epistles, or Revelation unless you lived to

---

one of two things: (1) give us an authoritative list of writings, dictated by an apostle, that would form the canon to provide certainty, so there would be no confusion, or (2) establish an infallible Church that could give us a list of infallible writings so we could be certain. He did not do the first, and the Protestant denies the second, leaving the Protestant position weak.

36 Compare Jude 17–18, where Jude writes, "But you must remember, beloved, the predictions of the apostles of our Lord Jesus Christ; they said to you, 'In the last time there will be scoffers, following their own ungodly passions.' " These words are nowhere recorded in the writings of the New Testament, but they were part of the tradition passed on by the apostles that Jude assumed all believers knew. Jude assumed his readers had an intimate knowledge of the words contained in the unwritten tradition. And what of the teachings of Andrew, Philip, Bartholomew, Matthias, Thomas, and the others?

37 Papias was probably appointed bishop by the Apostle John. The *Introductory Note to the Fragments of Papias* (Alexander Roberts and James Donaldson, eds., *The Ante-Nicene Fathers*, arr. A. Cleveland Coxe [Grand Rapids, Mich.: Eerdmans, 1985], 1:151) says, "Papias has the credit of association with Polycarp, in the friendship of St. John himself, and of 'others who had seen the Lord'. . . . Later writers affirm that he suffered martyrdom, some saying [in] Rome. . . . He was a hearer of the Apostle John, and was on terms of intimate intercourse with many who had known the Lord and His apostles."

38 J. B. Lightfoot, ed., *The Apostolic Fathers* (Grand Rapids, Mich.: Baker Book House, 1984), 531.

be eighty or ninety years old. Chances are you would not have read all or even most of Paul's writings. Paul's epistles were written many years after the life of Christ, and John's Gospel was not written until about a.d. 100—over *seventy* years after the Resurrection. Written copies of these precious documents were extremely rare, each having been copied by hand on expensive parchment or papyrus. To complicate matters, very few people in the first centuries were literate; in fact, "Literacy in the [Roman] empire, by very rough estimate, did not exceed 10 percent on average."[39] Moreover, there was no established collection of inspired writings until the end of the fourth century.

The first-century Christian would have been without the New Testament, but he would not have been without the apostolic tradition, preserved by the Church and passed on to the next generations.[40] Suddenly an amazing thing occurred to me: even without the final collection and ready availability of the New Testament as we know it, the early Church existed and thrived by means of the apostolic tradition preserved within the Church.[41] As one who had based everything solely upon the leather-bound Bible under my arm, I found this discovery shook the very foundation of my Protestant belief in *sola Scriptura* and caused a deep curiosity about what else I might learn from my first brothers and sisters in Christ. I had to ask myself: Since

---

39 Wayne A. Meeks, *The Moral World of the First Christians* (Philadelphia: Westminster Press, 1986), 62.

40 2 Tim 2:2; Jn 17:20; 1 Cor 15:1–8; Jude 3. Irenaeus wrote, "When, therefore, we have such proofs, it is not necessary to seek among others the truth which is easily obtained from the Church. For the apostles, like a rich man in a bank, deposited with her [the Church] most copiously everything which pertains to the truth; and everyone whosoever wishes draws from her the drink of life. Let us suppose that the apostles had left us no written records. Would we not have been able to follow the precepts of the tradition that they handed down to those to whom they entrusted the Churches? It is this precept of tradition that is followed by many barbarian nations that believe in Christ who know nothing of the use of writing, or ink" (*Against Heresies*, 3, 4, 1).

41 The primitive Church appealed to the tradition and apostolic succession as her basis for truth and her weapon against the heretics. This was the universal teaching of the Church. Even if one does not accept apostolic tradition, one *must* accept the fact that Irenaeus and the early Church used succession and tradition as their authority. They firmly believed that the apostolic teaching would be sustained through the apostolic succession in the churches.

their trust was in an authoritative Church, where did this "doctrine" of *sola Scriptura* come from, anyway?

Sola Scriptura and Private Interpretation of the Bible Bring Disunity

When I was a Fundamentalist, I believed that the Catholic Church had dreamed up new doctrines and revelations that were considered equal to, or above, the Bible.[42] Wasn't it common knowledge that the Catholics had innumerable human doctrines added to the word of God? And, of course, we Evangelicals thought we were untainted by such things.[43] It must be noted here parenthetically that the Cath-

42 The Second Vatican Council stated in *Dei Verbum*, no. 4, "The Christian dispensation as the new and definitive covenant will never pass away, and we now await no further new public revelation before the glorious manifestation of our Lord Jesus Christ." Public revelation ceased with the death of the last apostle, and the Magisterium is not able to "create" new revelation. The Magisterium is not superior to the word of God, as is clearly stated in section ten of *Dei Verbum*: "This teaching office is not above the Word of God, but serves it, teaching only what has been handed on, listening to it devoutly, guarding it scrupulously and explaining it faithfully in accord with a divine commission and with the help of the Holy Spirit."

43 As an Evangelical Protestant I joined the bandwagon, denouncing Catholics for adding things to the Bible. The Catholic rightly acknowledges the need for doctrinal development and readily looks with confidence to the doctrines developed during the first centuries: the doctrine of the Trinity, the deity and humanity of Christ, etc. The development of these doctrines over the centuries is readily accepted as foundational in Evangelical circles as well. Upon further reflection, I realized that Protestants, myself included, had added many unbiblical words, doctrines, and practices to their repertoire—doing so with joyful abandon. Here are a few words and practices added or developed by Protestants that are not found in the Bible: "age of accountability," "total depravity of man," "ask Jesus into your heart" (can you recall Paul emphasizing this concept?), the "Rapture" (from a prophetic revelation in Scotland in the nineteenth century), "clothed in the righteousness of Christ" (a phrase never found in the New Testament, cf. Rev 19:8), "invisible Church," emphasis on a "personal relationship with Christ," "accepting Christ as personal Lord and Savior," "enthroning the Bible in your heart" (*Halley's Bible Handbook*), limited atonement, the "altar call," rededication, tent revivals, inerrancy, eternal security, denominations, "folding hands" to pray, faith *alone*, *sola Scriptura*, devotions, missionaries, full-time ministry, seminaries, church buildings (New Testament worship was in private homes, e.g., Rom 16:5; Col 4:15) with the building referred to as a "church," baptism and

olic Church has always taught that public revelation ended with the death of the last apostle. There can be no additional public revelation. The Scriptures of the Old and New Testaments are the only divinely inspired writings of God given to his Church. They are infallible and inerrant. There is no conflict here with Protestants. The conflict occurred only when the word *sola* was put in front of the word *Scriptura. Sola Scriptura* had never been taught by the apostles, the Fathers, or the Church. It is never taught in Scripture, and the error of this Reformation teaching cut Christians off from the divinely instituted Church, whereby God had intended his truth to be known in its fullness.[44] This fractured the unity of the one, holy, catholic, and apostolic Church into thousands of splinter groups,[45] each claiming a sliver of truth based on its private interpretations of the Bible yet denying the unity that God desired for his Church.

The Reformation principle of "each man with a Bible and his own

---

the Eucharist as mere symbols, Sunday school, the Christian flag (on most Protestant platforms), and many, many more. And since the New Testament canon itself is never mentioned in the Bible, the New Testament (as a book) is, in reality, an unbiblical addition.

44 No one claims the Catholic Church has been perfect; no one denies she needed great reformation during the sixteenth century. Much like the nation of Israel, she has gone through periods of decline and then great repentance and renewal. God always reforms his people. Israel never ceased to be God's people or his nation. The prophets never taught the people to ignore the traditions and interpret the Torah the way they individually wanted to. They were never encouraged to leave Israel during times of decline and establish their own "little Israels." Separating from the visible unity of Israel would have been unthinkable to Jews. Their visible, organic unity was a crucial foundational element of their covenant. Now that the covenant has expanded to include all men and not merely the Jews, why do we think that the covenant would be qualitatively different? Why should it be assumed that the covenant people would not continue to be a visible society with recognizable leadership? The Scriptures and the history of the early Church give no basis for such a covenantal deviation.

45 Swiss Reformer John Calvin (1509-1564) wrote to Philip Melanchthon (1497-1560, Luther's theologian): It is indeed important that posterity should [not] know of our differences; for it is indescribably ridiculous that we, who are in opposition to the whole world, should be, at the very beginning of the Reformation, at issue among ourselves" (Patrick F. O'Hare, *The Facts about Luther*, rev. ed. [1916; Rockford, Ill.: Tan Books, 1987], 293).

interpretation" has brought about the tragic results we see today.[46] The results are everywhere, obvious and devastating, as the "Reformation" has spun out of control.[47] Luther, Calvin, Zwingli, Hus, Wycliffe, Farel, Bucer, Melanchthon, and the other Reformers would not be pleased with their legacy today.[48]

---

46 In his *Commentary on the Psalms*, Martin Luther wrote, "*Scriptura sui ipsius interpres*", or, in English, "The Bible is its own interpreter." It is not difficult to see where that idea led. Even Luther quickly saw the devastating effect. He wrote, "There are almost as many sects and beliefs as there are heads; this one will not admit Baptism; that one rejects the Sacrament of the altar; another places another world between the present one and the day of judgment; some teach that Jesus Christ is not God. There is not an individual, however clownish he may be, who does not claim to be inspired by the Holy Ghost, and who does not put forth as prophecies his ravings and dreams" (cited in Leslie Rumble, *Bible Quizzes to a Street Preacher* [Rockford, Ill.: Tan Books, 1976], 22). See also O'Hare, *Facts about Luther*, 208. In a letter to Henrich Swingli, Martin Luther conceded that reformers would again have to take refuge in the Church councils in order to preserve the unity of the faith on account of the many interpretations that were given to the Scriptures (see *Epis. ad Zwingli*).

47 The legacy of the Reformation is more than twenty-three thousand different sects and schisms (denominations), with a new one starting every day, according to the *World Census of Religious Activities* (New York: U.N. Information Center, 1989). Any unity now would be possible only through a sovereign act of God. The unity of the Church in the New Testament, and for the first ten centuries, was understood to be an organic, visible unity. Apostolic tradition and the teaching authority of the Church were the internal "cement." The visible unity was to be maintained in love by an authoritative (not to be confused with authoritarian) teaching office. It was to be the observable basis upon which the world could draw the conclusion that the Father had sent the Son. Jesus asked the Father that his followers might "become perfectly one" (Jn 17:20-23). What good is an "invisible unity?" Can the world see an invisible, intangible unity? The visible and organizational unity of the early Church inspired the fear and admiration of the whole Roman Empire and eventually won it over.

48 In writing to Pope Leo X, Luther said, "I never approved of a schism, nor will I approve of it for all eternity. . . . That the Roman Church is more honored by God than all others is not to be doubted. . . . Though nowadays everything is in a wretched state, it is no ground for separating from the Church. On the contrary, the worse things are going, the more should we hold close to her, for it is not by separating from the Church that we can make her better. . . . There is no sin, no amount of evil, which should be permitted to dissolve the bond of charity or break the bond of unity of the body" (letter of Martin Luther to Pope Leo X, January 6, 1519, more than a

Reformation theologies radically changed the definition of "the Church". It was now understood to be a "nonvisible Church" with a mystical and unseen unity. I discovered this to be absolutely foreign to all biblical and early Church teaching, just as it is foreign to the wishes of Christ expressed in his High Priestly prayer.[49] The new and radical theology of the "invisible Church" would have been strange indeed to second-century Christians. The early Muratorian Fragment (written between 155 and 200) declares that "there is one Church spread abroad throughout the whole world," and it later refers to Timothy as "holy in the Catholic Church, in the ordering of churchly discipline."[50] There was no concept of denominations. There was one Catholic Church, which was a unified organization around the known world. In 180 the great theologian Irenaeus wrote,

> As I have already observed, the Church, having received this preaching and this faith, although scattered throughout the whole world, yet, as if occupying but one house, carefully preserves it.[51] She also believes these points of doctrine just as if she had but one soul, and one and the same heart, and she proclaims them, and teaches them, and hands them down, with perfect harmony, as if she possessed only one mouth.

---

year after the *Ninety-Five Theses*; quoted by Patrick O'Hare in *The Facts about Luther*, 356).

49 Jn 17:20–23: "I do not pray in behalf of these only, but also for those who believe in me through their word; that they may all be one; even as thou, Father, art in me, and I in thee, that they also may be in us; that the world may believe that thou didst send me. The glory which thou hast given me I have given to them; that they may be one, even as we are one; in them, and thou in me, that they may be perfectly one [perfected in unity], so that the world may know that thou hast sent me and hast loved them even as thou hast loved me." Notice that Jesus prays for the future generations of Christians, that they be "one" and "perfected in unity," not ripped apart by divisions and denominations. I realized that the divisions in Christendom were ripping and tearing the Body of Christ. I had always been appalled that people could have crucified Christ, yet I was inadvertently party to the tearing asunder of his Body, the Church. Paul also condemns factions and divisions in the Church (see 1 Cor 1:10–14; 11:18; 12:25).

50 Quoted by Jurgens, *Faith of the Early Fathers*, 1:108.

51 Irenaeus clearly presents the early Church as one, organic, visible unity, with a recognizable leadership. Protestantism is like a nation that divides into tens of thousands of competing, disagreeing factions but that still claims to have an invisible unity.

For, although the languages of the world are dissimilar, yet the import of the tradition is one and the same.[52] For the churches in Germany do not believe or hand down anything different, nor do those in Spain, nor those in Gaul, nor those in the East, nor those in Egypt, nor those in Libya, nor those which have been established in the central regions [Palestine] of the world.[53].

The Scriptures teach us that no prophecy is a matter of private interpretation[54] and that many distort Paul's writings to their own destruction.[55] The Bible was never meant to be read in a cavalier manner, outside the tradition and teaching of the Church. As Evangelicals, it was our practice to sit together and study the Bible, with the most important question being routinely asked: "How do you feel about this verse?" or "What does this passage mean to you?" The Scriptures were meant to be read, interpreted, and practiced within the community of the Church, under the leadership of the Magisterium (teaching office of the bishops), and in light of apostolic tradition. For me, reading these ancient writings of the primitive Church

52 Here we see the beauty of the Church's sacred tradition, deposited by the apostles, carefully preserved, and passed down from one generation to the next (2 Tim 2:2; 2 Th 2:15). It is of interest that at this point in time, the New Testament would not be formally collected and its canon determined for another two hundred years.

53 *Against Heresies*, 1, 10, 2, in Roberts and Donaldson, *Ante-Nicene Fathers*, 1:331. Notice it is not the New Testament that Irenaeus appeals to. It is the tradition passed on by the apostles and their disciples (e.g., 2 Tim 2:2). Can anyone extract from this passage any idea of denominationalism? The churches making up the one Church were "scattered throughout the whole world, yet, as occupying one house," being unified and taught by "the rulers" (1 Tim 5:17) of the Church. This position is diametrically opposed to my Protestant background, where no matter how much we conflicted and dissented among the various denominations and sects, we always had some vague notion of an abstract, "invisible" unity.

54 2 Pet 1:20–21: "First of all you must understand this, that no prophecy of scripture is a matter of one's own interpretation, because no prophecy ever came by the impulse of man, but men moved by the Holy Spirit spoke from God."

55 2 Pet 3:15–16: "So also our beloved brother Paul wrote to you according to the wisdom given him, speaking of this as he does in all his letters. There are some things in them hard to understand, which the ignorant and unstable twist to their own destruction, as they do the other scriptures."

was a revolutionary endeavor, especially as I was a Protestant who had never been confronted with the reality of these historical documents. It was especially enlightening for me because I had always considered these first Christians to be Evangelicals like me, adhering to the same "Protestant" teachings that I held so dear. It seems that the Protestant denominations, as a whole, have been sheltered from the first centuries of the Church, considering them "Catholic history." They are therefore liable to skip from the Book of Acts all the way to Martin Luther. This tendency is explained by Robert McAfee Brown, in *The Spirit of Protestantism*: "Emphasis on *sola Scriptura* has been the distinctive grandeur of Protestantism, but it has been the source of distinct misery as well. For it has often been based on the faulty assumption that it is possible to 'leapfrog,' as it were, over 1,900 years of Christian history, and read the Bible as though nothing had happened since the documents themselves were composed. Even if this were desirable, it is impossible. The 'leapfrog' is doomed to failure" (215). The famous Baptist preacher Charles Spurgeon said, "It seems odd that certain men who talk so much of what the Holy Spirit reveals to them should think so little of what He has revealed to others."[56] The Church and her saints have been teaching and defending the faith for two thousand years, and I, as a Protestant, was never taught to study them, much less to revere and emulate them.

Scripture, Tradition, and the Canon of Scripture

What basis do Protestants have for trusting the twenty-seven writings that make up the New Testament? The answer comes back, "We trust them because they are inspired." Yes, but how do we know they are inspired?[57] There were many hundreds of writings and epistles pass-

56 Walter A. Henrichsen, *A Layman's Guide to Interpreting the Bible* (Grand Rapids, Mich.: Zondervan, and Colorado Springs: NavPress, 1978), 41.

57 2 Tim 3:16; 2 Pet 1:20–21. Not only does the Catholic Church readily agree about the inspiration of the twenty-seven books, but she has been the primary defender of the fact of that inspiration and has affirmed it constantly for two millennia. The word "inspired" means "God-breathed." God superintended the writings and is their primary author, though he worked through the instrumentality of men (see CCC 105–7). It should be noted that the early Church did not use inspiration as a criterion for determining the canon. The term was used loosely in the first centuries. The primary basis for determining which books to include in the canon was the Church's authority and her

ing from hand to hand, city to city, province to province in the Roman empire. There was the *Gospel of Thomas*, the *Shepherd of Hermas*, the *Didache*, the *Epistle of Clement*, the *Acts of Peter*, the *Acts of John*, the *Gospel of the Hebrews*, the *Secret Gospel of Mark*, the *Protoevangelium of James*, and hundreds more. Who decided which ones were inspired and which were not? To say it was the Holy Spirit, not men, who chose the twenty-seven writings is to sidestep the real question—and is not an honest answer. The Holy Spirit also authored the Bible, but he used men to write it. Likewise, he used men, the Church, to collect and close the canon.

As I indicated before, neither Jesus nor the apostles told us which books belong in the canon of Scripture and which ones do not. In fact, the New Testament gives us no help at all. Some, like Martin Luther, held that if Christ is preached in a document, it is therefore inspired; but this falls quickly and hard since spurious writings speak of Christ and references in certain portions of the New Testament seem sparse in this regard. This is why Luther had such great animosity toward the Epistle of James.

Many of the Reformers, when faced with this obvious problem, reduced their answer to a claim of an "internal witness" that confirmed that the twenty-seven writings were inspired and therefore canonical.[58] Others felt that documents were inspired if they were

---

tradition. According to historian Henry Chadwick (in John McManners, ed., *The Oxford Illustrated History of Christianity* [New York: Oxford Univ. Press, 1990], 29),"The criterion for admission [of books into the canon] was not so much that traditions vindicated an apostolic authorship as that the content of the books was in line with the apostolic proclamation [tradition] received by the second-century churches." Protestants, whether they realize it or not, have to trust Catholic tradition to know which books are in their canon.

58 Swiss Reformer John Calvin wrote: "Let it therefore be held as fixed, that those who are inwardly taught by the Holy Spirit acquiesce implicitly in Scripture; that Scripture, carrying its own evidence along with it [self-authenticating], deigns not to submit to proofs and arguments; but owes the full conviction with which we ought to receive it to the testimony of the Spirit. Enlightened by him, we no longer believe, either on our own judgment or that of others, that the Scriptures are from God; but in a way superior to human judgment, feel perfectly assured . . . in holding it, [that] we hold unassailable truth; not like miserable men, whose minds are enslaved by superstition, but because we feel a divine energy living and breathing in it" (*Institutes of the Christian Religion* [Grand Rapids, Mich.: Eerdmans, 1983], 1:72–73). He

inspiring to the reader. But how inspiring is Leviticus, Philemon, or 3 John? By comparison, many ancient and modern writings are much more moving and inspiring. Should we eliminate Leviticus and include *Pilgrim's Progress* in the canon of Scripture? Another criterion used by Protestants is apostolicity; in other words, it is inspired *if* it was written by an apostle. However, we have in our New Testament the book of Hebrews, whose authorship is unsure and disputed to this day.[59] Mark and Luke were not apostles, yet almost one quarter of the New Testament was written by them. Since their names are not included in the text, how do we know that Matthew wrote Matthew, or that John wrote John? Jude indicates that he is not an apostle.[60]

---

says that the knowledge of what is Scripture comes to each individual from "heavenly revelation." Using Calvin's principles, each person would have the authority to determine his own canon of Scripture. This is the means used by Mormons to verify the inspiration of the *Book of Mormon*. They claim to know the *Book of Mormon* is true and inspired by God, because, when they read it, they get a "burning in the bosom," which is an internal witness to verify the inspiration. In the *Book of Mormon* we read, "And when ye shall receive these things, I would exhort you that ye would ask God, the Eternal Father, in the name of Christ, if these things are not true; and if ye shall ask with a sincere heart, with real intent, having faith in Christ, he will manifest the truth of it unto you, by the power of the Holy Spirit. And by the power of the Holy Ghost ye may know the truth of all things" (*Moroni* 10:4–5 [Salt Lake City: Church of Jesus Christ of the Latter-Day Saints, 1981], 529). How are these two "self-authenticating" procedures different? The Mormons authenticate their *Book of Mormon* using Calvin's methodology of an internal witness. Based on this subjective method alone, it is difficult to dispute their conclusions that the *Book of Mormon* is God's word.

59 Heb 2:3: "How shall we escape if we neglect such a great salvation? It was declared at first by the Lord, and it was attested to us by those who heard him." Not only is the author of Hebrews basing his knowledge on oral tradition, but he is also implying that he himself never heard the Lord Jesus in person but was only speaking from the oral tradition passed on to him secondhand by the apostles. We learn from Fr. John Laux that "from the earliest times there has been a wide difference of opinion respecting the authorship of the Epistle to the Hebrews. . . . The style is certainly not the style of St. Paul. . . . The Biblical Commission declared (July 24, 1914) that the *Epistle to the Hebrews* is of Pauline origin; but it is not necessary to assume that St. Paul himself was the author of its external form" (*Introduction to the Bible* [1932; Rockford, Ill.: Tan Books, 1990], 291–92).

60 Jude 17: "But you must remember, beloved, the predictions of the apostles of our Lord Jesus Christ; they said to you, 'In the last time there will be

The last two epistles of John claim to be written by an elder, not by an apostle. The majority of the New Testament seems to fall short of the "apostolic" test. From a Protestant perspective, there is no satisfactory answer to this basic question of the canon, which is absolutely foundational. The crisis pierces the very heart of Protestantism.[61] As we cited earlier, the classical Protestant position as explained by R. C. Sproul is: The Protestant has "a fallible collection of infallible books."[62]

It is not commonly realized that, until the late *fourth century*, there was *no* final list of canonical books, *no* established New Testament. The span of time between the crucifixion and the determination of the canonization of Scripture was equivalent to the time between the Pilgrim's *Mayflower* sailing from Plymouth, England, to our current day. Christians did not have a collected New Testament for almost *four hundred years after the Resurrection of Christ!* Compare that to another recent example from American history. It has been only two hundred years since the American Revolution, but it seems to be ages ago. Imagine if the founding documents of the United States were still uncertain—not yet collected and codified. What would be the basis for jurisprudence and constitutional government today? In the early Church, books, epistles, and writings were disputed; no sure list of canonical books was agreed upon. How did the Christians survive without a leather-bound New Testament under their arms? How did they blossom and spread throughout the inhabited world? How did they convert the whole Roman Empire? Was *their* foundational and

---

scoffers, following their own ungodly passions.'"

61 It is a matter of apostolic authority. Those who deny *any* authority in the Church have no reference point or absolute outside of themselves and are left competing with everyone else's finite, fluctuating feelings and conclusions. Along with the Bible, the Catholics have the apostles and their successors, commissioned by the risen Christ; the Protestants have the Bible alone. The Catholic Church has both the authority of the Church (Christ's Body on earth, his continuing Incarnation) and, therefore, the authority of the infallible Word. In denying one, the Protestant loses both; in affirming the one, the Catholic retains both.

62 When a Baptist minister stands up to deliver a sermon based on Jude, can he be certain that he is preaching from an inspired text? How does he know? To be honest, the pastor should say, "Today I will be preaching on a text from Jude, which I hope - I think - is the inspired word of God."

operative principle *sola Scriptura*? What sufficient rule of faith did they have to govern the Church, teach the catechumens, and resist heresy, all of which they did so well? The answer to all these questions is, in short, the apostolic tradition, preserved through apostolic succession within the Catholic Church. The apostolic writings were an integral part, but only a small part, of the entire deposit of faith.

Protestants are dependent upon the tradition of the Catholic Church for their current New Testament.[63] It was not until the authoritative voice of the Church spoke that the New Testament was declared a canon with the current twenty-seven books. This was accomplished at the Council of Hippo and the Third Council of Carthage. The Church and all the world then had the first official list of canonical books—the writings sanctioned for reading in the Catholic Church.[64] Protestants have by necessity trusted the determination of the Catholic Church. Protestants *must* trust the declaration of the infallible Church to know which books make up their infallible New Testament. This is a great irony. It was the tradition and the authority of the Catholic Church that established *their* canon. However, while rejecting all the other decrees of the councils as nonauthoritative, Protestants arbitrarily accept without question the tradition establishing the canon of the New Testament.

---

63 Martin Luther wrote, "We concede—as we must—that so much of what they [the Catholic Church] say is true: that the papacy has God's word and the office of the apostles, and that we have received Holy Scriptures, Baptism, the Sacrament, and the pulpit from them. What would we know of these if it were not for them?" (*Sermons on the Gospel of John*, chaps. 14–16 (1537), in vol. 24 of *Luther's Works* [St. Louis, Mo.: Concordia, 1961], 304).

64 "The Council of Hippo (393 a.d.) was probably the first church council to lay down the limits of the canon of scripture: its enactments are not extant, but its statement on the canon was repeated as Canon 47 of the Third Council of Carthage (397 A.D.). The relevant words are these: 'And further it was resolved that nothing be read in church under the name of the divine scriptures except the canonical writings. The canonical writings, then, are these:. . . .Of the New Testament: The four books of the gospels, the one book of the Acts of the Apostles, the thirteen epistles of the apostle Paul, the one [epistle] to the Hebrews, by the same, two of the apostle Peter, three of John, one of James, one of Jude, John's Apocalypse—one book. . . .Let it be permitted, however, that the passions of martyrs be read when their anniversaries are celebrated' " (F.F. Bruce, The Canon of Scripture [Downers Grove, Ill.: InterVarsity Press, 1988], 232-33).

If the Church had no authority to recognize and decide which writings were inspired and to close the canon, then we would have no guarantee that these writings are, in fact, inspired. These documents would simply become equal to all other writings that claim to be inspired by God. If there is no final authority, then any person or sect who claims the ability to discern what is inspired becomes, by necessity, freed from the New Testament canon—rejecting or accepting books at will. The subjective "inner witness" that so many groups claim to possess makes the individual equal to the Scriptures— the personal judge of Scripture. To be honest, those who recognize no binding ecclesiastical authority able to close the canon must respect *any* canon. This authority is the prerogative of Christ's Church as founded by Christ and carried on by the succession of bishops under the guidance and protection of the Holy Spirit.

Likewise, if the Church has no teaching authority by which to interpret these inspired writings, then everyone's individual and contradictory interpretation or opinion is equally valid (since it claims to be from the Holy Spirit), and this completely nullifies and denies any existence of unity or sanity in the Body of Christ and makes a mockery of absolute truth and unity. If private interpretation is the final criterion, who has the right to condemn the Mormons or the Jehovah's Witnesses, who are interpreting the Bible according to *their* own principles and private judgment? By necessity, moreover, each must deny that the other has the Spirit. "If you had the Holy Spirit leading you into all truth, you would certainly agree with me, since the Holy Spirit led me to this contradictory interpretation." We are thus brought back to the question, "What does this Bible verse mean to you?"

In light of this, it is very interesting that there are major movements afoot at this very moment to challenge and reopen the canon of Scripture.[65] Since there is no real authority in the Protestant camp,

---

65 Even Luther thought he could redefine the canon of Scripture. No longer restrained by the authority of the Catholic Church, Luther began to rearrange the New Testament, placing the "suspected" books in the back, namely, James, Hebrews, Jude, and Revelation. He raised the Gospel of John above the other three Gospels. "The Epistle of St. James, Luther denounced as 'an epistle of straw.' 'I do not hold it,' he said, 'to be his writing, and I cannot place it among the capital books' " (O'Hare, *Facts about Luther*, 202–3). Lu-

there is no one there who can authoritatively resist such a challenge. Upon what basis would the Protestant object to reopening the canon for the inclusion of additional "inspired" writings? Upon the basis of an internal witness? Whose internal witness?

As a Protestant, I had allowed the "traditions of men" to invalidate the word of God. Protestants have insisted on an *either/or* mentality that puts everything at odds. An example of this is "You can trust *either* the Bible *or* tradition." The Catholic has a *both/and* approach, which says "You can trust *both* the Bible *and* the tradition." The Protestant position is like saying "You can love *either* your wife *or* your children," instead of saying "You can love *both* your wife *and* your children." Take a look at this distinction in other areas of Catholic teaching and Protestant theologies, and you will find it is consistent throughout.

I apologize for this prolonged portion of the story, but it is crucial and foundational. These issues were a major motivation for my move to Catholicism. These were the cracks that finally led to the crumbling of the Fundamentalist wall that had kept me from seeing the truth of the Catholic Church.

Our Struggle with Other "Catholic Issues"

Just as the very idea of "tradition" had once repulsed us, since we considered it a biblical compromise,[66] so there were many other Catholic issues that repelled us. Unfortunately, our whole perception of the Catholic Church was a grotesque caricature, learned from exclusively

---

ther denied Hebrews any apostolic authority. Luther removed the so-called "apocrypha" that had been part of the canon since the Septuagint used by Christ and the apostles. When challenged on any of his views of Scripture, Luther said, "Thus I will have it, thus I order it, my will is reason enough. . . . Dr. Luther will have it so, and . . . he is a Doctor above all Doctors in the whole of Popery" (Henry Acinar, *Luther's Own Statements*, 3d ed. [New York: Benziger Bros., 1884], 25).

66 In Colossians 2:8 we read, "See to it that no one makes a prey of you by philosophy and empty deceit, according to human tradition, according to the elemental spirits of the universe, and not according to Christ." Is this referring to all "tradition"? Obviously not, since Paul refers to his teaching as "tradition" (2 Th 2:15; 3:6; 1 Cor 11:2). So what tradition is Paul referring to? He is denouncing the tradition of men (in this case the Gnostics) that is opposed to the apostolic traditions deposited in the Church.

anti-Catholic Protestant sources. We had never allowed the Church to speak for herself; we had not been honest in our investigations.

To our amazement, the very things that had once repelled us now became compelling arguments *for* the Roman Catholic Church: the universality of the Church in both space and time, her visible unity, her survival in spite of all her problems and tares, her undefiled orthodoxy and moral teaching in the midst of rampant heresy and schism.[67] (Two of these factors are discussed in great detail later in this book: baptism and the Eucharist.) I found that Catholics weren't stupid after all, that they hadn't abandoned the faith of our fathers. The truth is that the Catholic Church knows the Bible and teaches it in such a manner as to avoid the contradictions we had to accept as Evangelicals. They knew what Evangelicals taught and rejected it for good and sufficient reasons. In fact, I found the Catholic Church has always been wonderfully intelligent and incredibly loyal to Scripture and the teaching of the Fathers in the early Church.

We had become good at tackling problematic issues—we had overcome the many obstacles to becoming a Christian in the first place, especially our questions with regard to the historicity of the scriptural accounts, the philosophic integrity of the Christian position, the Virgin Birth and the Resurrection, the inspiration of Scripture, the opposition of secular society, and so on. Not only had we overcome the obstacles, but we had helped many others understand the beauty of the Christian faith. But now we had to decide what the "Church" was. Protestants strongly emphasize the doctrine of salvation but do not have a coherent doctrine of the church.

---

67 G.K. Chesterton writes of the romance of orthodoxy in this way: "People have fallen into a foolish habit of speaking of orthodoxy as something heavy, humdrum, and safe. There was never anything so perilous or so exciting as orthodoxy. It was sanity: and to be sane is more dramatic than to be mad. It was the equilibrium of a man behind madly rushing horses, seeming to stoop this way and to sway that, yet in every attitude having the grace of statuary and the accuracy of arithmetic. The Church . . . swerved to left and right, so exactly as to avoid enormous obstacles. . . . To have fallen into any one of the fads from Gnosticism to Christian Science would indeed have been obvious and tame. But to have avoided them all has been one whirling adventure; and in my vision the heavenly chariot flies thundering through the ages, the dull heresies sprawling and prostrate, the wild truth reeling but erect" (*Orthodoxy*, in *The Collected Works*, I:305-6).

Janet and I already had the writings of the early Church, the apostolic and Church Fathers in thirty-eight volumes. They had been sitting on our shelves for ten years, and I had used them only periodically to research such issues as the deity of Christ or abortion. I had taken little interest in them otherwise. We began methodically to search through the Scriptures and the teaching of these first Christians. We investigated the "Catholic traditions" one at a time. The issue of Scripture and tradition was the first one I challenged. I was going to prove the Catholics wrong. Becoming Catholic was the last thing we wanted to do. I was shocked to find out, as I have already mentioned, that the Catholic Church had held unwaveringly to the truth from the beginning. It was we Evangelicals who had deviated, set up *sola Scriptura*, and left the ancient teaching of the Church.

Janet began reading about worship and liturgy in the first four centuries. Before long she found out the Catholic Church was profoundly on target again, faithfully teaching and practicing the faith and liturgy[68] of the early Church.

Two issues down, a hundred to go. Even if the Church was right on these two issues of tradition and worship, we were sure she must be wrong on all the others. We would extricate ourselves from any possible entanglement with this Catholic Church yet. More obstacles loomed ahead of us. Janet and I examined them one at a time, drawing on all our resources to discredit the Catholic teachings but attempting to be honest and fair at the same time. We found to our utter amazement that these many bogeymen were not barriers at all; rather, we had been misled by our Protestant past. These looming hurdles slowly melted away as we carefully approached them: Mary, purgatory, the papacy, confession, bishops, the Eucharist, baptismal regeneration, contraceptives,[69] justification by "faith working through

68 The liturgy of the Roman Catholic Church is rich with meaning, loaded with Scripture, centered in Christ—a profound and glorious service of worship to God.

69 The issue of contraceptives is often the largest problem for Evangelical couples as they consider conversion to the Church. Prior to our marriage, an Evangelical pastor had counseled us about birth control, recommending several methods of contraception. After eighteen years of marriage, a couple settles into a comfortable routine together, so it can be very traumatic to accept the Catholic teaching as dogma. The pope is in that this was in the top three "biggies" for us. Since our conversion and submission to the Church,

love," veneration of saints, the Mass, and all the other Catholic teachings and practices we had mistrusted, disputed, and despised.

Why had we so profoundly misunderstood these teachings of the Catholic Church? We had assumed without question that they were all wrong-headed and unbiblical. G. K. Chesterton seemed to address the same issue when he wrote, "The happy Protestants were not worried about it at all, but told lies from morning to night as merrily and innocently as the birds sing in the trees."[70] I never realized the degree of dishonesty and lack of integrity I had as a Protestant "anti-Catholic" until I started rereading the books and listening again to tapes mass-produced by anti-Catholics and comparing them with the actual, historical teaching of the Catholic Church. I had misrepresented the Church's teachings, not out of malice, but out of ignorance and prejudice. We are saddened now by the many people who unwittingly take these caricatures of the Catholic Church so seriously. Our Protestant prejudices blinded us. We are grateful to God for giving us the courage to be honest and the honesty to be fair in our investigations. There is a unifying factor among all Protestants that they seem unaware of, at least I was unaware of it. This unifying factor is a monolithic rejection of the Catholic Church and the primacy of Rome. I found it to be ironical, though not coincidental, that it is the Catholic Church by which others define themselves—like saying, "It's the Cadillac of. . . ." Protestants, and especially Fundamentalists, define themselves by their opposition to the Church. They are protesting still, and it says a lot when something becomes the standard by which all others are measured. The Protestants[71] refute this,

---

we have not regretted our obedience; in fact, our relationship has blossomed to heights we never experienced before.

70 *Catholic Church and Conversion*, 75.

71 In speaking of Protestants, I am referring to myself first, to the historical movement begun by Martin Luther (followed by Calvin, Zwingli, and others) second, and, third, to the Fundamentalists, Evangelicals, and "Bible-believing" Christians who trace their roots back to, and still hold to, the foundational principles of the Protestant Reformation. There are many strains of Protestants, ranging from fringe cults like Moonies and Jehovah's Witnesses to the Anglicans and other liturgical churches that still maintain some similarities with the Catholic Church. I came from a Baptist heritage and later associated with Evangelical Presbyterian denominations. Janet was raised Presbyterian. We were married in a "New Testament Assembly," and later we

saying they define themselves by the Bible alone. Their very name, "Protestant," however, is significant: they define themselves in their protest, not in their affirmations. Archbishop Fulton Sheen rightly observed, "There are not over a hundred people in the United States who hate the Catholic Church. There are millions, however, who hate what they wrongly believe to be the Catholic Church— which is, of course, quite a different thing."[72]

We Begin to Discover the One, Holy, Catholic, and Apostolic Church

The Protestant Reformation was actually an act of negation. Protestants overreacted and cut too much flesh away from the bone. What resulted was a mere skeleton of the Church Christ had intended. They had no patience and no confidence in the ability of the Holy Spirit to reform the Church. Schisms and factions were soundly condemned in the New Testament[73] and by all subsequent generations. The concept of "denominations" was unheard of and unthinkable.[74] The early Church fought with all her strength and resources to keep the Lord's command and prayer for unity. She could never have conceived of the sad condition we see today. The only way I could justify myself as a Protestant was to reinterpret the Bible's words and in-

---

associated with Evangelical and nondenominational Bible churches.

72 *Radio Replies* (1938; Rockford, Ill.: Tan Books, 1979), 1:ix.

73 1 Cor 1:10, 3:3, 12:25; Jn 17:21–26, to mention only a few. The word"schism" used in 1 Corinthians 1:10 is the same word, *rent*, used to describe the tearing of cloth. The Fathers understood the seamless robe of Christ (Jn 19:23–25) as a type of the visible unity of the Church—the Body of Christ clothed with the seamless white robe of holiness and unity. The seamless robe has now been rent and torn, not by Roman soldiers, but by those who bear the name of the Christ himself.

74 Just as one cannot imagine the Jews ever being told to leave Israel during times of corruption or wrongdoing, to start a "new nation," so it was unthinkable in the early Church to divide or break off into denominations (1 Cor 1:10–13).

When problems arise in the Church, as in the nation of Israel, everyone should pray for repentance and reformation from within. Men impatiently see things from a finite perspective, whereas God sees things eternally—all generations simultaneously. It is Christ's Church, and it is his job to preserve and purify her. It is our job to strive for purity and unity.

tent, conceiving an "invisible" Church with an "invisible unity." The majesty of the Church has been reduced to thousands of beggarly groups disputing doctrine and competing for members. Using the Lord's criterion, we might ask if the world could observe the disunified churches today and believe that the Father sent the Son (Jn 17:22–23)? Again we see a radical negation and reductionism. The Reformers set out to reform, for reform was needed, but they forgot the Church they were trying to remedy. It is as though in rekindling the fire they forgot about the fireplace! The fire of reform took on a life of its own and failed to accomplish its goal—the purifying of the one, holy, catholic, and apostolic Church.[75] Instead, a most grievous sin was introduced to God's Church, prideful and arrogant division, more evil than the elements reform had meant to remedy. It violated, worse yet, it treated with disdain and contempt the unity of Christ's Body and his express desire for visible oneness. The stage was set for the unhappy disintegration and splintering of Christendom we see today, with the exponential multiplication of confusion, sects, schisms, and false teaching.

Eusebius wrote that "the splendor of the Catholic and only true Church, always remaining the same and unchanged, grew steadily in greatness and strength, shedding on every race of Greeks and non-Greeks alike the majestic, spotless, free, sober, pure light of her inspired citizenship and philosophy."[76] That splendor has been torn asunder and rent into innumerable schisms. There is no longer a united front —the organic, visible unity—that once demanded the respect and fear of the Roman Empire and turned a pagan society into a Christian civilization. This lost unity is the very thing that could

75 The Reformation severed the "one," making it divided; fouled the "holy" and brought in great sinfulness (see the following quotation); divided the "catholic," making it sectarian and denominational; and rejected the "apostolic," by making everyone his own "apostle" or "pope," needing no authority or continuity of succession. The result of the Reformation was *not* an outbreak of holiness and righteous living. From many available citations, this one from Martin Luther must suffice: "The world by this teaching becomes only the worse, the longer it exists . . . the people are more avaricious, less merciful . . . and worse than before under the Papacy" (Heinrich Denifle, *Luther and Lutherdom*, trans. Raymund Volz, vol. 1, pt. 1 [Somerset, Ohio: Torch Press, 1917], 47).

76 Eusebius, *History of the Church* 4, 7, p. 110.

shake our modern world to the core and again convert the world to Christ. Just imagine!

My wife and I gradually discovered that the perceived obstacles that kept us from considering the Catholic Church were simply theological realms where Catholic teaching was so expansive, biblical, all-encompassing, and rich that our minds, so denominationally entrenched, were unable to comprehend it, much less embrace it. Our reading and wealth of discoveries brought endless exclamations of excitement and sharing: "Janet, read this verse; I wouldn't have believed it!" Or, "Steve, look what I found in a first-century epistle!" We delighted in lengthy discussions of the Marian doctrines,[77] the primacy of Rome, the unity of the Church, "salvation by "faith alone" or "works" (so-called), "worshiping" statues,[78] infant baptism, the Eucharist, tradition and Scripture, and so on.

Should We Accept Church Authority?

For the Protestant, the major obstacle, overshadowing all others, is the issue of authority. He has the Bible alone and can be his own authority. The hierarchical structure of the Catholic Church is more than an Evangelical can tolerate. Evangelical friends have chided us,

---

77 There are two great misconceptions in this regard. The first is that the Marian doctrines were unbiblical inventions of the Catholic Church in the Middle Ages. These teachings on the Blessed Virgin can be found in the earliest centuries. The second misconception we had was that the intention of the Marian doctrines was to glorify Mary and set her up as equal to her Son (something like a fourth person in the Trinity). This is absolutely not the case. The Catholic teachings on the Blessed Virgin were universal, and they were emphasized, especially in the first centuries, to refute heresies denying the full humanity of Jesus. Marian doctrines are a moat, a bulwark, to defend the doctrines regarding the Person of Christ. They built a defense around the Person and natures of Christ in the battle to defend the orthodox teachings of the Church against various heresies (e.g., Docetism, Arianism, Nestorianism). We Protestants had always considered such Marian doctrines to be additions to the gospel and thought they sanctioned idolatry, but when I studied the Fathers and their teachings on Mary, I was embarrassed about my earlier ignorance.

78 The teaching of the Catholic Church forbids the worship of statues.
A statue or icon is a likeness of someone who is to be remembered and appreciated; it is similar to a treasured picture of one's grandfather. Veneration (reverence) is not worship, it is respect. Only God is to be worshiped.

"So, you're crossing the Tiber to submit to the yoke of Rome."[79] Though the question was sarcastically asked, the answer, quite frankly, is Yes, we are. For us it was a matter of Scripture, history, and objective truth, an educated submission to Christ in his Church—the glorious Body of Christ.

Authority doesn't sit well with the twentieth-century mind-set. It smacks of weakness, slavery, and subservience, especially in a society that values unlimited personal freedom as a birthright. Submission to authority can come about in one of two ways: *first*, as an act of insecure subservience or groveling, which is brought about by a lack of nerve, a reluctance to be responsible for one's own choices and acts or an unwillingness or inability to act independently.

The *second* reason for submission to authority is the exact opposite of the first and a seeming paradox—it is an act of decisive independence. The strong, secure, and independent person can, as a supreme act of his independence, accept the authority of one who is worthy to exercise it. Consider the great warriors and knights of old, who willingly, and of their own accord, swore allegiance and obedience to a king who was by his very character and title deserving of honor and submission. Submission to Christ in his Church is not an act of blindness, weakness, conformity, or groveling. It is rather an act of courage, intelligence, and decisiveness—a willing choice made from the very essence of emancipation.[80] We realized that the Catholic Church

79 The Tiber River flows to the west and the north of the city of Rome, only a few minutes' walk from the burial site of St. Peter under St. Peter's Basilica. Anyone approaching Rome from the north must cross the Tiber River to enter the city. "Crossing the Tiber" is used figuratively for accepting and converting to the Roman Catholic Church.

80 Janet and I had already accepted, for good and sufficient reasons, the authority of the Scriptures. This was not an act of blind faith but one of reasoned conviction. In a broader view, and in light of the current discussion, once one is aware of Christ's Church on earth, submission to that Church, the vehicle and repository of the Scriptures and salvation, is not a difficult thing to accept; in fact it is the wise thing to do and is incumbent upon us as his creatures, his subjects, and his children. We had believed in Christ for many years, but to find his Church was to find the other side of the same coin. Finding the "Church side" of the coin was just as exhilarating as finding the "Christ side." Like a husband and wife, they are one flesh. Though they can be separated, it does great violence to the visible and mystical union.

was God's authority, his Kingdom represented visibly in space and time. Once we recognized the truth and historical solidity of the Church's claims, we had no choice but gladly to swear allegiance and pledge our fealty.

The Next Important Crossroads: Catholic or Orthodox?

Even though we had traversed what seemed to be a million miles, we did not decide immediately to join the Catholic Church. In fact, in light of the obstacles mentioned earlier, we seriously considered joining one of the Eastern Orthodox churches. There seemed fewer obstacles between us and Orthodoxy. What are the Orthodox churches?[81] A bit of background is in order at this point. The apostles, in obedience to the commission of the Lord Jesus (Mt 28:18–20), preached the gospel and gave birth to churches throughout the known world. The churches were all together one Church in an organic, visible society. The early Fathers make this abundantly clear. For the first thousand years, this unity prevailed under the hierarchy of the bishops in union with the See of Rome. Throughout the first one thousand years of Christian history there was only one Church—the Catholic Church. In other words, the creeds held, and the unity prevailed. Of course, there were heretics and schismatics, but they left the one Church or were excommunicated, and they were therefore no longer part of the Catholic Church. The Church of Rome, and her bishop in succession from St. Peter, have *from the first century* held a place of preeminence, the See of Peter.[82] To my great surprise, I found that the

---

81 For the sake of simplicity and truthfulness I will refer to the Eastern Orthodox churches in the plural, not in the singular. There is no central leadership to tie the various jurisdictions into one coherent whole. Each jurisdiction is headed by a patriarch, but there is no single, overall hierarchical structure as in the Catholic Church. The Orthodox have always depended upon the secular ruler, the emperor, to call the various Orthodox churches together for ecumenical councils. Since there is no emperor representing all the Orthodox churches, they have been unable to come together as a unified whole for more than one thousand years. They hold to the same ancient traditions as Catholics but have no mechanism for unification into one cohesive whole. Therefore, they are in actuality churches, in the plural.

82 Mt 16:17–19; Jn 21:15–17. The clear testimony of Scripture and history demonstrates the primacy of Peter and the subsequent primacy of Rome.

primacy of Peter in the See of Rome was acknowledged universally by the Orthodox Christians, even in the earliest centuries. Loyalty and obedience to the bishop of Rome was loyalty to Peter.[83] The Eastern churches have continued to affirm the primacy of Rome, but only as a first among equals. The Eastern churches were Greek speaking, the Western Church spoke Latin; the Eastern churches were mystical, the Western was more legal minded; the East accepted things as mysteries, the West was more concerned to define the mysteries in order to counteract heresies and to develop doctrine further.[84] In the year 1054, for a number of reasons, the unfortunate split between East and West took place.[85] Even though they recognized each other as having legitimate apostolic succession and valid sacraments, they were separated. This was the first major split in the first thousand years of the Church. With this short explanation, we will go on, but we will come back to the Orthodox churches again in our story.

By this time Janet and I knew we were no longer Protestants and

---

Peter was clearly appointed as the rock upon which Christ would build his Church, and even Protestant scholar J. Jeremias acknowledges that "only in Jn 21:15–17, which describes the appointment of Peter as a shepherd by the risen Lord, does the whole Church seem to have been in view as the sphere of activity" (Gerhard Kittel and Gerhard Friedrich, eds., *Theological Dictionary of the New Testament* [Grand Rapids, Mich.: Eerdmans, 1968] 6:498).

83 St. Cyprian (martyred in 258) said, "There is one God and one Christ, and one Church, and one Chair founded on Peter by the word of the Lord. It is not possible to set up another altar or for there to be another priesthood besides that one altar and that one priesthood. Whoever has gathered elsewhere is scattering" (*Letter of Cyprian to All His People,* 43 (40), 5, in Jurgens, *Faith of the Early Fathers*, 1:229).

84 Development of doctrine is a key and crucial responsibility of the Church. The Bible is not a doctrinal textbook or manual. Systematic definition of doctrine is needed. The doctrine of the Blessed Trinity, as formulated in the Nicene Creed, is an excellent example. The word "Trinity" is not used in the Bible. It was not coined until the year 180, by St. Theophilus of Antioch. It was simply defined at the Council of Nicaea in 325 and more firmly defined by later councils of the Catholic Church.

85 There were a number of reasons for the final split, which was only exacerbated by geographical distances, language, and culture. The major issues were the *filioque* in the Creed (which stated that the Holy Spirit proceeded from the Son as well as from the Father) and the primacy of the pope, bishop of Rome.

never could be again with a clear conscience—but what were we? We knew what we *weren't*, but we didn't know what we *were*. We had gone through a passageway, leaving a familiar homeland behind, but we didn't know what land we now inhabited. We were sojourners and aliens. We quit going to Protestant churches, though we were chastised for it by our Protestant brethren. For a while we just stayed home on Sunday mornings, raised our family, homeschooled our children, studied the Scriptures, managed our family business, and met regularly with Christian friends. Before our initial studies on the Catholic Church, we had never considered any other alternatives to Evangelical Protestantism; or, I should say, based on what we had known, there were no other alternatives. Through our whole Evangelical experience, the Catholic Church was not even on our radar screen. We had always placed the Catholic Church in the same category as the Jehovah's Witnesses, the Moonies, and the Mormons. Now we had crossed over a line, and there was no return; we were without a "homeland." I find this is a common experience with those who begin approaching the Catholic Church. The comfortable homeland of American Evangelicalism begins to drop out from beneath them, leaving the poor souls with the unsettled feeling of being lost.

The Final Stages of Our Journey

We have known Al and Sally Kresta since 1983, and we've always relished our friendship. The hours we've spent discussing theology, history, society, and related issues over the years would number in the hundreds. We first met them at Trinity House Theater in Livonia, Michigan, which was sponsored by Trinity Baptist Church. Six actors impersonated six famous theologians. Al Kresta played the role of my hero, Dr. Francis Schaeffer—complete with graying beard and knickers. Janet and I were quite impressed with Al's accuracy and eloquence as he played the part. Al pastored an Evangelical church in the Detroit area and was the talk-show host of the most popular Christian radio program in the area. In 1990 Al sorrowfully resigned his pastorate, and on Holy Thursday in 1992 he quietly joined the Catholic Church.[86] Janet and I were shocked! What a strange thing to

86 Al Kresta's conversion story can be read in *Surprised by Truth*, ed. Patrick Madrid (San Diego, Calif.: Basilica Press, 1994).

do, we thought. We'll watch and wait. Watching was easy, because Al and Sally never pushed the issue, never attempted to proselytize, and said very little about it.

They started a tumult in our lives, though, with two simple actions: they answered a question for Janet,[87] and they gave us a book to read. The book was entitled *Evangelical Is Not Enough*.[88] Janet read the book each evening and shared it with me as she read. At the time I wasn't very interested. I had already resolved to be a "Lone Ranger" Christian. Finding a Church that would fit the Scriptures and the early Church seemed out of the range of possibility.

As Janet read the book, something beautiful and profound clicked inside her, like a light switch; but me . . . no, not me. I was too busy to pursue such a wild-goose chase, and there was no way I was going to join the crazy Catholic Church, so why waste time reading the book? Janet continued for some time to read and pursue the issues raised in the book before I had the least spark of interest. She found other books and quietly read them, informing me each evening of her discoveries. I'm not sure I would have pursued the Catholic faith as I

87 Janet asked Al, "How can you justify praying to Mary?" Al thought for a moment and answered, "Think of it as praying with Mary instead of praying to her." Janet realized immediately what he meant. As Evangelicals, we just automatically thought that those who have died are gone. An Evangelical recently asked me, "Where does it say in the Bible we should pray to dead saints?" to which I responded, "Where in the Bible does it say saints are dead?" Arguing with the Sadducees, Jesus said, "You are wrong, because you know neither the scriptures nor the power of God. . . . Have you not read what was said to you by God, 'I am the God of Abraham, and the God of Isaac, and the God of Jacob'? He is not God of the dead, but of the living" (Mt 22:29–32). Jesus again proved the saints are still alive by talking with Moses and Elijah on the Mount of Transfiguration. As a Protestant I used to argue that there is only one mediator between God and man (1 Tim 2:5); therefore we could not appeal for the intercession of the saints or Mary. However, I failed to realize that every time I asked a friend to pray for me, I was asking him to be a mediator by interceding for me. Why had we been taught that this "great cloud of witnesses" (Heb 12:1) doesn't really exist and that they don't care about us on earth still fighting the good fight?

88 Thomas Howard, *Evangelical Is Not Enough* (San Francisco: Ignatius Press, 1984). This book was written before Howard himself converted to the Catholic Church. For the full story of his conversion, read his *Lead, Kindly Light* (Steubenville, Ohio: Franciscan Univ. Press, 1994).

have if Janet had not opened the door and taken the first steps over the threshold. Janet described *Evangelical Is Not Enough* in this way, "Thomas Howard put into words what I have deeply felt over the last years but didn't know how to verbalize. He said what I sensed and knew but didn't understand."

On one occasion, about a year later, when the Krestas were over for the afternoon, we cautiously brought up the topic of their conversion again and with a somewhat sarcastic smile asked Al and Sally if they regretted their decision to become Catholics. You see, we had a pretty good idea that they would regret their ill-advised adventure after the first year. Their answer, however, surprised us and sent us on an extended adventure of our own. They both responded, "No, we don't regret it. In fact, it is one of the best decisions we have ever made." Al became more serious, and Sally lit up like a light bulb. Should we drop the discussion and change the subject, or should we open the door farther and ask them *why* they were so happy about being Catholics? Janet and I took a deep breath and looked hesitantly at one another. It was a dangerous move, but someone had to do it. I asked Al why . . . . And the ancient Church arose that day for the first time as a real alternative, as the country we longed for and could now enter ourselves. Not only was she an alternative, but, after a long day of questions, discussions, and scriptural study, she became a very viable alternative. But there were many obstacles—big obstacles. We knew we were no longer Protestants—that was a painful realization we had come to quite a while before—and now we discovered there was an "ancient Church." But it still wasn't that easy. Which ancient Church? We now faced another dilemma.

Our First Move Is Toward the Eastern Orthodox Churches

Now we come back to our discussion of the Orthodox churches. There are three basic branches of Christianity: Roman Catholicism, Eastern Orthodoxy,[89] and Protestantism. We knew we were no longer

89 The Eastern Orthodox churches shared the common heritage and structure of the Catholic Church for the first one thousand years. Though they divided over the primacy of Rome and the filioque, Catholics and Orthodox share the same doctrines of the sacrificial nature and the Real Presence of Christ in the Eucharist, baptismal regeneration, liturgical worship, the hierar-

Protestants, so now the problem grew slightly less complicated. Now there were only two choices, not the twenty-three thousand choices within Protestant denominations.[90] Our search now came down to the remaining two, and the Orthodox route seemed easier and less complicated. The Orthodox do not define all the Marian doctrines as dogma, they do not forbid contraceptives, and they do not have a pope. Maybe more important, most Evangelicals don't know who or what they are, so you can join an Orthodox church without making a big scene. *Everyone* thinks he knows what the Catholic Church is. Our experience has shown that when you announce you are going to an Orthodox church, people simply say, "That's nice. I haven't really heard of them; where do they meet?" Conversely, when you announce you have become Catholic, people gasp, roll their eyes, and blurt out, "Oh no, you've got to be kidding. I remember those nuns from school days. Why are you joining that corrupt organization when all the real Bible Christians are leaving for a real church?" You can slip into the Orthodox churches, have all the advantages of the Eucharist, apostolic succession, confession, and the rest, yet be free of the "recognition factor" you must bear if you join the Catholic Church.

Francis Schaeffer's son Frank came to speak in the Detroit area in the fall of 1993. I had heard him speak many times before on the issues of abortion and the decline of our Western culture, and he always promoted Evangelical Christianity as the solution to the problems. To my utter amazement he had recently become an Eastern Orthodox Christian. An odd thing for the son of Francis Schaeffer to do, we thought. What would his dad think? We went with a few friends to hear him speak of his conversion, and they were just as skeptical as we were. We were intrigued from the opening statements. Janet and I were very impressed, and we discussed these radical ideas with our friends late into the night. These ideas had a historical continuity and a compelling magnetism—we were strongly attracted. In the months to come we bought and read all the Orthodox books we

---

chical structure of the Church with bishops, priests, and deacons, apostolic succession, holy tradition, veneration of saints, devotion to the Virgin Mary, icons, the teachings of the early ecumenical councils, etc.

90 See Frank Schaeffer's book *Dancing Alone* (Brookline, Mass.: Holy Cross Press, 1994), 4.

could find.

My daughter Cindy and I went to our annual father/teen daughter canoe trip in October 1993. My backpack was filled with books; I was really interested now and was reading everything I could get my hands on, including a book by Peter Gillquist titled *Becoming Orthodox*.[91] During free times I would grab this book and read about how he and his group had become Eastern Orthodox Christians. I was minding my own business but was routinely "attacked" by several other campers. They told me I was foolish for reading such a book—those liturgical churches were idolatrous and following the traditions of men. I was forced to explain my reasons for doing this kind of reading and was soon defending the basic tenets of the ancient Church. Entirely new to the topic, I found myself in an uncomfortable but exhilarating position. It compelled me to put my thoughts and impressions into words. It also gave me an indication of what I might expect if someday, heaven forbid, I were to convert to one of these ancient churches.

Janet's and my curiosity and fascination were increasing rapidly, so one Saturday we had Al and Sally over for dinner again. They arrived early, and for ten straight hours we asked hundreds of questions and got into intense discussions. "Why Catholicism instead of Orthodoxy? Why do you accept the pope when the Orthodox don't? What are the pros and cons of the two similar traditions?" I called my friend Paul Brandenburg[92] in Lansing. I asked, "Paul, why are *you* a Catholic and not an Evangelical? Why aren't you Orthodox?" We talked for a long time; he was very helpful. It was his opinion that anyone really serious about the doctrine of ecclesiology—the Church would eventually find himself in the Catholic Church. He sent me a set of tapes by two other converts: Peter Kreeft and Thomas How-

91 Peter Gillquist, *Becoming Orthodox* (Ben Lomond, Calif.: Conciliar Press, 1992). This book details the journey of a large group of Christians from their Evangelical roots as leaders in Campus Crusade for Christ to Eastern Orthodoxy. Many congregations, numbering in the hundreds, joined en masse.

92 Paul and I had been friends in Detroit when we were still toddlers. We kept in touch over the years. In 1976 he was hitchhiking near my parents' home and stopped in. I gave Paul a pile of books (along with my excitement), and he took them back to his university and became a Christian. He graduated with a degree in law and became an attorney. I was grieved when I found out he had become a Catholic.

ard. I finished reading *Evangelical Is Not Enough*, along with a pile of other books from both Catholic and Orthodox perspectives. We attended a five-week study series promoting Orthodoxy, which was taught by three Orthodox priests from the Detroit area. We visited Russian, Romanian, and Greek Orthodox churches.

We Take the Plunge

We were realizing that "Lone Ranger" Christianity was not an option our Lord had left us. He had established a Church and expected us to be in the visible fold. We could not sit on the fence forever, dwelling in no man's land. Does one ever have exhaustive information at his fingertips? No, but one can have enough assurance to make a decision. When it boiled down to a choice, we couldn't become Eastern Orthodox and had to go with the Roman Catholic Church. The choice was not marginal, however; it was overwhelming and unequivocal. Without going into great detail, our choice was finalized by several issues: the development of doctrine of the Catholic Church and her Western experience and influence, the concept and theology of ecclesiology and the unity of the Church, the Magisterium as a principle of unity and finality, the intellectual approach of the Western Church, the two-thousand-year continuum through Peter to the present day, and the primacy of Rome, among many others.[93]

When we first read the postscript to *Evangelical Is Not Enough*, we considered it something of a weak sidestep, an attempt to avoid the

93 I have an informal list put together by Al Kresta entitled "Why I Didn't Go into the Orthodox Church." Some of the reasons mentioned are a history of frequent lapses into heresy (confirmed by Orthodox historian Timothy Ware in *The Orthodox Church*, 2d ed. [London and New York: Penguin Books, 1993]), the Orthodox churches' unfamiliarity with the West, overemphasis on ethnicity, lack of clear authority and unity, jurisdictional confusion, frozen theological development, closed or seclusive mentality of indifference (Gillquist's experience in Greece, for example), and seeming inability to deal with modernity. In addition to the above, Janet and I also had secondary reasons, such as the lack of activities and private schools for the children and the shortage of scholarly reading material. All of these matters played a part in our turning from Orthodoxy to the Catholic Church. I have nothing against the Orthodox churches and feel tremendous goodwill toward then. I rejoice in their loyalty to the truth and our mutual faith and traditions; and I feel free to enjoy fellowship with them. I also pray for the restored unity of these great segments of Christendom.

issues in a tough decision. Thomas Howard wrote,

> It would strike a partisan note which I have no wish to strike here if I were to embark on a detailed account of the steps which took me from Canterbury to Rome. Perhaps the simplest way of putting the matter would be to say that it is the same old story which one finds in Newman, Knox, Chesterton, and all the others who have made this move. The question, What is the Church? becomes, finally, intractable; and one finds oneself unable to offer any very telling reasons why the phrase "one, holy, catholic, and apostolic," which we all say in the Creed, is to be understood in any way other than the way in which it was understood for 1,500 years. I am sharply aware of the fissure between the Latin and Orthodox churches in this matter, and on this point I must dodge behind a manifestly flimsy shield, namely, that I, as a solitary layman, cannot untangle what these churches have been unable, for 1,000 years, to untangle. I am a Western Christian, for good or ill. But I have no quarrel—no quarrel at all— with anyone who will own the name "Christian" with all that that noble name has meant since the Day of Pentecost. Yes—I believe that the Roman Catholic Church is the Ancient Church. I accept its claims. I believe that here one finds the *fullness* ("catholicity") of the Faith.[94]

Now, having struggled with the same decision, Janet and I acknowledge and accept the wisdom of his words.

The Dawn of a New Year

I will get back to our story: we were still delving into the Scriptures and the writings from the first centuries of the Church to be sure we were on the right track. On December 31, 1993, we were reading books and discussing our findings. When darkness arrived, we drove two country miles to spend New Year's Eve with some longtime friends and fellow Evangelicals. The discussion inevitably gravitated toward our "lunacy": "You're not really serious about this whole thing, are you?" Yes, we were, and we admitted it. Tradition and Scripture became the heated topic that brought in the New Year. As we sipped champagne and watched our children running around, we argued the Catholic issues—we had a long and deep friendship. We had always

---

94 Howard, *Evangelical Is Not Enough*, 157.

discussed important matters as really good friends are wont to do. After the fireworks were over, we slowly drove home. On the way home, I said, "Janet, I think I've finally argued myself right into the Catholic Church without meaning to do so." We went to bed and got up the next morning, both deep in thought. The tapes Paul Brandenburg had sent were still on my desk, waiting to be listened to, so we popped them into the tape deck. Peter Kreeft and Thomas Howard were telling the tale of their Fundamentalist Protestant backgrounds, their godly families, and their eventual conversions to the Church. Within a few minutes we were listening intently—laughing and crying—as we moved through all three tapes. We were traversing similar territory, and their stories rang loud and true. A spiritual transformation was taking place in my mind and heart and I knew it; a struggle between my Evangelical Protestant tradition and the ancient and universal tradition of the Church was raging in my soul. When the last tape came to an end, I turned to Janet. After a few moments' reflection and a deep sigh of relief I calmly declared, "I am a Catholic." My sense of joy and relief can never be described. The mental turmoil and searching were over. I was home.[95] Tears were streaming down my face. The sense of having "arrived" filled my whole being—I was a fulfilled Christian! Janet understood but responded with some alarm, "Oh, yeah, I'm not quite ready to commit myself to that yet."

I felt like old Scrooge on Christmas morning, after he finally emerged from the nightmares, dancing and singing— "giddy like a schoolboy." I quickly grabbed the phone and dialed Al Kresta. "Al, guess what, I'm a Catholic!" There was a stunned silence on the other end of the line, then a stuttering "Well, well, that's really good. Wow, what a surprise. Are you sure? What happened?" I explained the events of the last twenty-four hours. He quickly gained his composure and asked if we would like to attend a Catholic church and go to

---

95 In my daily journal for January 1, 1994, I wrote, "I have basically crossed the line, I had, in arguing with others, argued myself right into the Catholic Church. I have mentioned these things [my investigations] to others over the last year, and they have immediately attacked with a barrage of clichés and arguments, trying to discredit the Catholic and Orthodox churches. I am not even a Catholic yet, and they attack my simple attempt to understand the 'other Christians'. I have been pushed repeatedly into defending a position that I have not yet accepted and, in the process, have argued myself right in."

Mass the next day. Wait a minute! Hold the phone! I had decided to be Catholic, but I had said nothing about going to a Mass! Neither Janet nor I had ever, ever set foot in a Catholic church, and we had never met a real Catholic priest. We'd only seen caricatures in the movies and on television. All of a sudden I realized the import of what I had announced to him. G. K. Chesterton wrote, "This process, which may be called discovering the Catholic Church, is perhaps the most pleasant and straightforward part of the business; easier than joining the Catholic Church and much easier than trying to live the Catholic life."[96] Being a Catholic "intellectually" led unremittingly to commitment. If I went through with this whole thing, it meant I would have to join the Catholic Church—I would have to go to Mass! I had been told horror stories about the Mass: pagan worship, the recrucifixion of Christ, prayers to statues, and the ever-stifling, dead liturgy with no Bibles in sight. Now it was my turn to stumble for words. I put my hand over the phone. "Janet, Al wants us to go to Mass tomorrow!" We nodded our heads at each other and told Al we would try it. He told us to meet him at Domino's Farm the next day, Sunday morning. I hung up the phone. Janet and I just stared at each other. What had we gotten ourselves into this time?

How can I explain our experience that morning? It is hard to relay all that happened, but I will do my best. We drove into the Domino's Farm parking lot at 10:45 a.m. Sunday morning, January 2, 1994. We were ready for anything and everything. Remember, neither of us had ever entered a Catholic church prior to that morning. We were so leery that we left our kids at home, not knowing what to expect. We wanted to enter late and sit in the back row—ready for a quick exit if my worst fears proved a reality; we had discussed it while driving. Al and Sally found us seats in the middle, right on the aisle—I'll never forget. We furtively looked around. The people all seemed to be normal, not much different from an Evangelical setting.

Al and Sally tried to make us feel comfortable. We had no idea what a missal was, so they quickly gave us a primer on the various sections, the readings, the prayers, and the Creed. The music started—violins, flutes, and guitars—and the robed priest with his entourage processed down the aisle right next to me. People began to

96 *Catholic Church and Conversion*, 91.

sing. Some hands went up in a gesture of worship. I recognized that the words of some of the songs were psalms from the Bible. I didn't think Catholics used the Bible in the Mass. Even after all the reading we had done, our old prejudices and misinformation bubbled to the surface. Where were the pagans and idol worshipers we were expecting to see? Was this the dry, dead liturgy we had heard so much about?

Then they began reading the Bible: three passages, with a psalm sandwiched between two of them. I lost track of everyone else in the room, including Janet. I began participating, listening to the Scripture readings, and worshiping God in the liturgy that millions upon millions of others were celebrating simultaneously. Then they recited the Nicene Creed, with which I was very familiar. They recited the Creed every week? I couldn't believe it!

About halfway into the liturgy, I suddenly realized that this exact *same* liturgy, with the exact same Scripture readings, was being celebrated around the world in Asia, Japan, Russia, New York, Israel, Egypt, South Africa, India, Rome, and everywhere else. I also realized, which compounded the thought, that this had been going on, not only all over the world, but in the *time* dimension as well, for two thousand years. This same ancient liturgy had been celebrated by the apostles, Polycarp, Tertullian, Irenaeus, Clement, Cyril, Athanasius, Augustine, and all the other saints and our predecessors in the early Church. Janet and I were taking part in a wondrous and marvelous historical event, and the profundity of the whole thing did not escape us; in fact, it enveloped and overwhelmed us with our first real sense of true worship—something we had never found in our past church affiliations.

To intensify our experience even further, we realized that the same liturgy is going on continuously in heaven before the throne of God. I was familiar enough with the Book of Revelation and its detailed explanation of the altar, the Lamb, the incense, the singing, and the worship to see the clear connection. In front of the throne of God stands the risen, victorious Lord, seen eternally as "a Lamb standing, as though it had been slain" (Rev 5:6). The risen Christ, the Lamb of God, the Bread of Life was here, right on the altar in the form of bread and wine! We were partaking of an eternal event, something that transcended space and time. We were joining in celebration and profound worship with the "one, holy, catholic, and apostolic Church" around the world and through all of time, even joining in with the hosts of heaven. I understood that we were all being transported up to the very royal chambers of God Almighty and that in his mercy and grace he had brought the heavenly liturgy, and the slain Lamb, right down into our very presence. Eternity piercing the veil of time, just as it had in the Incarnation.

The people around us were raising their hands to the Lord Jesus, singing out loud in obvious worship to the Creator of the universe, singing out loud with adoration. These were supposed to be pagans and statue worshipers, idolaters and the "unsaved." Janet and I were angry about the lies we had been fed and at the same time overjoyed to find a Church to match what we had read about. I must admit, Janet and I wept. I had quit singing and following along in the missal. Al leaned over in an attempt to help me find my place, thinking my lack of singing indicated I was lost in the liturgy. I blubbered out that it was the lump in my throat and the tears in my eyes that had silenced me.

Janet and I have never gotten over the experience of this first Mass. I will never forget the seat that I sat in. We drifted out in a daze and had lunch afterward, enchanted with the liturgy we had just experienced. We couldn't wait to return the following week to Christ the King Catholic parish. We had no idea that Masses were celebrated every day of the week in hundreds of thousands of locations. We thought you could go only on Sunday. Our children quickly joined in our enthusiasm and have grown to love the Church as we do. Fr. Ed Fride was the first Catholic priest we had ever met. We have come to love him for his dedicated service, his sincerity, and his genuine love for Jesus and the Church.

We Finally Come Home on Pentecost Sunday, 1994

Our excitement and joy did not wane over the next months. After visiting Christ the King for several weeks we asked how we could join. To our dismay, we discovered you can't just "join" the Catholic Church as you can an Evangelical church. We were told we would have to take what they called R.C.I.A. classes. "How long will that take?" we asked. They told us it would take many months, and then we could be received into the Church in about a year. We were stunned. "Look at this pile of books we've read over the last year. What else do we need to learn? We learned enough to cross the impassable chasm; isn't that enough to prove we really want to join? You don't have to take us through a year of classes to convince us. We are already Catholics!" Dennis Walters, chairman of the parish education commission, faithfully visited our home every Sunday evening for twelve weeks, teaching us the many facets of Catholic belief, life, and practice. He interceded with Fr. Ed Fride on our behalf so we could enter the Church by Pentecost Sunday.[97] I think we probably drove the poor man crazy with our phone calls and inquiries—rushing to get into the Church—but he was always patient, always smiling, and always ready to help.

The day we were received into the Roman Catholic Church will always be remembered as one of the greatest days of my life: Pentecost Sunday, May 22, 1994. Our children were baptized and confirmed. Al and Sally Kresta acted as sponsors for us and our daughter Charlotte; John McAlpine sponsored Cindy; Dennis and Suzie Walters sponsored Jesse; and my childhood friend Paul Brandenburg and his wife Trudie sponsored our daughter Emily. Joining the Church that day with us was a convert from a long line of Baptist missionaries, our newfound friend Rob Corzine.

And so our long journey came to an end—but really it was just the beginning. I can honestly say the thrill has not diminished. There hasn't been a Sunday Mass yet when Janet and I haven't had tears in our eyes and lumps in our throats. Every Sunday it's nearly impossible for me to get through special line of the Nicene Creed—dry-eyed, that is—that affirms our belief in "one, holy, catholic, and apostolic Church." We have not reduced our reading. How could we, when there is so much to learn. The Church is full of untold riches: saints, martyrs, confessors, bishops, depths of devotion, prayers of gold, traditions of inestimable value, a treasure chest of writings, history, stories of love, truth, and courage in which to immerse oneself. It is

97 Fr. Ed gave us a very thorough theology exam to see what we knew. It was the test theology teachers are required to take before they qualify to teach theology in the Catholic diocesan high school. We never did find out how we did on that test. After we were received into the Church, we asked Fr. Ed about the test, and all he would say is, "You're in, aren't you?"

impossible to describe the pleasure of finding our roots—our wonderfully exciting history—once treated as irrelevant and denigrated as "Catholic history." Consider someone suffering from amnesia and imagine the ecstasy he would experience when his memory was restored and he found that he was a king. Denominations frantically dig new ponds each generation and wade around splashing in the shallow eddies, but the Catholic Church has a depth that is unfathomable. It fills the soul with a thirst to read, read, read and to pray, pray, pray. There is no end to the pleasures awaiting the orphan who repatriates to the "one, holy, catholic, and apostolic Church." The more information we gather and study, the more our decision is confirmed, and the more we want to shout it from the housetops.

The closer we drew to the Church and to our final decision to cross the Tiber, the more we realized how hollow and uninformed the clamor against the Church is. G. K. Chesterton describes the opposition as "rags and tatters of stale slander and muddleheadedness which I am obliged to put first as the official policy of the opposition to the Church. These stale stories seem to count for a great deal with people who are resolved to keep far away from the Church. I do not believe they ever counted with anybody who had begun to draw near to it."[98]

Concluding Remarks

This has been but a simple outline, a skeletal framework, a bare-bones summary of a few of the thoughts and reasons why we have converted to the Catholic Church as proclaimed in the ancient creeds. Friends, family, and acquaintances have received our conversion with mixed reactions, from dismay to joy, from disbelief to anger. A few have asked questions and been interested in our decision, but most, unfortunately, have been defensive and hurt. Some think it was a move to "find ourselves" or "to get some meaning into our lives." That had nothing to do with it; our life was certainly not devoid of meaning. We were already Christians, so that was not the motivation. Others think our decision was a big mistake and that we'll "come around" sooner or later. Our conversion certainly cannot be reduced to such superficial explanations. The reasons behind it are plenteous

98 *Catholic Church and Conversion*, 84.

and multifaceted, and the discussion will carry on into the future.

As for ourselves, we are pleased and overjoyed with our decision and at perfect peace with the results. Our children have taken to the Church like fish take to water, often thanking me for bringing our family into the Church. One gets nowhere in life without taking risks and going on adventures. Those who sit safely within the fire's ring of light know nothing about the thrill of discovery, adventure, and danger. Bilbo Baggins broke the mold set for hobbits and experienced daring adventures; he was never the same again. We will never be the same either—blessed be God forever!

We will soon enter the next millennium. Times change, ideas change . . . our world acts as though *everything* were relative, as though there were no abiding truth, no absolutes to build upon. Everything is decided by relativism and the tyranny of the majority. If there are no absolutes, society becomes absolute. The twentieth century, the "enlightened century," has produced more horror, terror, bloodshed, and war, more inhumanity and decay, than all the preceding centuries put together. Those who believe we have made great progress with our philosophy of materialism and those who believe mankind is basically good by nature and without the flaws of sin have some explaining to do. No doubt we have advanced in wealth and technology, but these are impotent when it comes to providing meaning, morals, kindness, love, generosity, compassion, loyalty, self-control, faith, joy, and all the other things that are the *real* treasures.

Catholicism is the voice of sanity; as Chesterton said, "Catholicism is the only thing that saves a man from the degrading slavery of being a child of his time."[99] Janet and I happily rest in the sanity, peace, truth, and salvation of the Catholic faith. We stand in visible unity and a most profound historical continuity with the Lord Jesus, the apostles, the Fathers, the martyrs, the saints, and the whole, glorious Catholic Church. Here I stand; I can do no other!

We are not the first to cross the Tiber, we won't be the last—we are in good company!

---

99 *Catholic Church and Conversion*, 110.

PART TWO

BAPTISM IN THE SCRIPTURES AND IN THE ANCIENT CHURCH

Introduction: The Origins of Baptism

"The doctrines of the Catholic Church are men's doctrines, derived from pagan sources, and they began to infiltrate the Church after it became secularized and Christianity was accepted by Emperor Constantine as the official religion of the Roman Empire." This is what you will learn about the Catholic Church if you attend your average Fundamentalist church or Evangelical Bible study. I heard it a thousand times. I taught it myself. The early Church, we would say, has nothing in common with the Catholic Church of today. Is this assessment correct?[1] You will be able to answer that question for yourself

1 Tim Staples, a recent convert, writes, "The confusion I discovered at Jimmy Swaggart Bible College, contrasted with the Catholic doctrine I had been studying, made Rome look that much more attractive. I intensified my study of the early Church Fathers. If the Catholic Church *was* the fourth-century syncretistic invention of Emperor Constantine, as Jimmy Swaggart taught and as I had always believed, perhaps writings of the earliest Christian theologians and apologists would clear up my Catholic delusions. This was my last hope. I took Jimmy Swaggart's challenge: 'We would like to challenge the Catholic church to demonstrate that the saints and martyrs of the first three hundred years accepted the beliefs and practices of the Catholic church as it exists today. . . . All of the Early Church fathers were evangelical and Pentecostal and had no association with what is now recognized as the Roman Catholic Church.' I acquired a copy of J. B. Lightfoot's *The Apostolic Fathers* and devoured it. I went to the library on campus and began to study the lives and works of other Fathers of the Church, reading their writings in the original Greek and checking their theological arguments against what the Greek text of Scripture said. I researched all of the early councils of the Church. To my dismay, all I found was Catholic truth. I could not believe Brother Jimmy could have read what I read and issued his 'challenge'. The writings of the Church Fathers clearly show that the early Church was Catholic long before

as you read the following scriptural passages and the historical survey of the first five centuries of Christianity. I approached the teachings of the Catholic Church as a cautious Evangelical; I firmly believed I would find my favorite Protestant ideas central in the writings of the Fathers. I assumed the Fathers would be devoid of Catholic doctrines and that "Catholic" corruptions had crept in like cockroaches in the night, infiltrating the primitive and pristine New Testament Church. I was in for a big surprise! These were a part of the studies that helped me span the great divide, the gapping chasm between Fundamentalist Protestantism and the Catholic Church. You will have the source material right at your fingertips. I have added footnotes for each quotation so that you will be introduced to the passage of Scripture or the writer and given an explanation of the thoughts and reasons expressed.

In my journey to the Catholic Church, my main interest, in addition to the Scriptures, was in the first five centuries of the Church. I decided to concentrate my study on that particular era of Christian history to discover the truth, using primary sources. I delved headfirst into the writings of the apostolic Fathers (the disciples of the apostles) and the subsequent Fathers of the Church.

In the following sections, we will tackle the Church's teaching on baptism. Immersion or pouring? Infant baptism or baptism of adults only? Symbolic or effective? A simple sign or the means to new birth? We'll carefully analyze the Protestant tradition—what I believed as an Evangelical—and what the earliest Christians believed, including those who wrote the inspired writings we know as the Bible.

Baptism Was a Pagan and Religious Rite

Baptism was a ritual of purification that was practiced among various pagan cultures and also among the Jews.[2] The word baptism comes

---

the time of the Emperor Constantine" (Tim Staples, *Surprised by Truth*, ed. Patrick Madrid [San Diego, Calif.: Basilica Press, 1994], 216).

2 Presbyterian theologian Francis Schaeffer wrote, "There are two other signs given to mark covenant promises—circumcision in the case of Abraham and baptism in the case of Christians. But neither of these two tokens was new. They had been used by many people before and were simply given a Jewish or a Christian meaning—a definite meaning from God Himself " (*Genesis in Space and Time* [Downers Grove, Ill.: Inter-Varsity Press, 1972], 148).

from the Greek verb *baptizo* (βαπτιζω), which means to dip, to immerse, or to plunge. The word *baptizo* was used by the Greeks for the dipping of a cup into a vessel of water, or for dipping cloth into a vat of dye.

"Sacral [holy or sacred] baths are found in the Eleusinian and similar cults, in Bacchic consecrations, in Egyptian religion and the worship of Isis outside Egypt."[3] The *Egyptians* practiced a form of baptism for kings and the dead, with a view to renewal of life. They believed ritual washing of the dead would renew the spark of life in the next world. Baptismal baths are also found "in the Mithras mysteries, in the Apollinarian games and in the festival of Pelusium. . . .[4] There are many early examples of sacral water ceremonies in Babylon, Persia, and India. With the Ganges the Euphrates came to have a religious significance comparable with that of the Jordan among the Jews and Christians."[5]

The *Roman* mystery religions, before and during the time of Christ, worshiped the gods of the Isis mysteries, an oath of which is preserved on papyrus. "Before initiation, a confession of sins was expected. The candidate sometimes told at length the story of the faults of his life up to the point of his baptism, which was commonly a part of the initiation ceremony, and the community of devotees listened to the confession. It was believed that the rite of baptism would wash away all the candidate's sins, and, from that point on, his life would be changed for the better, because he had enrolled himself in the service of the savior god."[6]

The *Jews* also practiced baptismal and washing rites for the ceremonial cleansing of Levites (Nb 8:6–13) and for certain initiation procedures.[7] New converts from paganism to Judaism had to fulfill

3 Gerhard Kittel, *Theological Dictionary of the New Testament*, trans. And ed. Geoffrey W. Bromiley, 10 vols. (Grand Rapids, Mich.: Eerdmans, 1983), 1:530–31.

4 Ibid., 1:531.

5 Ibid.

6 S.v. "Mystery Religions," in *Encyclopedia Britannica*, vol. 12 (Chicago: Encyclopedia Britannica, 1981), 781–82.

7 Also priests washing hands (Ex 30:17–21), purification (Lev 11:24– 40), cleansing after contact with a corpse (Nb 19:11–22), leprosy (Lev 13– 14), after sexual situations (Lev 12, 15), etc.

certain obligations, which included the study of the Torah, circumcision, and a ritual bath to wash away the impurities of the Gentile background.[8] Various baptisms and washings were practiced among the Essenes in Qumran as early as 100 b.c. in the wilderness of Judea, where the Essenes emphasized the internal repentance that accompanied the outward act of washing.

The baptism of *John* was "a baptism of repentance for the forgiveness of sins" (Lk 3:3). John the Baptist was a Levite[9] in the line of Aaron and was performing a priestly and prophetic role. There is no certainty about the origin of John's baptism, whether it was instituted through divine revelation or developed from Jewish ceremonial washings; possibly it was borrowed from pagan sources (redeemed and consecrated for God). Whichever the case, John's baptism was, first of all, to turn the Jews from sin, back to their holy God, as a penitent people ready for their Messiah. Second, John's baptism looked forward to the Christian baptism for the forgiveness of sins and regeneration through the Holy Spirit. Third, we know it was through his baptism that the Lamb of God was revealed to John and proclaimed to the world.[10]

Baptism, therefore, was not a new invention of the Christian Church after Pentecost. It was preceded by pagan rites, Jewish ceremonies, Roman mystery religions, and John's baptism of repentance. After accepting the baptism of John, Jesus imbued the rite with power as a sacrament, developing it further with his apostles as the initiatory sacrament and the means of new birth.

---

8 Walter Elwell, ed., *Baker Encyclopedia of the Bible* (Grand Rapids, Mich.: Baker Book House, 1988), 1:257.

9 We read in Luke 1:5–6 that John's father was named Zechariah, a priest in the division of Abijah, a descendant of the high priest Aaron, from the line of Levi (1 Chron 24). Even John's mother was a daughter of Aaron. In this capacity, John was of the priestly line himself and a very appropriate person to recognize, baptize, and "ordain" Christ for his priestly ministry.

10 Jn 1:31–34: "I myself did not know him; but for this I came baptizing with water, that he might be revealed to Israel. And John bore witness, 'I saw the Spirit descend as a dove from heaven, and it remained on him. I myself did not know him; but he who sent me to baptize with water said to me, "He on whom you see the Spirit descend and remain, this is he who baptizes with the Holy Spirit." And I have seen and have borne witness that this is the Son of God.' "

Christ Redeems What Is Pagan and Makes It Holy

Everything belongs to God, the earth and all it contains, the people, the days, the times and seasons (Ps 89:11). God takes what has been corrupted or adulterated by sin and redeems it for himself. He can take pagan rituals and transform them through consecration to be used for his holy purposes. He takes sinful, pagan people, redeems them, and brings them into his Church. If God is not able to take sinful or pagan elements and redeem them for his use, we are all in big trouble. We as sinners saved by grace are excellent examples of this process of God's redemption.

Originally, Easter was the celebration of *Eastre*, the pagan goddess of spring, who brought new life after the death of winter. Her festival came at the spring equinox and was called *Eastron* (plural for *Eastre*). English-speaking Christians have appropriated the pagan name of Easter, in commemoration of Christ's Resurrection.[11] The Church, following the example of her Lord and the apostles, has the authority to continue redeeming the world, the peoples, and customs, giving them new meanings, consecrating them and making them holy to the Lord.[12] Even Protestants use the same marriage rituals and ceremonies of the pagan Romans (rings, veils, and so on), yet since these rituals are now sanctified by their Christian usage, Protestants feel no compunction about using them.

Jesus instituted baptism himself, both by his example and by his instruction.[13] The apostles and their successors within the early Church, having learned the doctrines of baptism from Jesus, obeyed Jesus' teaching and passed this rite of salvation and initiation on to

11 Joseph T. Shipley, *Dictionary of Word Origins* (New York: Philosophical Library, 1945), 131.

12 There are whole books written to "expose" the "fact" that the Catholic Church incorporated pagan practices and, in so doing, became a pagan religion. They conclude that the Catholic Church is therefore pagan, the figurative city of Babylon referred to in Revelation. Examples of such books include *The Two Babylons*, by Alexander Hislop, and *Babylon Mystery Religion*, by Ralph Woodrow. History shows the ludicrous nature of this argument. We ourselves were pagans at one time. Did we corrupt the Church as we entered, or did she, through the redemptive grace of God, redeem and purify us for God's service?

13 Mk 1:9–11; Jn 3:3–7, 22; 4:1–2; Mt 28:19; Acts 1:3.

the next generations of the Church, the Body of Christ.[14]

Scripture and the Church: A Unified Teaching

When surveying the Scriptures and the early Church, one cannot but be impressed with the unity of thought and consistency of doctrine and practice regarding baptism and regeneration. The following selections show the absolute consistency of the doctrine of baptism, not only in time, through the first fifteen centuries, but also in all corners of the known world where the Church had spread. Some may say that only the quotations that support the sacramental nature of Baptism are being represented in these selections. The answer again is: Not so; all mouths and pens spoke the same words. It was only heretics, Gnostics, schismatics, and unbelievers who denied the regenerating and renewing powers of water baptism. These would also be the ones who denied the Trinity, the deity of Christ, and the organic unity of the Church. Not until the late Middle Ages, after the German Reformation in the sixteenth century, did any in the Church accept and espouse contrary teachings, views that contradicted the clear and unwavering witness of the whole Catholic Church.

These profound gleanings from the universal, Catholic Church of the first centuries speak clearly for themselves. Some may say, "I don't really care what the apostolic Fathers and the early Church taught; if it were important enough for me to know, God would have put it in the Bible." I would ask them, "Is the Bible a doctrinal textbook—a comprehensive Church manual that clearly explains everything about the faith, with no ambiguities?" The answer is, obviously, No! There are many things, including important details of worship, hymn singing, marriage, child rearing, and even the books to be included in the New Testament, that are not taught in the New Testament. It was the apostolic tradition that taught and grounded the early Church, keeping her on course during the first centuries of growth and martyrdom.

Baptism vs. Faith

One last comment, even though it will be discussed in more detail later: there is no attempt here to pit baptism against faith, or belief

---

14 CCC 1114, 1210.

against baptism. Things are rarely that simple. Faith and baptism are two sides of the same coin. Are we saved by faith or by baptism? Are we saved by believing or by the Spirit? These are false dichotomies that should have no place in our thinking.

How does one receive salvation, justification, new birth, and eternal life?
By *believing* in Christ (Jn 3:16; Acts 16:31)?
By *repentance* (Acts 2:38; 2 Pet 3:9)?
By *baptism* (Jn 3:5; 1 Pet 3:21; Titus 3:5)?
By the work of the *Spirit* (Jn 3:5; 2 Cor 3:6)?
By *declaring* with our mouths (Lk 12:8; Rom 10:9)?
By coming to a knowledge of the *truth* (1 Tim 2:4; Heb 10:26)?
By *works* (Rom 2:6, 7; James 2:24)?
By *grace* (Acts 15:11; Eph 2:8)?
By his *blood* (Rom 5:9; Heb 9:22)?
By his *righteousness* (Rom 5:17; 2 Pet 1:1)?
By his *Cross* (Eph 2:16; Col 2:14)?

Can we cut any *one* of these out of the list and proclaim it *alone* as the means of salvation? Can we be saved without faith? without God's grace? without repentance? Without baptism? Without the Spirit? These are *all* involved and necessary; not *one* of them can be dismissed as a means of obtaining eternal life. Neither can *one* be emphasized to the exclusion of *another*. They are all involved in salvation and entry into the Church. The Catholic Church does not divide these various elements of salvation up, overemphasizing some while ignoring others; rather, she holds them all in their fullness.

What Does Baptism Do? Who Believes What?

The doctrine of baptism has been nearly lost in Protestant sentiments and theology. We must examine the place of baptism as the sacramental means of salvation and as the door into the "one, holy, catholic, and apostolic Church." While I was in the Protestant camp, there was such a fear of attributing *powers* to baptism (that baptism actually *did* something), that we always reduced it to a symbol only. Its sole purpose was to make a statement. This minimalist view arose, for the most part, in reaction to the Catholicism of the sixteenth century.

Where did this "symbolic view" of baptism come from? Where did it originate? You will see as you read that it did not come as a result of careful Bible study; nor did it begin with the apostles or in the early Church; nor did it originate in the Middle Ages. It was invented and developed as a doctrine of the Anabaptist movement, which broke away from Martin Luther's reform efforts.

The traditions of the ancient Church, as maintained in Roman Catholicism and Eastern Orthodoxy, hold to the sacramental and efficacious nature of baptism. These two most ancient branches of the Christian world concur. For the first fifteen hundred years there were no other doctrinal positions. However, a large segment of the *newest* wing of Christianity, the Protestants, denies the efficacy of baptism, holding to the recent Protestant tradition that baptism is an empty symbol, a mere statement of belief. This tradition was the result of a severe reaction to the past—it was reactionary. It was the result of a certain bias being inductively read into Scripture and into history.

As We Begin Our Journey into the Past

You can decide for yourself. We now proceed with our journey into the past, to uncover the teaching of the apostles and the Fathers of the Church who still had the preaching of the apostles ringing in their ears and the authentic tradition before their eyes. We will discover how the apostles' doctrine unfolded as the Church grappled with the issues of salvation and the sacrament of baptism. You will also want to consult the suggestions for further reading at the end of this book.

Baptism as Taught in Scripture

Genesis 1–3

"In the beginning God created the heavens and the earth. The earth was without form and void, and darkness was upon the face of the deep; and the Spirit of God was moving [hovering, fluttering] over the face of the waters. And God said, 'Let there be. . . .' And God saw everything that he had made, and behold, it was very good."[15]

---

15 Genesis unfolds the very beginning of the world as we know it. The world started out in darkness, without form, void and empty; much like a person without Christ, outside his Church. The pagan and those of the world are said to be in darkness (2 Cor 4:6; 6:14; Eph 4:18). The surface of the earth was covered with water, and God's Spirit was hovering over the water. Out

Genesis 6–8

"The Lord saw that the wickedness of man was great in the earth, . . . and it grieved him to his heart. So the Lord said, 'I will blot out man whom I have created from the face of the ground'. . . . But Noah found favor in the eyes of the Lord. . . . And God said to Noah . . . 'Make yourself an ark of gopher wood. . . . I will bring a flood of waters upon the earth, to destroy all flesh . . . ; everything that is on the earth shall die. But I will establish my covenant with you; and you shall come into the ark, you, your sons, your wife, and your sons' wives with you. . . . ' Noah did this; he did all that God commanded him. . . . And they that entered . . . went in as God had commanded

---

of the darkness God created light, and then from the waters he brought forth his first creation, the physical world. As the waters were gathered into their place, the land "rose" from the water, and from the land which had been under the water came forth plants, animals, and from the ground God formed man. A new world was brought forth from the water, by the agency of the Holy Spirit hovering over the waters. St. Theophilus of Antioch (d. *c.* 185) said, "Those things which were created from the waters were blessed by God, so that this might also be a sign that men would at a future time receive repentance and remission of sins through water and the bath of regeneration" (*To Autolycus*, in William A. Jurgens, *The Faith of the Early Fathers*, 3 vols. [Collegeville, Minn.: Liturgical Press, 1970–1979], 1:75). We will see the parallels to baptism, as God establishes his second creation, his Church. We know from Scripture and the Creed that Christ was the source of the first creation, since "through him all things were made." At his baptism, we see him creating again, as the firstborn of many brethren (Rom 8:29). Jesus in his earthly body was baptized, and the Spirit again hovered over the water and lighted on Jesus, initiating the second and new creation. So it is with each of us, as we are baptized and become new creations, "born from above," and placed in the Body of Christ.

St. Ambrose tells us in his treatise *On the Mysteries* 3, 8–11, "What did you see [in the baptistry]? Water certainly, but not water alone; you saw the deacons ministering there, and the bishop, asking questions and hallowing. . . . Believe, then, that the presence of the Godhead is there. . . . Consider, however, how ancient is the mystery [of baptism] prefigured even in the origin of the world itself. In the very beginning, when God made the heaven and the earth, 'the Spirit,' it is said, 'moved upon the waters.' He Who was moving upon the waters, was He not working upon the waters? . . . The water, then, is that in which the flesh is dipped, that all carnal sin may be washed away" (Philip Schaff, ed., *The Nicene and Post-Nicene Fathers*, 2d series, trans. H. De Romestin [Grand Rapids, Mich.: Eerdmans, 1983], 10:318).

him; and the Lord shut him in. . . . The flood continued forty days upon the earth; and the waters increased, and bore up the ark, and it rose high above the earth. . . . And all flesh died that moved upon the earth. . . . Only Noah was left, and those that were with him in the ark."[16]

Genesis 17, Exodus 12

"[And God said to Abraham:]'. . . This is my covenant, which you shall keep, between me and you and your descendants after you: Every male among you shall be circumcised. You shall be circumcised in the flesh of your foreskins, and it shall be a sign of the covenant between me and you. He that is eight days old among you shall be circumcised; every male throughout your generations, whether born in your house, or bought with your money from any foreigner who is not of your offspring, both he that is born in your house and he that is bought with your money, shall be circumcised. So shall my covenant be in your flesh an everlasting covenant.' "[17]

---

16 The story of Noah is a picture of baptism (1 Pet 3:20–22), as we will discover as we proceed in this historical survey. It is mentioned frequently not only in Scripture but in the writings and teachings of the Fathers. Notice not only the symbolism of salvation through water, through the agency of the ark, but also the dove alighting on the ark (like the dove on Jesus after his baptism) with an olive branch in its beak, which symbolizes renewal and peace. "The olive leaf has symbolized peace and heralded new life and hope ever since the early history of mankind, as so aptly expressed in the biblical story of the flood" (Michael Zohary, *Plants of the Bible* [London and New York: Cambridge Univ. Press, 1982], 56). Is the raven a type or prefiguring of sin that leaves the ark after the flood [baptism] and does *not* return?

St. Cyprian (martyred in 258) wrote, "For as, in the baptism of the world in which its ancient iniquity was purged away, he who was not in the ark of Noah could not be saved by water, so neither can he appear to be saved by baptism who has not been baptized in the Church which is established in the unity of the Lord according to the sacrament of the one ark" (*The Epistles of Cyprian* 73, 11, in Alexander Roberts and James Donaldson, eds., *The Ante Nicene Fathers*, arr. A. Cleveland Coxe [Grand Rapids, Mich.: Eerdmans, 1985], 5:389).

17 Gen 17:10–13. The covenant of God with his people Israel was a physical sign, applied to their bodies. Removal of the foreskin eight days after birth was the outward sign that actually *brought about what it signified* and made the baby a child of the covenant. We will see later that circumcision in the Old Covenant corresponds to water baptism in the New Covenant (Col 2:11–13).

"And when a stranger shall sojourn with you and would keep the passover to the Lord, let all his males be circumcised, then he may come near and keep it; he shall be as a native of the land. But no uncircumcised person shall eat of it."[18]

Exodus 14
"Then Moses stretched out his hand over the sea; and the Lord drove the sea back by a strong east wind all night, and made the sea dry land, and the waters were divided. And the people of Israel went into the midst of the sea on dry ground, the waters being a wall to them on their right hand and on their left. . . . Thus the Lord saved Israel that day from the hand of the Egyptians."[19]

The Second Book of Kings (period from 722 to 586 b.c.)
"Naaman, commander of the army of the king of Syria . . . was a mighty man of valor, but he was a leper. Now the Syrians on one of their raids had carried off a little maid from the land of Israel, and she waited on Naaman's wife. She said to her mistress, 'Would that my lord were with the prophet who is in Samaria! He would cure him of his leprosy.' . . . So Naaman came with his horses and chariots, and

---

The sign of circumcision prefigures that "circumcision of Christ," which is baptism.

18 Ex 12:48. Here we are presented with the two great ceremonies of the Old Covenant: circumcision, which is the initiation into the covenant people of God, and the Passover. These two correspond to the great sacraments of the Church instituted by Christ: baptism as the initiation into salvation and the Church; and the Eucharist, our Pasch, remembering the Body and Blood of the Lord, our Lamb of God. No one was allowed to eat the Passover until he had the seal of circumcision, and in the Church no one is allowed to eat the Eucharist until he has the seal of baptism. We know from St. Paul that circumcision in the Old Covenant has been replaced with baptism in the New Covenant (Col 2:11–12).

19 Ex 14:21–22, 30. The crossing of the Red Sea by the Israelites is a picture of Christian baptism (1 Cor 10:2). Their slavery in Egypt (symbolic of slavery to sin, the world, and the devil) was put to an end when they passed through the waters of baptism in the Red Sea and came out to eat spiritual food and spiritual drink from the spiritual rock that followed them, and that rock was Christ. Here we have two great sacraments of the Church: baptism and the Eucharist. We will discuss this further when we touch on 1 Corinthians 10 later in this study.

halted at the door of Elisha's house. And Elisha sent a messenger to him, saying, 'Go and wash in the Jordan seven times, and your flesh shall be restored, and you shall be clean.'

"But Naaman was angry, and went away, saying, 'Behold, I thought that he would surely come out to me, and stand, and call on the name of the Lord his God, and wave his hand over the place, and cure the leper. Are not Abana and Pharpar, the rivers of Damascus, better than all the waters of Israel? Could I not wash in them, and be clean?' So he turned and went away in a rage. But his servants came near and said to him, 'My father, if the prophet had commanded you to do some great thing, would you not have done it? How much rather, then, when he says to you, 'Wash, and be clean'? So he went down and dipped himself seven times in the Jordan, according to the word of the man of God; and his flesh was restored like the flesh of a little child, and he was clean."[20]

The Prophet Ezekiel (592–572 b.c.)[21]

20 2 Kings 5:1–14. What an amazing story. Here we have a non-Jew, a pagan, who recognizes his disease and corruption. A servant girl, one of the Lord God's people, directs him to the prophet, who sends him to the Jordan River to cleanse himself. He claims the waters in Syria's rivers are preferable, so why bathe in the Jordan? When he does bathe, he is cleansed and his flesh is as new as a little child's. Notice the parallels and see why the early Church understood this event as an Old Testament picture or type of baptism. The unbeliever—the Gentile—is brought to the prophet of God by the girl, a picture of the Church that brings sinners to the sacraments. He denies that this water can do him any good. What is there about this water that can heal me? He is too blind and proud, too "secular," to believe water can do any such thing. He is challenged to try and does so. He is cured of his leprosy, cleansed of his sin, and is left with the flesh and conscience of a little child. Through baptism he is cleansed of his corruption and made clean and new, regenerated, born again. What a beautiful picture of the Church, her sacraments and the grace of God. (See St. Ambrose, *On the Mysteries* 3, 16, where he uses Naaman as an example of baptism.) Ephraem the Syrian refers to Naaman being cleansed and relates it to baptism, where our secret misdeeds are forgiven (*Hymns for the Feast of Epiphany* 5, 6). Also, notice Irenaeus' comments on Naaman later in this study.

21 Ezekiel was the third and last of the major Old Testament prophets, the successor of Isaiah and Jeremiah. Around 599 b.c., when he was about twenty-three years old, he was taken into captivity to Babylon along with all the Jewish people. Part of his prophetic ministry was to pronounce God's prom-

"Therefore say to the house of Israel, Thus says the Lord God . . . I will sprinkle clean water upon you, and you shall be clean from all your uncleannesses, and from all your idols I will cleanse you. A new heart I will give you, and a new spirit I will put within you; and I will take out of your flesh the heart of stone and give you a heart of flesh. And I will put my spirit within you, and cause you to walk in my statutes and be careful to observe my ordinances."[22]

The Prophet Zechariah (*c.* 520 b.c.)
"On that day there shall be a fountain opened for the house of David and the inhabitants of Jerusalem to cleanse them from sin and uncleanness."[23]

---

ise of future restoration, purification, and obedience of God's laws.

22 Ezek 36:22, 25–27. Almost six hundred years before Christ, Ezekiel explains what the New Covenant, the future covenant, will look like. Ezekiel tells the Jewish people what God will do and how he will do it. This passage seems to look backward to Israel's laws of purification and forward to the salvation in Christ. The Lord God says that he will "sprinkle clean water on you," which seems to harken *back* to the sprinkling of purification in the Law of Moses (e.g., Nb 8:7: the purification of Levites; Nb 19:17: the ashes of a burnt heifer are mixed with "running water" and sprinkled over people and objects in order to make them "clean"), and *forward* to the promised Messiah (e.g., Is 52:15: the coming Messiah will "sprinkle many nations," which seems to predict Matthew 28:19; the correlation with Jesus' words in John 3:3–5 cannot be missed). In Matthew 28:19, Jesus commands the disciples to "make disciples of all nations, baptizing them in the name of the Father, the Son, and the Holy Spirit."

23 Zech 13:1. The allusion to the coming of Christ, who would open a fountain of forgiveness for sin, is unmistakable. In *The Bible Knowledge Commentary*, ed. John F. Walvoord (Wheaton, Ill.: Victor Books, 1985), we read, "That day refers to the future day of the Lord. The phrase 'on that day' occurs 16 times in these three closing chapters. On the day of Christ's crucifixion the fountain was opened potentially for all Israel and the whole world. . . . This spiritual cleansing of the nation is associated in other passages of Scripture with Israel's spiritual regeneration and the inauguration of the New Covenant." We all know that the sign of the New Covenant is water baptism.

The eighteenth-century Protestant Matthew Henry, commenting on Zechariah 13:1, writes, "This fountain opened is the pierced side of Jesus Christ, spoken of just before, for thence came there out blood and water, and both for cleansing. And those who look upon Christ pierced, and mourn for their sins that pierced him, and are therefore in bitterness for him, may look again upon Christ pierced and rejoice in him, because it pleased the Lord thus

The Gospel of Mark (written in the last half of first century; event *c.* 30)
"John the baptizer appeared in the wilderness, preaching a baptism of repentance for the forgiveness of sins. And there went out to him all the country of Judea, and all the people of Jerusalem; and they were baptized by him in the river Jordan, confessing their sins. Now John was clothed with camel's hair, and had a leather girdle around his waist, and ate locusts and wild honey. And he preached, saying, 'After me comes he who is mightier than I, the thong of whose sandals I am not worthy to stoop down and untie. I have baptized you with water; but he will baptize you with the Holy Spirit.' "[24]

The Gospel of Matthew (written in the last half of first century; event *c.* 30)
"Then Jesus came from Galilee to the Jordan to John, to be baptized by him. John would have prevented him, saying, 'I need to be bap-

---

to smite this rock, that it might be to us a fountain of living waters" (Matthew Henry, *Matthew Henry's Commentary* [Peabody, Mass.: Hendrickson Publishers, 1991], 4:1464). We know from Paul (1 Cor 10:1–4) and the Fathers that the spiritual drink flowing from the rock was the Eucharist; we know as well that the water and blood flowing from Christ's side were understood to represent the sacraments of baptism and the Eucharist.

In their ten-volume *Commentary on the Old Testament* (Grand Rapids, Mich.: Eerdmans, 1978), Protestants C. F. Keil and F. Delitzsch explain, "By this water we have to understand not only grace in general, but the spiritual sprinkling-water, which is prepared through the sacrificial death of Christ, through the blood that He shed for sin, and which is sprinkled upon us for the cleansing of sin in the gracious water of baptism" (10:392). Martin Luther wrote, "This fountain might well and properly be understood as referring to Baptism, in which the Spirit is given and all sins are washed away" (*Luther's Works*, ed. Jaroslav Pelikan [St. Louis: Concordia, 1973], 20:331).

24 Mk 1:4–8 (parallel accounts in Mt 3:1–12; Lk 3:2–20; Jn 1:19–28). John testified that he baptized with water only but that the one who came after him, the Messiah, would baptize with the Holy Spirit. In other words, it would no longer be just symbolic but would be a sacrament. "Celebrated worthily in faith, the sacraments confer the grace that they signify. They are efficacious because in them Christ himself is at work: it is he who baptizes, he who acts in his sacraments in order to communicate the grace that each sacrament signifies" (CCC 1127). Not only would it be an outward sign, as the ceremonies of the Old Covenant were, but it would be a powerful inner transformation, brought about by Christ through the Holy Spirit.

tized by you, and do you come to me?' But Jesus answered him, 'Let it be so now, for thus it is fitting for us to fulfill all righteousness.' Then he consented. And when Jesus was baptized, he went up immediately from the water, and behold, the heavens were opened and he saw the Spirit of God descending like a dove,[25] and alighting on him; and lo, a voice from heaven, saying, 'This is my beloved Son, with whom I am well pleased.' "[26]

John the Baptist as recorded in the Gospel of John (written by St. John *c.* 90–100; event *c.* 30)

---

25 See the footnote for Genesis 6–8. The dove is often used in Scripture as a symbol of the Holy Spirit. Thus, the Holy Spirit, at the baptism of Christ, alighted on Christ as a dove. His baptism is our example (obvious from the context and the placement of John 3:3–5), and the Holy Spirit descending at baptism brings new life and peace—as on the ark.

26 Mt 3:13–17 (parallel accounts in Mk 1:9–11; Lk 3:21–22; Jn 1:31– 34). The most amazing thing happens—the sinless Jesus, God in the flesh, is baptized by John. Why? Jesus said it must be done "to fulfill all righteousness." This could be understood to mean "fulfill everything laid down by God." This might include: *first*, associating fully with mankind and the Jewish nation and complying with the purification rites of the Old Covenant; and *second*, initiating his ministry (he was thirty years old) with the descent of the Holy Spirit and the verbal confirmation of his Father from heaven. Heaven *made contact with earth*, so to speak, and the new creation, the Church, was under way. *Third*, and most important for this study, Jesus was baptized to set the example of baptism, which he would later teach as the means of being born again (Jn 3:3–5) for entry into the Kingdom of God. He was the firstborn of many brethren. He also made water baptism more than a mere symbol; it was now a sacrament, an outward sign that also works an inward grace. A *fourth* effect of Jesus' baptism, confirmed by many Fathers of the Church, was the sanctification of water for the purpose of the newly instituted sacrament.

The Trinity is revealed here in a clear and unmistakable demonstration: Jesus is baptized, the Spirit alights upon him, and the Father's voice is heard from heaven. Christian baptism is solemnly performed in the name of the three Persons of the Trinity: the Father, and the Son, and the Holy Spirit. At the moment of a catechumen's baptism, the three Persons of the Trinity work their grace upon the new believer: Jesus in redemption through his propitiatory sacrifice, the Spirit in regeneration, and the Father in declaring us righteous and in adopting us as his sons. Can anyone contemplate anything more glorious and profound?

Notice, especially for the remainder of this study, that there are two distinct elements in Jesus' baptism: water and the Spirit.

"John answered them, 'I baptize with water; but among you stands one whom you do not know, even he who comes after me'. . . . This took place in Bethany beyond the Jordan, where John was baptizing. The next day he saw Jesus coming toward him, and said, 'Behold, the Lamb of God, who takes away the sin of the world! This is he of whom I said, "After me, comes a man who ranks before me, for he was before me." I myself did not know him; but for this I came baptizing with water, that he might be revealed to Israel.' And John bore witness, 'I saw the Spirit descend as a dove from heaven, and it remained on him. I myself did not know him, but he who sent me to baptize with water said to me, "He on whom you see the Spirit descend and remain, this is he who baptizes with the Holy Spirit." And I have seen and have borne witness that this is the Son of God.' "[27]

Jesus Christ as recorded in the Gospel of John

"Now there was a man of the Pharisees, named Nicodemus, a ruler of the Jews. This man came to Jesus by night and said to him, 'Rabbi, we know that you are a teacher come from God; for no one can do these signs that you do, unless God is with him.' Jesus answered him, 'Truly, truly,[28] I say to you, unless one is born anew [from above],[29] he

---

27 Jn 1:26–34. This is John the Baptist's account of Jesus' baptism. He did not know who the Messiah was but was to recognize him when he was baptized and the Spirit of God descended upon him. Jesus was recognized in baptism, just as he was later recognized by the disciples in Emmaus in the "breaking of the bread." Jesus intended that we recognize him in the sacraments he gave his Church.

Here again we see water and the Spirit working together. In the beginning, the Spirit hovered over the water and brought about the first creation. Here again, the Spirit hovers over the water and, working through Jesus, begins the second creation of God. We go through the same event ourselves when we are joined to Christ through baptism and initiated into his one Body, the Church.

28 "Truly, truly" ("Amen, amen" in the Greek) sets the stage for a very profound and earth-shaking statement. It was a way of highlighting something—emphasizing it with capital letters. The double *Amen* is used only in the Gospel of John. Jesus uses it three separate times in his discussion with Nicodemus.

29 The Greek word ἀνωθεν can be translated in two ways: either "from above" or "again." It seems Jesus intended the meaning "from above," because later in the same context, in verse 31, he says, "He who comes from

cannot see the kingdom of God.' Nicodemus said to him, 'How can a man be born when he is old? Can he enter a second time into his mother's womb?' Jesus answered, 'Truly, truly, I say to you, *unless one is born of water and the Spirit,*[30] he cannot enter the kingdom of God. That which is born of the flesh is flesh, and that which is born of the Spirit is spirit. Do not marvel that I said to you, 'You must be born anew [from above].' "[31] . . .After this Jesus and his disciples went into the land of Judea; there he remained with them and baptized."[32]

---

above [ἄνωθεν] is above all." It seems that Nicodemus misunderstood Jesus' meaning, so Jesus immediately refers to an event still fresh in everyone's mind: his baptism. At his baptism, they had witnessed the "Spirit descend as a dove from heaven." This was birth from above— ἄνωθεν. (See also Jn 3:31; 8:23.)

30 Notice that Jesus does not create an *either/or* conflict, rather he explains a *both/and* reality. It is not *either* water *or* the Spirit; Jesus says it is *both* water *and* the Spirit. Fundamentalists have built watertight compartments, excluding elements that should work together. Why deny that God can work through the material means of water? As Oscar Cullman says, "It is important for the author here, as throughout the whole Gospel, that the Spirit is present in material elements just as the *Logos* became flesh" (*Early Christian Worship*, trans. A. Stewart Todd and James B. Torrance [Philadelphia: Westminster Press, 1953], 76).

31 How is one born from above? Water and the Spirit. What does Jesus mean? First, what had just happened to Jesus? A few days earlier Jesus had been baptized, and as he came out of the *water*, the *Spirit* came down from heaven. Here we have, within the contextual flow of St. John's Gospel, the baptismal example of Jesus, which clearly explains the *water* and the *Spirit.* Second, what does Jesus do immediately *after* his discourse with Nicodemus? "After this Jesus and his disciples went into the land of Judea; there he remained with them and *baptized*" (Jn 3:22). This is the only time Scripture mentions that Jesus baptized. It is significant within the context of John's narration about *water* and the *Spirit* that he concludes the discourse with the comment that Jesus then went out and baptized.

32 Jn 3:1–7, 22 (emphasis added). Jesus' meaning was clearly understood by the disciples (and all of the early Church), which we will see as we progress. The discussion with Nicodemus concerning baptism as the means of new birth is framed in a marvelous baptismal framework that could not have been missed by John. In fact, it appears to be quite intentional. We see Jesus baptized, with water and the Spirit, then his discourse with Nicodemus about water and the Spirit, followed immediately by the baptizing of his followers in the Jordan. How is it that some persist in denying the baptismal context and meaning behind the words of Jesus as recorded by the Apostle John almost

Jesus Christ as recorded in the Gospel of Mark[33]
"And he said to them, 'Go into all the world and preach the gospel to the whole creation. He who believes and is baptized will be saved; but he who does not believe will be condemned.' "[34]

Jesus Christ as recorded in the Gospel of Matthew[35]
"And Jesus came and said to them, 'All authority in heaven and on earth has been given to me. Go therefore and make disciples of all nations, baptizing them in the name of the Father and of the Son and of the Holy Spirit, teaching them to observe all that I have com-

---

seventy years later at the turn of the century? There is no doubt that John's readers understood these words to apply to water baptism as the sacrament of new birth, birth from above.

33 The oldest Greek manuscripts of Mark do not contain verses 9–20 of the sixteenth chapter. Walter Wessell explains it this way: "The best solution seems to be that Mark did write an ending to his Gospel but that it was lost in the early transmission of the text. The endings we now possess represent attempts by the church to supply what was obviously lacking" (*The Expositor's Bible Commentary*, ed. Frank Gaebelein [Grand Rapids, Mich.: Zondervan, 1984], 8:793). George Montague, S.M., agrees but concludes, "While not from Mark either, this [longer] ending appears in many ancient manuscripts and is considered as belonging to the canonical inspired scriptures. . . . The longer ending does contain important teaching, and it is accepted as the inspired word of God" (*Mark* [Steubenville, Ohio: Franciscan Univ. Press, 1992], 189–90).

34 Mk 16:15–16. Notice the clear parallel with Matthew 28:19–20, with the emphasis on teaching and baptizing. This passage does not suggest that baptism is an option or merely a symbol but rather that baptism, along with faith, is an indispensable prerequisite for obtaining salvation. This was the universal teaching of the early Church and continues in the Catholic Church to this day, which teaches, not either faith or baptism, but both faith and baptism. Baptism is called "the sacrament of faith" (CCC 1236).

35 We know that Jesus spent forty days with the disciples between his Resurrection and his Ascension. During these forty days, he taught them and gave them his commands ("instructions and commands to be done," used in both Acts 2:2–3 and Matthew 28:20). Jesus relayed instructions and commands "through the Holy Spirit to the apostles he had chosen" as to all they were to know, do, practice, and teach in making disciples and in establishing the Church. These oral instructions (traditions) were then carried out by the apostles in obedience to the Lord. See Jn 14:26.

manded you; and lo, I am with you always, to the close of the age.' "[36]

Peter preaching on the day of Pentecost in the Acts of the Apostles (written by Luke in the last half of the first century)
"Now when they heard this they were cut to the heart, and said to Peter and the rest of the apostles, 'Brethren, what shall we do?' And Peter said to them, 'Repent, and be baptized every one of you in the name of Jesus Christ for the forgiveness of your sins; and you shall receive the gift of the Holy Spirit. For the promise is unto you, and to your children[37]. . . . So those who received his word were baptized,

---

36 Mt 28:18–20. The authority mentioned here by Jesus is reminiscent of the keys of the kingdom given to Peter. How do the commissioned apostles make disciples? By teaching and baptism, based on their practice while with Jesus. "Jesus was making and baptizing more disciples than John (although Jesus himself did not baptize, but only his disciples)" (Jn 4:1–2). Baptism was the outward sign that also brought about the inward regeneration. It was not *apart from* faith and the grace of God but in conjunction *with* them. Many within the Anabaptist tradition downplay the necessity of baptism, but the Scriptures are clear about its importance and necessity, a teaching universally held by the Church. For example, St. Irenaeus, the disciple of Polycarp, who was himself the disciple of St. John, wrote, "And again, giving to the disciples the power of regeneration into God, He said to them, 'Go and teach all nations, baptizing them in the name of the Father, and of the Son, and of the Holy Spirit'" (*Against Heresies* 3, 17, 1, in Roberts and Donaldson, *Ante-Nicene Fathers*, 1:444).

37 Martin Luther understood this passage to include infants in the baptismal initiation. He taught: "Who is to be baptized? All nations, that is, all human beings, young and old, are to be baptized. . . . Little children should be baptized when they are brought to Baptism by those who have authority over them. How do you prove that infants, too, are to be baptized? Infants, too, are to be baptized because they are included in the words 'all nations'; [and] because Holy Baptism is the only means whereby infants, who, too, must be born again, can ordinarily be regenerated and brought to faith (Mk 10:13; Jn 3:5–6)" (*Luther's Small Catechism*, rev. ed. [St. Louis, Mo.: Concordia, 1965], 172–73). When the Anabaptists began to conflict with Luther, he appealed to the "*totius orbis constans confessio*," or the "constant confession of the whole Church."

John Calvin, the sixteenth-century Swiss reformer, also held unwaveringly to the necessity of infant baptism. In his *Institutes of the Christian Religion* (1536; trans. Henry Beveridge), Calvin devotes the whole of chapter 16 to paedobaptism (infant baptism) and defends the ancient sacrament most vociferously. He concludes the twenty-six page defense by stating, "Doubtless

and there were added that day about three thousand souls."[38]

Philip as recorded in the Acts of the Apostles

"But when they believed Philip as he preached good news about the kingdom of God and the name of Jesus Christ, they were baptized, both men and women."[39] "And behold, an Ethiopian, a eunuch, a minister of Candace, the queen of the Ethiopians, in charge of all her treasure, had come to Jerusalem to worship and was returning; seated

---

the design of Satan in assaulting infant baptism with all his forces is to keep out of view, and gradually efface, the attestation of divine grace which the promise itself presents to our eyes. . . . Wherefore, if we would not maliciously obscure the kindness of God, let us present to him our infants, to whom he has assigned a place among his friends and family, that is, the members of the Church" ([Grand Rapids, Mich.: Eerdmans, 1983], 2:554).

38 Acts 2:37–41. This is the first full-fledged "Gospel message" ever preached in obedience to the "Great Commission." The hearers are told to repent and be baptized *for the forgiveness of their sins!* Peter preaches that baptism is a prerequisite for the forgiveness of sins and a time at which they would receive the promised Spirit, as Jesus had at his baptism. We see the same elements again: belief, water, and the Spirit. This is the fulfillment of the Old Testament types we have noticed: creation, the flood, the Red Sea, Naaman, Ezekiel's prophecy, followed by Jesus' baptism and Jesus' discourse with Nicodemus. "Water and Spirit" is the repeated message of the Scriptures. It is interesting to note that Peter does not call on the crowd to have "faith alone" but exhorts them to repent and be baptized. Belief is assumed to be a prerequisite. In the same manner, when one is called to believe, baptism is assumed as a corollary. Would a Fundamentalist conclude from this verse that *faith* is not important because *it* is not explicitly mentioned? Of course not. Neither should he be unbalanced in the other direction, concluding that baptism is not necessary when belief is mentioned as shorthand for the whole initiatory package. Belief and baptism form one act of salvation: baptism is the sacrament of faith. This passage presents great difficulties for some Protestant commentators because they reject the clear import of Peter's words. F. F. Bruce quotes Professor N. B. Stonehouse: "Acts 2:38 assuredly confronts the interpreter with weighty problems" (F. F. Bruce, *The New International Commentary on the New Testament: The Book of the Acts* [Grand Rapids, Mich.: Eerdmans, 1984], 75). Why not just listen to what Peter says? There were no weighty problems for the first hearers or for the whole early Church. The confusion occurred only later, for those who accepted the novel views that denied the universal teaching of the Church. These Fundamentalist traditions emerged and became popular with the Anabaptist groups who sprang up in the sixteenth century.

39 Acts 8:12.

in his chariot, he was reading the prophet Isaiah. And the Spirit said to Philip, 'Go up and join this chariot.' So Philip ran to him, and heard him reading Isaiah the prophet, and asked, 'Do you understand what you are reading?' And he said, 'How can I, unless some one guides me?' And he invited Philip to come up and sit with him. . . . Then Philip opened his mouth, and beginning with this scripture he told him the good news of Jesus. And as they went along the road they came to some water, and the eunuch said, 'See, here is water! What is to prevent my being baptized?' And he commanded the chariot to stop, and they both went down into the water, Philip and the eunuch, and he baptized him."[40]

Peter as recorded in the Acts of the Apostles

"At Caesarea there was a man named Cornelius, a centurion of what was known as the Italian Cohort. . . . While Peter was still saying this, the Holy Spirit fell on all who heard the word. And the believers from among the circumcised [Jews] who came with Peter were amazed, because the gift of the Holy Spirit had been poured out even on the Gentiles. For they heard them speaking in tongues and extolling God. Then Peter declared, 'Can any one forbid water for baptizing these people who have received the Holy Spirit just as we have?' And he commanded them to be baptized in the name of Jesus Christ."[41]

---

40 Acts 8:27–38. It seems apparent that the apostles and first deacons (Acts 6:5) taught baptism as an elementary prerequisite for salvation. How did the eunuch know baptism was necessary if Philip had not explained it to him? Philip had apparently preached to him as Peter had preached on Pentecost: "Repent and be baptized for the remission of your sins." Notice also, in passing, that the eunuch recognized his need of an authoritative interpretation of the Scriptures.

41 Acts 10:1, 44–48. Here again we see the water of baptism and the Spirit of God, but in the reverse order. Why was the order switched? In the historical context, it had been ten years since the crucifixion, and only Jews had been baptized into the faith of the Church. Cornelius was the first Gentile (non-Jew) to become a Christian. Peter and the Jewish Christians could not get it through their heads that God was also the God of the Gentiles. God's family covenant with the Jewish nation was now expanding to become the covenant with *his Church*, which is made up of Jew *and* Gentile (Eph 2:11–13). Peter had a vision of unclean animals that God told him to kill and eat; God told him that nothing is unclean that he declares clean, referring to the Gentiles (Acts 10:9–20). When Peter preached to Cornelius the Gentile, he still did not

Luke (on the conversion of the Philippian jailer) in the Acts of the Apostles
"About midnight Paul and Silas were praying and singing hymns to God, and the prisoners were listening to them, and suddenly there was a great earthquake, so that the foundations of the prison were shaken; and immediately all the doors were opened and every one's fetters were unfastened. When the jailer woke and saw that the prison doors were open, he drew his sword and was about to kill himself, supposing that the prisoners had escaped. But Paul cried with a loud voice, 'Do not harm yourself, for we are all here.' And he called for lights and rushed in, and trembling with fear he fell down before Paul and Silas, and brought them out and said, 'Men, what must I do to be saved?' And they said, 'Believe in the Lord Jesus, and you will be saved, you and your household.' And they spoke the word of the Lord to him and to all that were in his house. And he took them the same hour of the night, and washed their wounds, and he was baptized at once, with all his family."[42]

Paul in his First Letter to the Corinthians (written *c.* 57)
"For the unbelieving husband is consecrated [sanctified] through his wife, and the unbelieving wife is consecrated [sanctified] through her

---

comprehend that Gentiles could become Christians and inherit the promise of the Spirit. And so, God dramatically demonstrated the fact to Peter. The Spirit descended, and Peter's eyes were opened to understand that Gentiles can receive salvation. The first thing he did was baptize Cornelius and his household (which would have included his servants and children). Again, water and Spirit.

42 Acts 16:25–33. The practice of baptizing the whole family, including children and infants, is in accordance with the practice of the apostles in the New Testament, who baptized whole households, which certainly included infants and servants. See Acts 11:14; 18:8; 1 Cor 1:16. It must be remembered that the Church was expressly Jewish for the first decade; the baptism of the first Gentile convert, Cornelius, took place about ten years after the Resurrection of Christ. The Jewish custom for circumcising proselytes into Judaism included the circumcision of children and infants along with the whole extended household. The Jewish converts to Christianity would have expected their children to be baptized into the Church with them—this was a new covenant, a better covenant—and being newer and better it would certainly not exclude children, who had been included in the old (see Ludwig Ott, *Fundamentals of Catholic Dogma* [Rockford, Ill.: Tan Books, 1960], 360).

husband. Otherwise, your children would be unclean, but as it is they are holy."[43]

The Acts of the Apostles (the conversion of St. Paul)
"And one Ananias, a devout man according to the law, . . . said to me, 'Brother Saul, receive your sight. . . . And now why do you wait? Rise and be baptized, and wash away your sins, calling on his name.' "[44]

43 1 Cor 7:14. According to the *Oxford Dictionary of the Christian Church*, many have seen in these words a reference to infant baptism, though this does not need to be seen as the only interpretation possible. "In the period of the New Testament, positive hints of Infant Baptism have been found in the fact that the children of Christian parents are said to be 'holy' whereas they might be 'unclean,' and that they are exhorted to obey their parents in the Lord (Col 3:20; Eph 6:1); and never is there a suggestion that they will have to seek baptism on reaching years of discretion" (F. L. Cross and E. A. Livingston, eds. [New York: Oxford Univ. Press, 1989], 701).

When the disciples blocked parents from bringing their children to Jesus, Jesus intercepted them and said, "Let the children come to me, and do not hinder them; for to such belongs the kingdom of heaven" (Mt 19:14). The parallel passage in Luke 18:15, "Now they were bringing even infants to him that he might touch them," uses the Greek word βρέφος, which means a "newborn infant in arms." Jesus does not want to keep children out of the Kingdom and demonstrates that his grace reaches to those of this age. He himself was circumcised on the eighth day in the initiatory rite of the covenant people of God, the Jewish nation (Lk 2:21). Baptism replaced circumcision (as we will see later) as the new initiation into the New Covenant, that of the Church. Many have considered this a foundational verse for infant baptism (e.g., John Calvin and Martin Luther).

44 Acts 22:12–16. Paul is stunned and blinded. What are the first recorded words he heard after seeing the bright light and falling to the ground? He heard Ananias say, "Be baptized, and wash away your sins, calling on his name." Was there any ambiguity in these words? Had God planned this whole event only to have Ananias get the gospel message theologically incorrect? Shouldn't Ananias have told Paul to have faith alone? The theology of Ananias was most assuredly correct, and he clearly presents the true apostolic teaching on baptism as it relates to faith and remission of sins—just as preached by Peter and Philip. This was the universal teaching of the New Testament Church. Paul would have understood this sacrament and its importance since he was a scholar of the Scriptures, a student of Gamaliel, and knew of the promised "sprinkling" and washing of the Messianic kingdom. Though the words of Ananias clearly state that the washing away of sins was a direct result of baptism, as a Protestant I resisted the word of God with reductionist statements such as: "His baptism was to be the outward and

Apostle Paul in the Letter to the Romans (written *c.* 58, twenty-eight years after the crucifixion)

"Do you not know that all of us who have been baptized into Christ Jesus were baptized into his death? We were buried therefore with him by baptism into death, so that as Christ was raised from the dead by the glory of the Father, we too might walk in newness of life."[45]

Paul in his First Letter to the Corinthians 10:1–4

"Our fathers were all under the cloud, and all passed through the sea [baptism], and all were baptized into Moses in the cloud and in the sea, and all ate the same supernatural food and all drank the same supernatural drink. For they drank from the supernatural Rock which

---

visible sign of his inward and spiritual cleansing." I was trying to reword the Scriptures to conform to my parochial tradition—yet I would have claimed to be a Bible Christian, the one who defended the literal interpretation of the New Testament. Since I *couldn't* reword Scripture, I resorted to "interpreting around" these passages to fit our preconceived ideas of what the Bible *should* say.

45 Rom 6:3–4. How seriously does Paul take the sacrament of baptism? Is it symbolic only, or is it symbolic with the sacramental ability, through God's action, to *perform* what it signifies? Notice Paul's allusion to John 3:5—new birth ("newness of life") brought about by our baptism. Paul is hearkening back to his own baptism and explains clearly to the Romans the power of baptism in our lives and in the unseen spiritual world. Some Fundamentalists deny that Paul refers to water baptism in this passage (e.g., Kenneth Wuest in *Romans in the Greek New Testament* [Grand Rapids, Mich.: Eerdmans, 1955]). But even the late Fundamentalist Harry Ironside, the famous author and pastor of Moody Memorial Church in Chicago, wrote, "Is this the Spirit's baptism? I think not. . . . It is establishment into the mystical Christ. Our baptism with water is a baptism unto Christ's death" (*Romans* [Neptune, N.J.: Loizeaux Bros.; 1973], 76). Protestant reformer John Calvin states, "Paul proves his previous assertion that Christ destroys sin in His people from the effect of baptism, by which we are initiated into faith in Him. It is beyond question that we put on Christ in baptism" (*Calvin's New Testament Commentaries*, 1540, trans. Ross Parker [Grand Rapids, Mich.: Eerdmans, 1980], 8:122). The *Catechism of the Catholic Church* states, "This sacrament is called Baptism, after the central rite by which it is carried out: to baptize . . . means to 'plunge' or 'immerse'; the 'plunge' into the water symbolizes the catechumen's burial into Christ's death, from which he rises up by resurrection with him, as a 'new creature' " (CCC 1214). This is clearly the belief of the Fathers regarding Romans 6 (see Tertullian's treatise *On the Resurrection of the Flesh* 47).

followed them, and the Rock was Christ."[46]

Paul in his First Letter to the Corinthians 6:9–11

"Do you not know that the unrighteous will not inherit the kingdom of God? Do not be deceived; neither the immoral, nor idolaters, nor adulterers, nor homosexuals, nor thieves, nor the greedy, nor drunkards, nor revilers, nor robbers will inherit the kingdom of God. And such were some of you. But you were washed, you were sanctified, you were justified[47] in the name of the Lord Jesus Christ and in the Spirit of our God."[48]

---

46 Here is a most interesting analogy from the Book of Exodus (which we referred to earlier in this study). How can one miss the clear reference to the sacraments in this passage? Again we are presented with *water* ("passing through the sea") and the *Spirit* ("the Lord was in the pillar of cloud by day and the pillar of fire by night"). Paul says "baptized . . . in the cloud and in the sea." Again we have the recurring theme of *water* and the *Spirit* working together to effect salvation and new birth from above. After their "baptism," the Israelites under Moses partook of the supernatural food and drink. Jesus makes the connection between the manna and his body in John 6 and turns water into wine in John 2. In the Church, one is first baptized for regeneration, and then one can partake of the Eucharist, the supernatural food of the Church. One passes through the sea (baptism) and then partakes of the spiritual food (Eucharist). Did Paul understand the sacraments? Of course he did, and he passed these great traditions on to the next generations (2 Tim 2:2).

Matthew Henry writes, "They had sacraments like ours. They were all baptized unto Moses in the cloud, and in the sea (v. 2), or into Moses, that is, brought under obligation to Moses' law and covenant, as we are by baptism under the Christian law and covenant. It was to them a typical baptism" (*Commentary*, 6:554).

47 These theological terms may appear to be in the wrong order for typical Evangelical definitions, since it is usually held that justification, the act of "being saved," comes first and is followed by sanctification, which is never really clearly defined but seems to be a move toward moral and spiritual change. There are considerable differences among Protestant groups concerning the nature of sanctification. Paul treats these terms synonymously in this passage and places sanctification in front of justification. But beyond that: Paul uses the aorist tense for these terms, which in the Greek portrays a completed action. We *were* washed, we *were* sanctified, we *were* justified.

48 Paul had heard this word "washing" before. It is the Greek word ἀπολούω, and it is used only twice in the New Testament: here in 1 Corinthians 6:11 and in Acts 22:16, describing Paul's own baptism. The word comes from *louo*, "to wash," and the preposition *apo*, "off" or "away." The Greek tense

Paul in his First Letter to the Corinthians 12:12–13
"For just as the body is one and has many members, and all the members of the body, though many, are one body, so it is with Christ. For by one Spirit we were all baptized into one body—Jews or Greeks, slaves or free—and all were made to drink of one Spirit."[49]

Paul in his Letter to the Galatians (written *c.* 50)
"For as many of you as were baptized into Christ have put on Christ."[50]

---

is aorist, which denotes one point in time. It is not a continuing or currently present activity. Paul understood what he was saying, for the words had been said to *him*, at *his* conversion, in reference to *his* baptism and the *washing away* of *his* sins. Here again we have the two elements expressed by Jesus in John 3:5: *water* and the *Spirit.* Notice also that God, Jesus, and the Spirit are all mentioned, a fact that probably ties this passage in with the trinitarian formula for baptism given by Jesus in Matthew 28:19.

Gerhard Kittel and Gerhard Friedrich's *Theological Dictionary of the New Testament* (ed. and abridged by Geoffrey W. Bromiley [Grand Rapids, Mich., and Exeter, England: Eerdmans and Paternoster Press, 1985], 539) comments, "In many verses there is a clear reference to baptism. In Acts 22:16, Ananias tells Paul to be baptized and wash away his sins. In 1 Corinthians 6:11, Paul reminds his readers that, being washed, they are to avoid fresh defilement." Many Protestant commentators attempt to avoid the obvious meaning of the text.

49 Can Paul possibly mean one, organic, visible Church? How can this passage be taken to mean anything else? How did the apostles and the early Church view the "unity of the Church"? It is through the act of the Holy Spirit, in the sacrament of baptism, that we are made a part of the one Body of Christ, his Church. As one reads the remainder of chapter 12, the Evangelical Protestant concept of an "invisible unity" seems hopelessly untenable and, as we will see later, an invention of the "Reformers" of the sixteenth century for the purpose of reinterpreting the clear apostolic teaching (and the clear intention of the Lord Jesus, Jn 17:20–23) concerning the "one, holy, catholic, and apostolic Church." Through baptism, one is born from above by the Spirit and placed in the Body of Christ as a member of the Church. Here again we have *water* and *Spirit.*

50 Gal 3:27. In his *Lectures on Galatians* in 1535, Martin Luther taught, "He must put off his old activities, so that from sons of Adam we may be changed into sons of God. This does not happen by a change of clothing or by any laws or works; it happens by the rebirth and renewal that takes place in Baptism, as Paul says: 'As many of you as were baptized have put on Christ'. . . .

Paul in his Letter to the Ephesians 4:4–6 (written from prison *c.* 62)
"There is one body and one Spirit, just as you were called to the one hope that belongs to your call, one Lord, one faith, one baptism, one God and Father of us all."[51]

Paul in his Letter to the Ephesians 5:25–27
"Husbands, love your wives, as Christ loved the church and gave himself up for her, that he might sanctify her, having cleansed her by the washing of water with the word, that he might present the church to himself in splendor, without spot or wrinkle or any such thing, that she might be holy and without blemish."[52]

Paul is speaking about a 'putting on', not by imitation but by birth. He does not say: 'Through Baptism you have received a token . . . that is what the sectarians [Anabaptists] imagine when they make Baptism merely a token, that is, a small and empty sign" (*Luther's Works*, 26:352–53).

"Baptism is the sacramental complement of faith, the rite whereby man achieves union with Christ and publicly manifests his commitment" (Joseph A. Fitzmyer, S.J., "The Letter to the Galatians," in Raymond E. Brown, Joseph A. Fitzmyer, and Roland E. Murphy, eds., *The Jerome Biblical Commentary* [Englewood Cliffs, N.J.: Prentice Hall, 1968], 2:243).

51 Following St. Paul, the Nicene Creed states, "We acknowledge one baptism for the forgiveness of sins." That this "one baptism" refers to *water* baptism is disputed by some Fundamentalists. Protestant scholar Andrew T. Lincoln challenges them: "The one baptism is water baptism, the public rite of confession of the one faith in the one Lord. The baptism is one . . . because it is the initiation into Christ, into the one body" (*Ephesians*, vol. 42 of *Word Biblical Commentary* [Dallas, Tex.: Word Books, 1990], 240).

In the second century, Tertullian wrote, "There is to us one, and but one, baptism; as well according to the Lord's gospel as according to the apostle's letters, inasmuch as he says, 'One God, and one baptism, and one Church. . . . We enter, then, the font once: once are sins washed away, because they ought never to be repeated. . . . Happy water, which once washes away; which does not mock sinners with vain hopes" (*On Baptism* 15, in Roberts and Donaldson, *Ante-Nicene Fathers*, 3:676).

52 Does this passage refer to baptism? Evangelical commentator A. Skevington Wood writes, "There seems to be little or no doubt that the reference is to baptism. The 'washing with water' is equivalent to the 'washing of rebirth' in Titus 3:5" (*The Expositor's Bible Commentary*, ed. Frank Gaebelein [Grand Rapids, Mich.: Zondervan, 1978], 11:77). Skevington then goes on to the disclaimer that this does not automatically a sacrament make, that no mere application of water can bring about new birth, to which the Catholic heartily

Paul in his Letter to the Colossians (written from prison *c.* 62)
"In him also you were circumcised with a circumcision made without hands, by putting off the body of flesh in the circumcision of Christ; and you were buried with him in baptism, in which you were also raised with him through faith in the working of God, who raised him from the dead."[53]

---

agrees. The *Catechism of the Catholic Church* (no. 161), quoting Vatican Council I, *Dei Filius* 3, says, "Believing in Jesus and in the One who sent him for our salvation is necessary for obtaining that salvation. 'Since "without faith it is impossible to please [God]" and to attain to the fellowship of his sons, therefore without faith no one has ever attained justification, nor will anyone obtain eternal life "but he who endures to the end." ' "

"The definite article (*the* washing in water) may well indicate a specific event, and the readers are scarcely likely to have taken this as anything other than a reference to their experience of baptism. . . . The explicit mention of water suggests not simply an extended metaphor for salvation but a direct reference to water baptism, not to baptism by the Spirit. . . . This writer sees the Church's cleansing from the moral pollution of sin being carried out not through baptism only but through baptism accompanied by the word which points to Christ. Sanctification takes place through water and the word" (Lincoln, *Ephesians*, 375–76).

F. F. Bruce, in his commentary on Ephesians (*The Epistles to the Colossians, to Philemon, and to the Ephesians* in the *New International Commentary of the New Testament* [Grand Rapids, Mich.: Eerdmans, 1984],
388–89), says, "The noun translated 'washing' occurs only one other place in the New Testament—in Titus 3:5, where Christ is said to have saved his people 'by the washing of regeneration and renewal in the Holy Spirit.' The reference is to Christian initiation, in which the bestowal of the Spirit and baptism in water play a central part—the baptism involving not only the external washing but [also] the inward and spiritual grace which it signifies. . . . The phrase 'with the word' in our present text: the 'word' is the convert's confession of the name of Christ as baptism is administered." Remember, Bruce was not a Catholic; he was a member of the Plymouth Brethren and a top notch Scripture and history scholar.

53 Col 2:11–12. In the Old Testament one was admitted into the covenant people of God through circumcision, the cutting away of flesh, as a divinely given seal of membership of the covenant people. In the New Testament baptism is "putting off the body of flesh in the circumcision [baptism] of Christ" (Col 2:11). Circumcision is for the Jew exactly what baptism is for the Christian; and, therefore, circumcision in the Old Testament was in that dispensation what baptism is in this. Colossians 2:11–12, is the final proof of this. John Calvin writes, "Hence it is incontrovertible, that baptism has been

Paul in his Letter to Titus (written *c.* 64)

"But when the goodness and loving kindness of God our Savior appeared, he saved us, not because of deeds done by us in righteousness, but in virtue of his own mercy, by the washing of regeneration and renewal in the Holy Spirit, which he poured out upon us richly through Jesus Christ our Savior, so that we might be justified by his grace and become heirs in hope of eternal life. The saying is sure."[54]

substituted for circumcision, and performs the same office" (*The Institutes of the Christian Religion*, 2:531). Baptism, like circumcision, occurs only once and acts as the initiatory rite into the covenant people of God, the Church. A Jew became a member of the Old Covenant through circumcision; a Christian becomes a member of the New Covenant through baptism. How simple! Martin Luther said, "We now have baptism instead of circumcision" (*Luther's Works*, ed. Abdel R. Wentz [Philadelphia: Fortress Press, 1959], 36:95, n.). Francis Schaeffer writes, "There is a flow between the circumcision of the Old Testament and the baptism of the New. The New Testament speaks of baptism as the Christian's circumcision. . . . We could say it this way, . . . 'You are circumcised by Christian circumcision, being baptized' " (*The Complete Works of Francis Schaeffer* [Westchester, Ill.: Crossway Books, 1982], 2:225).

54 Titus 3:4–7. The "washing of regeneration" is a powerful phrase referring to water baptism. William Arndt and F. Wilbur Gingrich interpret this phrase literally as "the bath that brings about regeneration" (*A Greek– English Lexicon of the New Testament and Other Early Christian Literature*, 2d ed., rev. and augmented [Chicago: Univ. of Chicago Press, 1969], 481). Paul adds this baptismal phrase, clearly understood by Jews and Gentiles alike, to his already formidable list of references to baptism. "Washing" (λουτρόν), which we discussed earlier (Eph 5:26), refers to "a bath". John Calvin understood this and displayed his irritation at having to admit to it. D. Edmond Hiebert, in Gaebelein, *The Expositor's Bible Commentary*, says, "God's salvation was mediated to us 'through the washing of rebirth and the renewal of the Holy Spirit.' 'Washing' speaks of our cleansing from the defilement of sin in regeneration. . . . In Eph. 5:26, the only other New Testament occurrence of the term, the natural meaning is 'washing' . . . [and] clearly asserts the washing as the means of rebirth. Most commentators take the washing as a reference to baptism" (11:445). Hiebert then attempts to refute what he has just exegetically concluded. Martin Luther, in his *Lectures on Galatians*, writes, "Paul adorns Baptism with magnificent titles when he calls it 'the washing of regeneration and renewal in the Holy Spirit'."

Most interestingly, and certainly to be expected, Paul teaches what Jesus had already said to Nicodemus—that new birth comes from above through water baptism and the Spirit. The word "regeneration" simply means "new birth". This is not coincidental. Water and the Spirit, baptism and the Spirit,

Letter to the Hebrews (written in the second half of the first century)
"Therefore let us leave the elementary doctrine of Christ and go on to maturity, not laying again a foundation of repentance from dead works and of faith toward God. . . . For it is impossible to restore again to repentance those who have once been enlightened, who have tasted the heavenly gift, and have become partakers of the Holy Spirit."[55]

Peter's First Epistle
"For Christ also died for sins once for all, the righteous for the unrighteous, that he might bring us to God, being put to death in the flesh but made alive in the spirit: in which he went and preached to the spirits in prison, who formerly did not obey, when God's patience waited in the days of Noah, during the building of the ark, in which a few, that is, eight persons, were saved through water. Baptism, which corresponds to this, now saves you, not as a removal of dirt from the body but as an appeal to God for a clear conscience, through the resurrection of Jesus Christ."[56]

---

regeneration and renewal. The same teaching appears over and over again, clearer each time. As an Evangelical Protestant, I tried to explain away the clear import of these texts. Why couldn't I see it—or, why did I refuse to see it? "He saved us . . . by the washing of regeneration and the renewal of the Holy Spirit." This has been the constant teaching of the Catholic Church for two thousand years.

55 Heb 6:1–4. If "enlightenment" is understood to refer to baptism, we then see the same initiatory pair—baptism and Spirit—being described by the writer of Hebrews as we have seen throughout. F. F. Bruce writes, "It is tempting to understand the verb here in the sense of baptism—a sense which it bore among Christians in Rome in the middle of the second century. The use of 'enlightenment' in the sense of baptism need not be a borrowing from the language of the mysteries; it is quite in line with New Testament teaching. At any rate, the enlightenment here is something which has taken place once for all—like baptism itself " (F. F. Bruce, *The Epistle to the Hebrews*, in the *New International Commentary on the New Testament* [Grand Rapids, Mich.: Eerdmans, 1988], 120).

56 1 Pet 3:18–22. Things seem pretty clear at this point regarding the apostles' teachings on baptism, based on the Old Testament and the teachings of Jesus, and I must say I am amazed at the mental gyrations many commentators go through to deny the sacramental aspect of baptism.

Baptism as Taught by the Fathers

The Didache, or The Teaching of the Apostles (written prior to some New Testament books)[57]

In his recent anti-Catholic book *The Gospel according to Rome* (Eugene, Ore.: Harvest House, 1995), James McCarthy says that "when Peter says that 'baptism now saves you,' he is speaking of the typological, or symbolic, significance of baptism. . . . It [the word "figure"] tells us that what follows, 'baptism now saves you,' is a figurative illustration that complements the symbolism of a preceding figure" (331–32). It seems he is saying that baptism is a figure of a figure instead of the fulfillment of a figure. *A Greek–English Lexicon of the New Testament and other Early Christian Literature* offers a different and more straightforward interpretation: "Baptism, which is a fulfillment (of the type), now saves you, i.e., the saving of Noah from the flood is a . . . 'foreshadowing' and baptism corresponds to it [fulfills it]" (75). McCarthy does go on to say: "This verse is part of one of the most difficult passages in the New Testament to interpret. Nevertheless, this much is clear: it does not support the Roman Catholic doctrine. . . . Admittedly, the passage is difficult" (331–32). The Roman Catholic interpretation explains the passage quite comfortably, without twisting the text from its clear meaning, accepting the literal meaning of the text and complementing the rest of New Testament teaching. It is difficult for McCarthy to interpret because he comes to the passage with an insurmountable handicap: his preconceived Fundamentalist bias. Protestant scholar J. N. D. Kelly explains, "the water of baptism is not the identical water which saved Noah but the sacramental water [of baptism] to which it pointed forward" (*A Commentary on the Epistles of Peter and Jude* [Grand Rapids, Mich.: Baker Book House, 1982], 160). In Scripture Paul tells us that Adam is a type of Christ; Christ is the antitype, or the fulfillment of the type. In the same way, Noah and the flood are a type of baptism; baptism is the antitype, or the fulfillment of the type, and baptism now saves us.

57 The *Didache* is an extremely ancient document with unquestioned historical integrity. This document was in existence and used by the primitive Church, most certainly during the lifetime of some of the apostles. The work was widely read and used in the first decades of the Christian Church to instruct catechumens (those undergoing training and instruction preparatory to Christian baptism). In *Early Christian Writings*, trans. Maxwell Staniforth (Harmondsworth, Middlesex, England: Penguin Books, 1968), Andrew Louth summarizes the introduction to the *Didache* by saying, "All this . . . points to a very early date . . . and many scholars would assign *The Didache* to a point somewhere in the latter half of the first century, earlier, that is, than much of the New Testament itself" (189).

58 Using Jesus as an example, those who ascribe to the tradition of "immersion only" as a means of baptism say that Jesus was immersed completely

"Baptize as follows: after first explaining all these points, baptize in the name of the Father and of the Son and of the Holy Spirit, in running water. But if you have no running water, baptize in other water; and if you cannot in cold, then in warm. But if you have neither, pour water on the head three times[58] in the name of the Father and of the Son and of the Holy Spirit. . . .[58]Let none eat or drink of your Eucharist but those baptized in the name of the Lord; for concerning this also did the Lord say: Do not give to dogs what is sacred."[59]

The Martyrdom of Polycarp (written *c.* 155)[60]

---

because the New Testament says, "And when Jesus was baptized, he went up immediately from the water" (Mt 3:16). They infer complete immersion from this verse. Concerning total immersion, Francis Schaeffer writes that "the Baptistic argument that 'Jesus went down into the water and came up out of the water' means nothing. One year we took our vacation at the seashore. One of my little daughters went down into the water and came out of the water every day, but she would not put her head under for all our coaxing. The simple fact is that the meaning of this passage is altogether fulfilled if Jesus went down until His feet were in the Jordan" (*Baptism* [Wilmington, Del.: Trimark Pub.], 11).

58 *Didache*, pt. 2: "A Church Manual," sec. 7, "Of Baptism," in Johannes Quasten, *Patrology* (Westminster, Md.: Christian Classics, 1993), 1:31. The *Didache* was written and used starting around a.d. 50 to 100. Notice the formula of the Trinity, in accordance with Jesus' teaching before his Ascension (Mt 28:19). After a thorough training in the Christian faith and in the apostolic tradition, the new convert was ready for baptism and acceptance into the Church. An interesting note: infusion, the pouring of water, was allowed as a legitimate form of baptism as early as the first century, during the lifetime of some of the apostles. This practice continues unabated in the Catholic Church.

59 Ibid., 9, 5. "From the beginning baptism was the universally accepted rite of admission to the Church; only 'those who have been baptized in the Lord's name' may partake of the Eucharist. . . . As regards its significance, it was always held to convey the remission of sins" (J. N. D. Kelly, *Early Christian Doctrines* [New York: Harper & Row, 1978], 193–94).

60 *The Martyrdom of Polycarp* is a vivid account of the ordeals surrounding the martyrdom of the aged bishop St. Polycarp in Smyrna (*c.* 70–155). Polycarp had been a believer since childhood and a disciple of the Apostle John. He was given up to death by beasts, fire, and finally the knife at the age of eighty-six. In *Against Heresies* 3, 3, 4, Irenaeus says of him, "Polycarp was not only instructed by apostles and conversant with many who had seen the Lord, but was appointed by apostles to serve in Asia as Bishop of Smyrna. I myself

"As Polycarp stepped into the arena there came a voice from heaven, 'Be strong Polycarp, and play the man.' . . . Finally he was brought forward for examination. . . . The Governor still went on pressing him. 'Take the oath, and I will let you go,' he told him. 'Revile your Christ.' Polycarp's reply was, 'Eighty and six years have I served Him, and He has done me no wrong. How can I blaspheme my King and my Savior?' "[61]

Ignatius of Antioch (*c.* 35–107)[62]

---

saw him in my early years, for he lived a long time and was very old indeed when he laid down his life by a glorious and most splendid martyrdom. At all times he taught the things which he had learned from the apostles, which the Church transmits, which alone are true" (Eusebius, *History of the Church*, 4, 14, p. 116).

61 *The Martyrdom of Polycarp* 9, 3, in *Early Christian Writings*, 128–30. The age of Polycarp is most certain evidence that he, a convert and disciple of the apostles, was baptized as an infant or small child. "From the *Martyrium Polycarpi* (9, 3: 'Eighty-six years I have served Him') it follows that Polycarp was baptized about the year 70 while a child. It is apparent from the *First Apologia* of St. Justin (15, 6) that the men and women of 60 or 70 years of age mentioned therein, 'who were disciples of Christ from childhood', were baptized between the years 85 and 95, as children" (Ott, *Fundamentals of Catholic Dogma*, 360). Polycarp was known as the father-figure of the Christians and was renowned throughout the entire region. Because he was unafraid of the lions, an attempt was made to burn him. He wouldn't burn, so he was finally killed with a dagger.

62 Ignatius of Antioch is a very important link to the teaching of the apostles. Peter presided as bishop over the church of Antioch in Syria and was then followed by Evodius, and then by Ignatius in about 96. (See Eusebius, *History of the Church* 3, 22, p. 83). Paul visited Antioch frequently and spent more than a year there in 44 or 45 (Acts 11:25–26). It is possible, and even likely, that Ignatius knew the Apostles Peter and Paul personally and worshiped with them in his younger days in Antioch. Ancient tradition says he knew St. John and was appointed as bishop of Antioch by Peter himself. He was also good friends with Polycarp. In about the year 106, Ignatius, as an old man, was arrested in Antioch for being a Christian and was chained to Roman guards. They escorted him from Antioch to Rome, where he was eaten by lions in the Roman Colosseum as a witness for his faith. This is how he assessed the situation: "I am His wheat, ground fine by the lion's teeth to be made purest bread for Christ" (*Epistle to the Romans* 4, in *Early Christian Writings*, 86). Ignatius is an invaluable witness to the teaching and beliefs of the first-century Church; he was intimately acquainted with the tradition of

"Follow your bishop, every one of you, as obediently as Jesus Christ followed the Father. Obey your clergy too, as you would the Apostles. . . . Make sure that no step affecting the Church is ever taken by anyone without the bishop's sanction. . . . Where the bishop is to be seen, there let all his people be; just as wherever Jesus Christ is present, we have the Catholic Church. Nor is it permissible to conduct baptisms or love-feasts without the bishop."[63] "For a shield take your baptism, for a helmet your faith, for a spear your love, and for body-armor your patient endurance; and lay up a store of good works as a soldier deposits his savings, so that one day you may draw the credits that will be due to you."[64]

"Under the Divine dispensation, Jesus Christ our God was conceived by Mary of the seed of David and of the Spirit of God; He was born, and He submitted to baptism, so that by His Passion He might sanctify water."[65]

---

the apostolic period.

63 Ignatius of Antioch, *Epistle to the Smyrnaeans* 8, 2, in *Early Christian Writings*, 103. This letter was written while he was in chains and in transit to Rome *c.* 106. Ignatius ties baptism in with the one Church; in fact, he begins section 8 by saying "Abjure all factions, for they are the beginning of evils." There is to be "one, holy, catholic, and apostolic Church" ruled over, in love, by the bishops. Baptism, the Eucharist, and the other sacraments are given to the Church and are to be administered by those within the apostolic succession, i.e., the bishops. Ignatius obviously understood and practiced the teaching of baptism as the initiatory rite into the Church. Again, the Catholic Church has taught this faithfully for two thousand years.

64 Ignatius of Antioch, *Epistle to Polycarp* 6, in *Early Christian Writings*, 111. The older man Ignatius writes words of encouragement and admonition to the younger Polycarp, bishop of Smyrna. He says the shield is a defensive piece of military equipment. Baptism was seen as a seal and the means of regeneration. Notice also the concept of good works, or credits, being stored up in a heavenly bank account.

65 Ignatius of Antioch, *Epistle to the Ephesians* 18, in *Early Christian Writings*, 66. Many wonder why Jesus was baptized if he had no sin. What did one who was taught by the apostles have to say? Jesus consecrated water, sanctified it, and by doing so set baptism as the sacrament of faith, as the door into the Church and into eternal life. From the point of Jesus' baptism on, the Spirit would honor true baptism by coming down upon the person who was baptized in faith, as he had done upon our Savior, Jesus Christ.

Eusebius (story of the Apostle John that took place after 96)
"In Asia there still remained alive the one whom Jesus loved, apostle and evangelist alike, John, who had directed the churches there since his return from exile on the island, following Domitian's death [fl. 51–96]. . . . Listen to a true account of John the Apostle, handed down and carefully remembered. When the tyrant was dead, and John had moved from the island of Patmos to Ephesus, he used to go when asked to the neighboring districts of the Gentile people, sometimes to appoint bishops, sometimes to organize whole churches. . . . So it happened that he arrived at a city not far off [Smyrna], and after settling the various problems of the brethren, he finally looked at the bishop already appointed, and indicating a youngster he had noticed . . . he said, 'I leave this young man in your keeping. . . .' He then returned to Ephesus, and the cleric took home the youngster entrusted to his care, brought him up, kept him in his company, looked after him and finally gave him *the grace of baptism.* After this he relaxed his constant care and watchfulness, *having put on him the seal of the Lord as the perfect protection.* [The story goes on for several pages and details the boy's fall into corruption, after which John pursues him and brings him to repentance.]

"Then [John] brought him back to the church, interceded for him with many prayers, shared with him in the ordeal of continuous fasting . . . and did not leave him, we are told, till he had restored him to the Church, giving a perfect example of true repentance and a perfect proof of regeneration, the trophy of a visible resurrection" (italics added for emphasis).[66]

---

66 This is an interesting account of an episode in the life of the aged Apostle John. It is recorded in Eusebius' *History of the Church* 3, 23, pp. 83– 85, and it was earlier recorded in *The Rich Man Who Finds Salvation*, as found in the writings of Clement of Alexandria. The genuine historicity of the episode is attested to by Irenaeus, Clement of Alexandria, and modern scholars. Besides the fascinating information on the Apostle John and on the workings of the early Church, we have an example of a young man receiving the "grace of baptism," the "perfect seal," who then falls under the spell of freedom and corruption, only to be returned to the faith through repentance. This is an example of "a perfect proof of regeneration" that was bestowed at baptism according to the narrative.

Justin Martyr (*c.* 100–*c.* 165)[67]

"And we, who have approached God through Him [Christ], have received not carnal, but spiritual circumcision, which Enoch and those like him observed. And we have received it through baptism, since we were sinners, by God's mercy; and all men may equally obtain it."[68]

"I will also relate the manner in which we dedicated ourselves to God when we had been made new through Christ. . . . As many as are persuaded and believe that what we teach and say is true, and undertake to be able to live accordingly, are instructed to pray and to entreat God with fasting, for the remission of their sins that are past, we praying and fasting with them. Then they are brought by us where there is water, and are regenerated in the same manner in which we were ourselves regenerated [reborn]. For, in the name of God, the Father . . . and of our Savior Jesus Christ, and of the Holy Spirit, they then receive the washing with water. For Christ also said, 'Except ye be born again, ye shall not enter into the kingdom of heaven. . . .' And for this [rite] we have learned from the apostles . . . in order that we may not remain the children of necessity and of ignorance, but may become the children of choice and knowledge, and may obtain in the water the remission of sins formerly committed, there is pronounced over him who chooses to be born again, and has repented of his sins, the name of God, the Father. . . ."[69]

67 Justin Martyr was an outstanding apologist of the early Church. He was born of pagan parents in Flavia, Neopolis (twenty-one miles from Thessalonica and thirty-four miles from Philippi, visited by Paul [Acts 16:11]). After a long search for truth in the pagan philosophies, Justin at last embraced Christianity about 130. For a time he taught at Ephesus, and then he moved to Rome, where he opened a Christian school, having Tatian as one of his students. He and some of his disciples were denounced as Christians in 165, and, on refusing to sacrifice to pagan gods, they were scourged and beheaded. Details of his martyrdom can be found in *Martyrium SS. Iustini et Sociorum*, based on official Roman court records. He is referred to by Eusebius as "an ornament of our Faith soon after the Apostles' time" (*History of the Church* 2, 13).

68 *Dialogue with Trypho the Jew* 43 (written *c.* 155), in Roberts and Donaldson, *Ante-Nicene Fathers*, 1:216. In this passage we have further confirmation that in the first centuries of the Church it was universally understood that circumcision in the Old Covenant was replaced by baptism in the New Covenant. Baptism is the door into the Church and the sign of the New Covenant.

69 Justin Martyr, *First Apology* 61 (written *c.* 148–155), in Roberts and Donald-

"And this food is called among us Εὐχαριστία [the Eucharist], of which no one is allowed to partake but the man who believes that the things which we teach are true, and who has been washed in the washing [bath] that is for the remission of sins, and unto regeneration, and who is so living as Christ has enjoined."[70]

Theophilus of Antioch (d. between 185 and 191)[71]

"Those things which were created from the waters were blessed by God, so that this might also be a sign that men would at a future time receive repentance and remission of sins through water and the bath of regeneration [new birth]—all who proceed to the truth and are born again and receive a blessing from God."[72]

---

son, *Ante-Nicene Fathers*, 1:183. Justin writes to Roman Emperor Antoninus Pius and to his adopted sons, Marcus Aurelius and Lucius Verus, explaining the Christian faith and defending the apostolic teaching of the Church. Notice the deep significance of baptism, which brings about regeneration. He draws on Isaiah 1:16–20, "Wash yourselves; make yourselves clean . . . though your sins are like scarlet, they shall be as white as snow." Justin again confirms the Church's universal teaching: that Jesus' words, "water and the Spirit" (Jn 3:5), refer to new birth through baptism. He informs us that the same procedures and teachings were applied to him when he was baptized near the end of the first century— possibly within the lifetime of the Apostle John. He claims this practice was directly given by the apostles.

70 Ibid., 66, in Roberts and Donaldson, *Ante-Nicene Fathers*, 1:185. When is one allowed to partake in the table of the Lord, the Eucharist? Only after he has been confirmed in the truth and baptized in the water of regeneration. This ubiquitous emphasis of the first Christians on the effectiveness and regeneration of baptism was completely unknown to me as an Evangelical Protestant.

71 St. Theophilus of Antioch was the seventh bishop of Antioch, the sixth successor of St. Peter. After carefully studying the Scriptures he was convinced of the truth of the Christian faith and converted from paganism to the Church. Theophilus is credited with introducing the word "Trinity" (τριας) as a description of the Father, the Son, and the Holy Spirit.

72 St. Theophilus of Antioch, *To Autolycus* 2, 16 (written *c.* 181), in Jurgens, *Faith of the Early Fathers*, 1:75. This is the only work of Theophilus to survive. It is an apologetic for the Christian faith in three volumes. The third volume contains a chronology of the world that ends with the death of Marcus Aurelius on March 17, 180. Theophilus is another witness to the apostolic teaching on baptism, especially as the means of rebirth.

Irenaeus (c. 130–c. 200)[73]

"But what really was the case, that they [Apostles] did record, that the Spirit of God as a dove descended upon Him; this Spirit, of whom it was declared by Isaiah, 'And the Spirit of God shall rest upon Him' as I have already said. . . . And again, giving to the disciples the power of regeneration into God, He said to them, 'Go and teach all nations, baptizing them in the name of the Father, and of the Son, and of the Holy Spirit.' "[74]

"For He [Jesus] came to save all through means of Himself—all, I say, who through Him are born again to God,— infants, and children, and boys, and youths, and old men."[75] "Thus there are as

73 St. Irenaeus, bishop of Lyons, says of himself, "When I was still a boy I saw you in Lower Asia in Polycarp's company, when you were cutting a fine figure at the imperial court and wanted to be in favor with him. I have a clearer recollection of events at that time than of recent happenings—what we learn in childhood develops along with the mind and becomes a part of it—so that I can describe the place where blessed Polycarp sat and talked, his goings out and comings in, the character of his life, his personal appearance, his addresses to crowded congregations. I remember how he spoke of his intercourse with John and with the others who had seen the Lord; how he repeated their words from memory; and how the things that he had heard them say about the Lord, His miracles and His teaching, things that he had heard direct from the eyewitnesses of the Word of Life, were proclaimed by Polycarp in complete harmony with Scripture. To these things I listened eagerly at that time, by the mercy of God shown to me, not committing them to writing but learning them by heart. By God's grace, I constantly and conscientiously ruminate on them" (Eusebius, *History of the Church* 5, 20, 5–7, p. 169).

74 St. Irenaeus, *Against Heresies* 3, 17, 1, in Roberts and Donaldson, *Ante-Nicene Fathers*, 1:444. Irenaeus recognizes the special authority that Jesus gave the apostles, the authority and power to bring new birth to sinners through faith and baptism; though faith is not mentioned in this immediate context, it is certainly implied and is a necessary ingredient.

75 Ibid., 2, 22, 4. This passage speaks of baptism, including infant baptism, which is confirmed by the fact that it is within the context of a baptismal discussion. A note in Roberts and Donaldson, *Ante-Nicene Fathers*, 1:391, says, "The reference in these words is doubtless baptism, as clearly appears from comparing book 3, 17, 1. It has been remarked by Wall and others, that we have here the statement of a valuable fact as to the baptism of infants in the primitive Church" (notes 8, 9). See Acts 16:31; Mt 19:14–15; Lk 2:21. There is no question that Irenaeus, and the whole Church spread abroad from Jerusalem to Gaul to Rome, considered baptism to be the agent of new birth, based on the teaching of the apostles (Titus 3:5) and the words of Jesus (Jn 3:5).

many schemes of 'redemption' as there are teachers of these mystical opinions. And when we come to refute them, we shall show in its fitting-place, that this class of men have been instigated by Satan to a denial of that baptism which is regeneration to God, and thus to a renunciation of the whole [Christian] faith."[76]

" 'And dipped himself,' says the Scripture, 'seven times in Jordan.' It was not for nothing that Naaman of old, when suffering from leprosy, was purified upon his being baptized, but it served as an indication to us. For as we are lepers in sin, we are made clean, by means of the sacred water and the invocation of the Lord, from our old transgressions; being spiritually regenerated as new-born babes, even as the Lord has declared: 'Except a man be born again through water and the Spirit, he shall not enter into the kingdom of heaven'."[77]

Consider Irenaeus' statement in fragment 33: "Being spiritually regenerated as new-born babes, even as the Lord has declared: 'Except a man be born again through water and the Spirit.' "

It should be noted that, when the first direct evidence of infant baptism shows up in the second century, it is presented, not as an innovation, but as a rite instituted by the apostles and universally practiced in the first and second centuries. As Reformed theologian R. C. Sproul writes, "The first direct mention of infant baptism is around the middle of the second century a.d. What is noteworthy about this reference is that it assumes infant baptism to be the universal practice of the church. If infant baptism were not the practice of the first-century church, how and why did this departure from orthodoxy happen so fast and so pervasively? Not only was the spread rapid and universal, the extant literature from that time does not reflect any controversy concerning the issue. . . . Those who dispute the validity of infant baptism make it less inclusive with respect to children, despite the absence of any biblical prohibition against infant baptism" (*Essential Truths of the Christian Faith* [Wheaton, Ill.: Tyndale House, 1992], 228).

76 Irenaeus, *Against Heresies* 1, 21, 1, in Roberts and Donaldson, *Ante- Nicene Fathers*, 1:345. This is a powerful testimony to the practice and beliefs of the first- and second-century Church. Only Gnostic heretics denied the "baptism which is regeneration," and there it is said to be an invention of Satan, a denial of the whole Christian faith. The Roman Catholic Church has faithfully carried the teachings and traditions of the apostles through the centuries down to our day. She has preserved the great deposit of "the faith which was once for all delivered to the saints" (Jude 3).

77 Irenaeus, fragment 34 of the lost writings of Irenaeus, in Roberts and Donaldson, *Ante-Nicene Fathers*, 1:574. Some see this as another reference to infant baptism, though it can be understood otherwise. This passage affords

Clement of Alexandria (*c.* 150–*c.* 215)[78]

"For thus He wishes us to be converted and to become as children acknowledging him who is truly our father, regenerated by water; and this is a different begetting than that of creation."[79]

"Being baptized, we are illuminated; illuminated, we become sons; being made sons, we are made perfect; being made perfect, we are made immortal. 'I', says He, 'have said that you are gods and all sons of the Highest' [Ps 81:6]. This work is variously called grace, illumination, and perfection, and washing; washing, by which we cleanse away our sins; grace, by which the penalties accruing to transgressions are remitted; and illumination, by which that holy light of salvation is

---

us another clear example of water, Spirit, and new birth based on the words of Jesus recorded in John 3:5: "Unless a man is born of water and the Spirit he cannot enter into the kingdom of God."

78 Clement of Alexandria was born of pagan extraction, probably in Athens, *c.* 150. After becoming a Christian he traveled widely, to Italy, Syria, and Palestine, among other places. He learned the faith from the most important and famous teachers of the Church. He remarks that he "was privileged to hear discourses of blessed and truly remarkable men." He was the head of the School of Catechumens in Alexandria, Egypt. His writings contain many historical events in the later life of the Apostle John. In the *Stromata* (1, 1), Clement claims a close and intimate association with the apostolic tradition. He writes, "Well, they preserving the tradition of the blessed doctrine derived directly from the holy apostles, Peter, James, John, and Paul, the sons receiving it from the fathers (but few were like the fathers), came by God's will to us also to deposit those ancestral and apostolic seeds. And well I know that they will exult; I do not mean delighted with this tribute, but solely on account of the preservation of the truth, according as they delivered it" (Quasten, *Patrology*, 2:27).

79 Clement of Alexandria, *Stromata* or *Miscellanies* 3, 12, 87, in Roberts and Donaldson, *Ante-Nicene Fathers*, 2:215. Notice again the absolute consistency of baptismal teaching, from one writer to the next, with no deviation. As we have moved through the first two centuries and approach the third, we have not seen the Evangelical understanding of a "symbolic only" baptism. Fundamentalist Protestants claim that later centuries swerved off the course laid out by the apostles and set up false traditions. However, with the monolithic consensus we are finding in our study, it is very clear that the early Church faithfully passed on the true teaching of the apostles, preserved in the tradition and in the Scriptures.

beheld, that is by which we see God clearly."[80]

Tertullian (*c.* 160–*c.* 225)[81]
"Happy is our sacrament of water, in that, by washing away the sins of our early blindness, we are set free and admitted into eternal life."[82]

---

80 Clement of Alexandria, *Paedagogus* or "The Instructor" 1, 6, 26, in Roberts and Donaldson, *Ante-Nicene Fathers*, 2:215. According to Johannes Quasten in *Patrology*, "It is hardly possible to give a better explanation of the adoption as children of God which takes place in the sacrament of regeneration [baptism]. Clement uses also the term 'seal,' 'illumination,' 'bath,' 'perfection,' and 'mystery' for baptism" (2:28). Having recently referred to the initiation of believers, the writer of Hebrews may have been alluding, as we have seen, to baptism when he used the word "enlightened" (Heb 6:4). In another passage (*Paedagogus* 3, 11, 59), Clement writes of "babes drawn out of the water," which is an apparent reference to infant baptism (Leighton Pullan, *Early Christian Doctrine* [London: Rivingtons, 1909], 75).

81 Tertullian, whose full Latin name was Quintus Septimius Florens, was born of pagan parents in Carthage, in northern Africa. He was a lawyer well-educated in rhetoric and literature. After becoming a Christian sometime before 197, he was a distinguished defender of the faith and wrote rigorous treatises on doctrinal and apologetic topics. Even though he later joined a fringe group called the Montanists, he was given the title of Father of Latin theology. In his thirty-one writings that still exist, he zealously defended Christianity, refuted heresy, taught the doctrines of the apostolic Church, morality, and church discipline.

82 Tertullian, *On Baptism* 1, in Roberts and Donaldson, *Ante-Nicene Fathers*, 3:669. Tertullian starts his treatise with these words, not as though he is trying to prove a new point (the efficacious nature of baptism), but to invoke a well-known, universally accepted doctrine and practice. Tertullian's treatise on the subject of baptism echoes what we have studied so far and is fascinating to read. After praising the "marvelous preaching of the 12 apostles and their immediate successors," Baptist J. M. Carrol states in his little booklet *The Trail of Blood* (Lexington, Ky.: Ashland Baptist Church, 1994), "So that it was in this period [first and second centuries] that the idea of 'Baptismal Regeneration' began to get a fixed hold in some of the churches" (13). With Tertullian we arrive at the end of the second century, two of the most glorious centuries in the Church's history, and we find him teaching the same doctrine of baptism as was taught by the "12 apostles and their immediate successors"—a wonderful continuity. Carrol claims these early Christians as his own, yet he refuses to face up to the fact that they taught distinctly Catholic doctrines that do not resemble his Fundamentalist teaching. Up to this point in our study we find no early voice of Christian orthodoxy teaching that baptism is only for adults, does not regenerate, is only by immersion, or does not wash away

"There is absolutely nothing which makes men's minds more obdurate than the simplicity of the divine works which are visible in the *act*, when compared with the grandeur which is promised regarding the *effect*; so that from the very fact, that with so great simplicity, without pomp, without any considerable novelty of preparation, finally, without any expense, a man is dipped in water, and amid the utterance of some few words, is sprinkled, and then rises again, not much (or not at all) the cleaner, the consequent attainment of eternity is esteemed the more incredible. . . . Is it not wonderful too, that death should be washed away by bathing?"[83] "And so, according to the circumstances and disposition, and even age, of each individual, the delay of baptism is preferable; principally, however, in the case of little children."[84]

sins. Tertullian's treatise *On Baptism* comprises eleven pages of small type in *The Ante-Nicene Fathers* and clearly summarizes many of the topics we have discussed so far, such as the hovering of the Spirit in "the beginning" and at baptism, water as a vehicle of divine operation, sacraments to infuse inward grace, the Flood, the Red Sea, and many others. This incomplete list gives an idea of the content of the whole treatise.

83 Ibid., 3:669, sec. 1. Tertullian chides and condemns those who dare to deny God's ability to regenerate and wash away sins with the waters of baptism. He writes, "Oh, miserable incredulity, which quite denies to God His own properties, simplicity and power! Take heed, those who deny the sacramental power of the waters appointed by God Himself!" (ibid., chap. 2). These are very strong words. The primitive Church speaks from the past—to our generation—warning against heresy and false teaching, censuring the very beliefs espoused by the Evangelical Protestants of today.

84 Ibid., 3:678, sec. 18. It has become abundantly clear that the ancient Church, from east to west, was baptizing infants and doing so with the conviction that they were obeying the direct commands of the apostles. According to *The Catholic Encyclopedia*, ed. Charles G. Herbermann et al. (New York: Robert Appleton Co., 1907), "While not denying the validity of infant baptism, Tertullian desired that the sacrament be not conferred upon them until they have attained the use of reason, on account of the danger of profaning their baptism as youths amid the allurements of pagan vice. In like manner, St. Gregory of Nazianzus (Or. xl, De Bapt.) thought that baptism, unless there was danger of death, should be deferred until the child was three years old, for then it could hear and respond at the ceremonies. Such opinions, however, were shared by few, and they contain no denial of the validity of infant baptism" (2:270). The few who recommended a later age for baptism, such as Tertullian, afford incidental proof that the Church had baptized infants from the beginning, for if infant baptism had been an innovation or heresy, these men who questioned it would have been delighted to point out

Origen (*c.* 185–*c.* 254)[85]

"The Church received from the Apostles the tradition [custom] of giving Baptism even to infants. For the Apostles, to whom were committed the secrets of divine mysteries, knew that there is in everyone the innate stains of sin, which must be washed away through water and the Spirit."[86]

---

that infant baptism was not an apostolic practice.

85 Origen was a man of profound abilities and stature in the first half of the third century. He was a biblical scholar, a theologian, and a spiritual writer. Christians from across the empire appealed to Origen on theological and biblical matters. Origen was born to Christian parents in Alexandria, Egypt, and during the persecution in Alexandria in 202, his father was martyred. Eusebius tells us, "There by their heroic endurance of every kind of torture and every form of death, they were wreathed with the crown laid up with God. Among them Leonides [Origen's father] was beheaded, leaving his son quite young." Origen insisted on suffering martyrdom with his father, but his mother intervened by hiding his clothes, so he could not leave the house. While his father was in prison, Origen exhorted him in a letter, "Mind you don't change your mind on our account" (Eusebius, *History of the Church*, 6:1, 2, p. 180).

Even though many question his allegorical method of biblical interpretation, the bishops from the whole Roman Empire and from around the world consulted him to settle theological disputes and correct doctrinal errors. A person no less than St. Jerome called him the second teacher of the Church after Paul. During the persecution of Decius in 250, Origen was imprisoned and subjected to prolonged torture, after which he survived only a few years. He was a prodigious writer and published commentaries on most books of the Bible. Historians say he may have written more than six thousand works. For more information on Origen, read chapter 6 of Eusebius' *History of the Church*.

86 Origen, *Commentary on Romans* 5, 9, in Jurgens, *Faith of the Early Fathers*, 1:209. Origen, the great biblical scholar and defender of the faith, born within a hundred years of the lifetime of the Apostle John, wrote confidently that infant baptism was a custom handed down from the apostles themselves. We know that Origen had documents and original sources from the apostolic period available to him that are no longer extant. If infant baptism had been an innovation or a deviation from the constant teaching of the Church, Origen and the other Fathers of the Church would have denounced the practice in no uncertain terms. Yet all we find is universal assent that infant baptism was of apostolic origin.

Francis Schaeffer wrote, "In the light of the teaching of the whole Bible, for us not to baptize babies there would have to be a clear command in Scrip-

"If you like to hear what other saints have felt in regard to physical birth, listen to David when he says, 'I was conceived,' so it runs, 'in iniquity and in sin my mother hath borne me,' proving that every soul which is born in the flesh is tainted with the stain of iniquity and sin. This is the reason for that saying which we have already quoted above, 'No man is clean from sin, not even if his life be one day long' (Job 14:4). To these, as a further point, may be added an inquiry into the reason for which, while the Church's baptism is given for the remission of sin, it is the custom of the Church that baptism be administered even to infants. Certainly, if there were nothing in infants that required remission and called for lenient treatment, the grace of baptism would seem unnecessary."[87]

"Let us remember the sins of which we have been guilty, and that it is not possible to receive forgiveness of sins without baptism."[88]

Cyprian of Carthage (martyred 258)[89]

ture not to do so. Instead of that, the emphasis is all the other way. Of the seven cases of water baptism mentioned in the New Testament, three were of families. . . . Origen was born about 180 a.d. and he was baptized as an infant. . . . The claim that infant baptism is a product of the Roman Catholic Church is totally mistaken. . . . Take advantage of this God-given privilege of infant baptism. . . . The Baptism of your infants is a part of your privilege as a Christian. Take it with thanksgiving along with the other good things God gives you" (*Baptism*, 19–24).

87 Origen, *Homilies on Leviticus* 8, 3, in Quasten, *Patrology*, 2:83. What a unity of thought among the whole primitive Church! What internal consistency! Origen expounds the doctrine of original sin, as held by the apostles and the Fathers and held today by the Catholic Church.

88 *Exhort. ad Martyr.*, n. 30, 293, in J. Berington and J. Kirk, *The Faith of Catholics*, ed. T. J. Capel (New York and Cincinnati: Fr. Pustet & Co., 1885), 2:113. Origen, very close to the time of the apostles, provides further confirmation of their teaching. As we have already seen, when those who first heard the gospel from the mouth of Peter asked what to do, Peter responded, "Repent, and be baptized every one of you in the name of Jesus Christ for the forgiveness of your sins; and you shall receive the gift of the Holy Spirit" (Acts 2:38).

89 Cyprian of Carthage was a pagan rhetorician who converted to Christianity in 246. Within the amazingly short period of two years he was appointed bishop of Carthage in northern Africa and had acquired a deep knowledge of Scriptures and the writings of Tertullian. During the Decian persecution that broke out in the autumn of 249, he was forced to flee. "He found a

"In respect to the case of infants, which you say ought not to be baptized within the second or third day after birth, and that the law of ancient circumcision should be regarded, so that you think that one who is just born should not be baptized and sanctified within the eighth day, we all thought very differently in our council. For in this course which you thought was to be taken, no one agreed; but we all rather judge that the mercy and grace of God is not to be refused to any one born of man . . . we ought to shrink from hindering an infant, who being lately born, has not sinned, except in that, being born after the flesh according to Adam, he has contracted the contagion of the ancient death at its earliest birth, who approaches the more easily on this very account to the reception of the forgiveness of sins—that to him are remitted, not his own sins, but the sins of another [Adam]."[90]

Athanasius (*c.* 296–373)[91]

---

safe refuge in the hills outside the city, from where, in comparative safety, he directed his flock by letters to his clergy" (Jurgens, *Faith of the Early Fathers*, 1:216). After returning at the conclusion of the persecution, he was recognized as a leading bishop and was embroiled in the controversy over heretic baptisms. Cyprian, exiled to Curubis in August of 257, was beheaded near Carthage on September 14, 258. He was the first African bishop to die a martyr's death.

90 In his *Epistle to Fidus* 64, in Quasten, *Patrology*, 2:378–79, Cyprian confirms the decision of a synod regarding the validity of baptism for infants, rooted in their common understanding of its sacramental essence as passed down from the apostles.

91 Athanasius was the greatest defender of the deity of Christ and the Holy Trinity and was instrumental in the doctrinal development that finally defined the trinitarian nature of God and the human and divine natures of Christ. The heresy of Arianism, which claimed that Jesus was a creature and not deity, was rampant in his day, especially in the East, and Athanasius was unrelenting in his defense of the truth. He often stood alone and was exiled five times, often being forced to live in caves. As a deacon he attended the Council of Nicaea, where the great Creed of the Church was hammered out, especially the phrase "begotten, not made, one in being with the Father." He also ardently defended the full deity of the Holy Spirit and the full humanity of Christ. Because of his efforts he was often slandered, banished into the desert, exiled from his bishopric. This man was a true hero of all orthodox Christendom, defending the deity of Christ against seemingly impossible odds, and at great personal risk. It is interesting to note that in the first centuries of the Church there were raging controversies regarding the deity of

"And these too hazard the fullness of the mystery, I mean Baptism; for if . . . [they] deny also the true Son, and name another of their own framing as created out of nothing, is not the rite [baptism] administered by them altogether empty and unprofitable, making a show, but in reality being no help towards religion?"[92]

"For it is time for them to think that the grace of the Font [baptism] is nothing, if some are found to despise it."[93] "The words of the Epistle to the Hebrews (vi. 4) do not exclude sinners from repentance, but demonstrate that there is but one, and no second, baptism in the Catholic Church. . . . Neither does he say, 'It is impossible to repent,' but, 'It is impossible for us to be renewed by means of penitence,' which is a very different thing. For he who repents ceases indeed from sinning, but he still has on him the scars of his wounds; whereas he who is baptized, puts off the old man, being born again by the grace of the Spirit."[94]

Christ, yet baptismal regeneration and infant baptism were never debated. They were universally accepted from the time of the apostles. Athanasius is another monumental witness to this fact. Do we take his view of baptism and the Eucharist lightly? We who take his Christology so seriously should take his counsel on the sacraments seriously as well.

92 *Four Discourses against the Arians*, discourse 2, 18, 42, in Schaff, *Nicene and Post-Nicene Fathers*, 2d series, 4:371. Athanasius is debating the Arians, those who deny that Christ is eternal and "one in being with the Father." Their baptisms, therefore, are invalid, for they do not baptize in the name of the true Father, Son, and Holy Spirit. Therefore the rite is empty and unprofitable for them, for the rebirth does not happen. Athanasius mentions the great mystery of baptism (in which we are regenerated) and the fact that the Arians "hazard the fullness" of baptism because of their heresy. Athanasius argues from a stance well accepted by all Christians (otherwise it would have been an unpersuasive argument) that there is a strong sacramental and efficacious reality to baptism. There are many *today* who make it only "a show" by denying the sacramental reality and reducing it (denigrating it) to an outward symbol only.

93 *Letter XLIX: to Dracontius*, written in 254 or 355, in Schaff, *Nicene and Post-Nicene Fathers*, 2d series, 4:558. When arguing with heretics, Athanasius frequently goes back to the source of our regeneration, the font of baptism. In this case, Athanasius is encouraging Dracontius to accept the office of bishop and not flee in the face of persecution. He is reminding Dracontius of the grace he has received, starting with baptism, which the unbeliever says "is nothing" and some "despise it."

94 *Ep.* iv. *ad Serap.* n. 13, t. I. part ii, 563, in Berington and Kirk, *Faith of Catho-*

Didymus the Blind (313–398)[95]

"The Holy Spirit renovates us in baptism, and in union with the Father and the Son, brings us back from a state of deformity to our pristine beauty and so fills us with His grace. . . . He frees us from sin and death and from the things of the earth; makes us spiritual men, sharers in the divine glory, sons and heirs of God. . . . He gives us heaven . . . and in the divine waters of the baptismal pool extinguishes the inextinguishable fire of hell. For when we are immersed in the baptismal pool, we are by the goodness of God . . . and by the grace of His Holy Spirit stripped of our sins as we lay aside the old man, are regenerated and sealed by His own kingly power. But when we come up out of the pool, we put on Christ our Savior as an incorruptible garment, worthy of the same honor as the Holy Spirit who regenerated us and marked us with His seal."[96]

Basil the Great (*c.* 330–379)[97]

---

lics, 2:117. When I was an Evangelical, St. Athanasius was one of my personal heroes. I admired his tenacity and fortitude in the long battles he waged with his nemesis Arius, the arch-heretic. I was amazed to discover that my hero, and all the early champions of the faith whom I loved as an Evangelical, believed in baptismal regeneration and the other distinctly Catholic teachings.

95 Alexandria was a major center of Christian thinking and activity. Not only was the Greek translation of the Old Testament (the Septuagint) translated there, but Alexandria also contained one of the largest libraries in the Western world. During the early third century b.c., the Alexandrian Library had almost five hundred thousand volumes, which was the largest collection of books in the ancient world. Didymus the Blind was a renowned head of the catechetical school in Alexandria in the fourth century a.d. He lost his sight at the age of four, but he was highly esteemed during his lifetime, even with his great handicap, for he amassed a great amount of learning and wisdom without ever going to school or learning to read. He had a tremendous mind with encyclopedic knowledge. His reputation is verified by the fact that Athanasius, bishop of Alexandria, placed him in the highest position, as head of the school. His students included Jerome and Rufinus. He was referred to as "a prophet" and "an apostolic man." He died at the age of eighty-five.

96 Didymus the Blind, *The Trinity* 2, 12, in Quasten, *Patrology*, 3:98. Baptism is absolutely necessary for salvation. There is little more to be said, for the passage speaks for itself in its fidelity to the constant teaching of the Church.

97 Basil the Great was appointed the bishop of Caesarea in Cappadocia in

"Whence is it that we are Christians? Through our faith, would be the universal answer. And in what way are we saved? Plainly because we were regenerate through the grace given in our baptism. How else could we be? . . . Whether a man have departed this life without baptism, or have received a baptism lacking in some of the requirements of the tradition, his loss is equal. . . . For if to me my baptism was the beginning of life, and that day of regeneration the first of days, it is plain that the utterance uttered in the grace of adoption [baptismal vows] was the most honorable of all. . . . How then are we made in the likeness of his death: In that we were buried with Him by baptism. What is the manner of this burial? And what is the advantage resulting from the imitation? First of all, it is necessary that the continuity of the old life be cut. And this is impossible unless a man be born again, according to the Lord's word [Jn 3:3–5]; for the regeneration, as indeed the name shows, is a beginning of a second life. . . . How then do we achieve the descent into hell? By imitating, through baptism, the burial of Christ. For the bodies of the baptized are, as it were, buried in the water. . . . Hence it follows that the answer to our question why the water was associated with the Spirit is clear: the reason is because in baptism two ends were proposed; on the one hand, the destroying of the body of sin, that it may never bear fruit unto death; on the other hand, our living unto the Spirit. . . . This then is what it is to be born again of water and of the Spirit, the being made dead being effected in the water, while our life is wrought in us through the Spirit."[98]

---

370 and was a vigorous opponent of Arianism and a defender of the faith against the Arian Emperor Valens. For the rest of his life he fought untiringly for the doctrine of the deity Christ and of the Holy Spirit against the attacks of the Arians. He was known for his eloquence, knowledge, and great personal holiness. He is one whose opinion should be of great importance to Christians today.

98 Basil the Great, *On the Spirit*, chaps. 10, 15, in Schaff, *Nicene and Post-Nicene Fathers*, 2d series, 8:17, 21–22. There are so many interesting and descriptive passages on baptism in Basil's writings that it is hard to reduce them to a few short selections. His treatise, and doctrine of baptism, follows the teaching of the apostles and is the same teaching practiced today by the Roman Catholic Church.

Gregory of Nyssa (*c.* 333–*c.* 395)[99]

"But Christ . . . assumes manhood in its fullness, and saves man, and becomes the type and figure of us all, to sanctify the firstfruits of every action, and leave to His servants no doubt in their zeal for the tradition. Baptism, then, is a purification from sins, a remission of trespasses, a cause of renovation and regeneration. By regeneration, understand regeneration conceived in thought, not discerned by bodily sight. For we shall not, according to the Jew Nicodemus and his somewhat dull intelligence, change the old man into the child, . . . but we do bring back, by royal grace, him who bears the scars of sin, and has grown old in evil habits, to the innocence of the babe. . . . And this gift it is not the water that bestows,[100] but the command of God, and the visitation of the Spirit that comes sacramentally to set us free. . . . 'Except a man be born of water and of the Spirit, he cannot enter into the kingdom of God' [Jn 3:5; Gregory calls this passage "the fountainhead"]. Why are they both named, and why is not the Spirit alone accounted sufficient for the completion of Baptism? Man, as we know full well, is compound, not simple: and therefore the cognate and similar medicines are assigned for healing to him who is twofold and conglomerate:—for his visible body, water, the sensible element—for his soul, which we cannot see, the Spirit invisible, invoked by faith, present unspeakably. . . . He [the Spirit] blesses the body that is baptized, and the water that baptizes. Despise not, therefore, the Divine laver, nor think lightly of it, as a common thing, on account of the use of water. For the power that operates is mighty, and wonderful are the things that are wrought thereby."[101]

99 Gregory of Nyssa, brother of Basil the Great, was also a great champion of the faith of the Nicene Creed, which taught that Jesus was fully God and fully man. He suffered greatly for his orthodox stand and was banished—deposed from his bishopric by the Arian heretics in 376.

100 Water apart from the Spirit has no ability to cleanse the soul; if it did, we would be reregenerated every time we took our morning baths. It is the water *and* the Spirit, working in conjunction, along with "the word" of faith spoken by the catechumen and the word of God spoken by the baptizer. Initiation into Christ and the Church cannot be reduced to one component. We are taught that there are several components working together: faith, water, confession, repentance, the Spirit, etc.

101 Gregory of Nyssa, *On the Baptism of Christ*, in Schaff, *Nicene and Post-Nicene Fathers*, 2d series, 5:519, written for Epiphany, January 7, 381, the day

Gregory Nazianzen (329–389)[102]

"The Word recognizes three Births for us; namely, the natural birth, that of Baptism, and that of the Resurrection. . . . Let us discourse upon the second. . . . And as Christ the Giver is called by many various names, so too is this Gift. . . . We call it, the Gift, the Grace, Baptism, Unction, Illumination, the Clothing of Immortality, the Laver of Regeneration, the Seal, and everything that is honorable. We call it the Gift, because it is given to us in return for nothing on our part; Grace, because it is conferred even on debtors; Baptism, because sin is buried with it in the water; . . . the Laver because it washes us; the Seal, because it preserves us."[103]

The Nicene Creed (325)[104]

---

commemorating the baptism of Christ. Here St. Gregory makes many fine distinctions and shows that a disregard for the regenerating aspect of water baptism is folly. He tells us to "despise it not" and later says that those who do not understand and don't give the baptismal laver its due are "dull minded" like Nicodemus.

102 St. Gregory was the son of the bishop of Nazianzus (also named Gregory), and he studied at the University of Athens. He was ordained a priest about 362 and later was called to Constantinople to subdue heresy and restore the faith of the Nicene Creed. He was a major figure in the final establishment of the Nicene Creed at the Council of Constantinople in 381. He was appointed bishop of Constantinople. He also wrote against the heresy of Apollinarianism (which held to the full deity of Christ but denied his full manhood).

103 Gregory Nazianzen, *Oration 40: Oration on Holy Baptism* 2, in Schaff, *Nicene and Post-Nicene Fathers*, 2d series, 7:360. This oration, which was preached at Constantinople on January 6, 381, is seventeen pages long in Schaff 's edition. How is it possible to distill this much information into a short paragraph? For anyone who wants to understand the early Church's teaching on baptism, this is an especially rich source.

104 The Nicene Creed was based upon the earlier Apostles' Creed and was accepted by the whole Catholic Church (which was *one*, visible unity), represented by 318 bishops from all over the known world. Many of the bishops attending the Council of Nicaea were maimed, blind, or crippled as a result of the persecutions, tortures, and sufferings they had endured for the Christian faith. St. Athanasius attended the council as a deacon, assisting his bishop. This Creed is universally accepted as the standard of orthodoxy and the statement of the faith of the Church. There is no question that it is a

"We acknowledge one baptism for the forgiveness of sins."

Cyril of Jerusalem (*c.* 315–386)[105]
"Let no one then suppose that Baptism is merely the grace of remission of sins, or further, that of adoption; as John's baptism bestowed only the remission of sins. Nay we know full well, that as it purges our sins, and conveys to us the gift of the Holy Spirit, so also it is the counterpart of Christ's sufferings."[106]

---

pinnacle of Christian thought, the essence of the Christian faith packed into a few lofty lines.

The Nicene Creed is recited every Sunday in every Catholic Mass celebrated around the world. The clause of the Creed regarding baptism is a sublime summation of all the teaching on baptism from Scripture and the early Church—the most profound of doctrines distilled into nine pregnant words. Notice there is no hint of baptism being "only symbolic," a simple "outward sign of an inward reality." A typical Fundamentalist Protestant theology textbook reads, "Water baptism does not effect the identification with Christ: it presupposes and symbolizes it" (H. C. Thiessen, *Lectures in Systematic Theology* [Grand Rapids, Mich.: Eerdmans, 1973], 424). This statement stands in stark contrast to the Scriptures and the universal teaching of the early Church, but the Fundamentalist *must* take this position if he wants to defend his teaching of "salvation by faith alone."

The Catholic Church, however, continues faithfully to teach the ancient doctrines of the primitive Church. "Basing itself on scripture and tradition, it teaches that the Church, a pilgrim now on earth, is necessary for salvation: The one Christ is mediator and the way of salvation; he is present to us in his body which is the Church. He himself explicitly asserted the necessity of faith and Baptism, and thereby affirmed at the same time the necessity of the Church which men enter through Baptism as through a door" (*Lumen gentium* no. 14, quoted in CCC 846).

105 Cyril of Jerusalem, bishop of Jerusalem, was banished from that city because of his strong stand against the heresy of Arianism, which claimed Jesus was simply a creature (the basic belief of the Jehovah's Witnesses today). St. Cyril is a Father and Doctor of the Church. The arch-heretic Arius once accused him of selling the treasures of his church to feed the poor in a time of famine; and for this the assembly deposed him—he was deposed and restored several times by heretics and Roman emperors alike. His writings are invaluable as a source of information on the Church of the fourth century and earlier because of his gleaning from earlier writings and customs. His writings consist of twenty-three treatises, eighteen of which are addressed to catechumens and five to the newly baptized.

106 Cyril of Jerusalem, *Mystagogical Catecheses* 2, 5–7, in Quasten, *Patrology*,

"Unless a man receive baptism, he has no salvation, excepting only martyrs, who receive the kingdom though they have not entered the [baptismal] font. For when the Savior was redeeming the universe by means of His cross and His side was pierced, 'forthwith come there out blood and water' [Jn 19:34], to show that in times of peace men should be baptized in water, and in time of persecution in their own blood."[107]

"Do not think of the font as filled with ordinary water, but think rather of the spiritual grace that is given with the water. For just as the sacrifices on pagan altars are in themselves indifferent matter and yet have become defiled by reason of the invocation made over them to the idols, so, but in the opposite sense, the ordinary water in the font acquires sanctifying power when it receives the invocation of the Holy Spirit, of Christ and the Father."[108]

Ambrose of Milan (*c.* 339–397)[109]

3:373. This passage rebukes those who believe baptism brings about only the remission of sins and adoption. He tells them it does much more; namely, it places the individual into the death and Resurrection of Christ as explained in Romans 6. In this short sentence Cyril captures the essence of Jesus' teaching on water and the Spirit and Paul's teaching on baptism as our incorporation into the death and Resurrection of Christ.

107 Cyril of Jerusalem, *Procatechesis* 16, in Quasten, *Patrology*, 3:374. Also in this work he calls baptism the "holy indelible seal," the "ransom for the captives, remission of offenses, death of sin," and the "regeneration of the soul." It should be noted here that the Church has always held that there are three baptisms: the baptism of water, of blood, and of desire. The baptism of blood, spoken of in this passage, occurs when a person is martyred before having the opportunity to receive water baptism, and the baptism of desire occurs when a person earnestly desires baptism but is unable to secure the sacrament for himself (e.g., the thief on the cross in Luke 23:39–43).

108 Cyril of Jerusalem, *Mystagogical Catecheses* 3, 3, in Quasten, *Patrology*, 3:374. Is it water or Spirit? It is not *either/or*. It is *both/and*. The Incarnation proves that God uses earthly material for spiritual ends. Is it not also recorded that Jesus took ordinary clay and spittle, and an ordinary washing with water, to heal a man's blindness (Jn 9:6–7)? He used his breath to "breathe" the Holy Spirit into his apostles (Jn 20:22). We should not deny God the use of his own creation.

109 Ambrose was the son of a Praetorian prefect in Gaul (modern-day France) and was himself a practicing lawyer before being chosen as a governor in Milan. Ambrose was appointed bishop of Milan in 374 to replace an

"After this the Holy of Holies [symbolic for baptistery] was opened to you, you entered the sanctuary of regeneration; recall what you were asked, and remember what you answered. You renounced the devil and his works, the world with its luxury and pleasures. That utterance of yours is preserved not in the tombs of the dead, but in the book of the living. You saw there the deacon, you saw the priest, you saw the High Priest [i.e., the bishop]. . . . What did you see? Water, certainly, but not water alone. . . . The Apostle taught you that those things are not to be considered 'which we see, but the things which are not seen, for the things that are seen are temporal, but the things which are not seen are eternal'. . . . The water then, is that in which the flesh is dipped, that all carnal sin may be washed away. All wickedness is there buried. . . . The reason why you were told before not to believe only what you saw was that you might not say perchance, I see water, which I have been used to seeing every day. Is that water to cleanse me now, in which I have so often bathed without ever being cleansed? By this you may recognize that water does not cleanse without the Spirit.

"Therefore read that the three witnesses in baptism, the water, the blood, and the Spirit [1 Jn 5:1], are one, for if you take away one of these, the Sacrament of Baptism does not exist. For what is water without the cross of Christ? A common element without any sacramental effect. Nor, again, is there the Sacrament of Regeneration without water: 'For except a man be born again of water and the Spirit, he cannot enter into the kingdom of God' (Jn 3:5). Now, even the catechumen believes in the cross of the Lord Jesus, wherewith he too is signed [sign of the cross]; but unless he be baptized in the Name of the Father, and of the Son, and of the Holy Spirit, he cannot receive remission of sins and not gain the gift of spiritual grace."[110]

Arian bishop. He was a famous preacher and a jealous upholder of orthodoxy, aggressively combating paganism and Arianism. He was instrumental in the conversion of St. Augustine, who always revered him.

110 Ambrose of Milan, *The Mysteries*, chaps. 2–4, in Schaff, *Nicene and Post-Nicene Fathers*, 2d series, 10:317–19. This book discusses the sacraments of the Church, given to her by her Savior, Jesus, through the apostles. Here we have a most eloquent presentation of the primitive Church's practice and teaching of the sacraments, as learned from the apostles and carried on faithfully by the Catholic Church from the beginning. Throughout the whole discourse St. Ambrose uses the magnificent passages of Old Testa-

John Chrysostom (*c.* 347–407)[111]
"Weep for the unbelievers! Weep for those who differ not a whit from them, those who go hence without illumination, without the seal![112] These truly deserve our lamentations and tears. They are outside the royal city with those who have been found guilty, with the condemned. 'Amen, I tell you, if anyone is not born of water and the Spirit, he shall not enter into the kingdom of heaven.' "[113]

"They are citizens of the Church. . . . You see how many are the benefits of Baptism, and some think its heavenly grace consists only in the remission of sins; but we have enumerated ten honors. For this reason we baptize even infants, though they are not defiled by sins [or, though they do not have sins]:[114] so that there may be given

---

ment Scripture to illuminate the sacrament of baptism: creation, Egypt and the Red Sea, the Tabernacle, Noah and the flood, the bitter waters of Marah, Naaman cleansed of leprosy, etc. All of these teach regeneration, cleansing of sin, and entrance into the Church and eternal life through water, which is the sacrament of baptism.

111 John Chrysostom, bishop of Constantinople and Doctor of the Church. After the death of his mother, for whom he had long cared during her illness, he lived in the desert as a hermit, in prayer and study. He was ordained a priest in 386 and was appointed to give special devotion to preaching (which is how he got his title, "Chrysostom", which means "golden-tongued"). His homilies on the books of the Bible earned him the title "the greatest of Christian expositors," and he held to a literal interpretation of the Scriptures as opposed to the allegorical method that had been employed by Origen. He was made bishop in 398. His combination of honesty, asceticism, and tactlessness got him into trouble: he spoke out against immorality, and this worked his ruin. After being banished and exiled, he was killed by being forced to walk a long distance in very severe weather. He is remembered for his personal holiness, excellent biblical preaching, and his moral and ecclesiastical reforms (see his treatise *On the Priesthood*).

112 In Chrysostom's writings the seal and illumination refer to baptism and confirmation after baptism. "For him Confirmation is inseparable from Baptism and is simply the crown on the baptismal rite" (Jurgens, *Faith of the Early Fathers*, 2:122, note 7).

113 John Chrysostom, *Homilies on Philippians* 3, 4, in Jurgens, *Faith of the Early Fathers*, 2:121. This course of fifteen homilies on Philippians was probably composed at Constantinople, between 398 and 404.

114 St. Augustine clearly demonstrated that St. John Chrysostom, in using the plural *sins*, meant personal sins, not the original sin of Adam (see Quasten,

to them holiness, righteousness, adoption, inheritance, brotherhood with Christ, and that they may be His members."[115]

"That the need of water is absolute and indispensable, you may learn in this way. On one occasion, when the Spirit had flown down before the water was applied, the Apostle did not stay at that point, but as though the water were necessary and not superfluous, observe what he says; 'Can any man forbid water, that these should not be baptized, which have received the Holy Ghost as well as we?' "[116]

" 'There flowed from his side water and blood' [Jn 19:34]. Beloved, do not pass over this mystery without thought; it has yet another hidden meaning, which I will explain to you. I said that water and blood symbolized baptism and the holy Eucharist. From these two sacraments the Church is born: from baptism, 'the cleansing water that gives rebirth and renewal through the Holy Spirit' [Titus 3:5], and from the holy Eucharist. Since the symbols of baptism and the Eucharist flowed from his side, it was from his side that Christ fashioned the Church, as he had fashioned Eve from the side of Adam. Moses gives a hint of this when he tells the story of the first man and makes him exclaim: 'Bone from my bones and flesh from my flesh!' As God then took a rib from Adam's side to fashion a woman, so Christ has given us blood and water from his side to fashion the

---

Patrology, 3:478). St. Augustine writes, "You see that he [John Chrysostom] certainly did not say, 'Infants are not defiled by sin', or 'sins', but, 'Not having sins.' Understand 'of their own' and there is no difficulty. 'But,' you will say, 'why did he not add "of their own" himself?' Why else, I suppose, if not that he was speaking in a Catholic church and never supposed he would be understood in any other way, when no one had raised such a question?" (Jurgens, *Faith of the Early Fathers*, 2:100–101). It was understood by Augustine that sins were individual sins, which each person personally commits, whereas sin, in the singular, is the original sin inherited from Adam. Therefore the infants have not yet committed sins, but they are affected by original sin, for which baptism is the remedy.

115 John Chrysostom, *Baptismal Catecheses*, Apud Aug., Contra Iul. 1, 6, 21, in Jurgens, *Faith of the Early Fathers*, 2:100. Instructions to the catechumens in Antioch in the years 388–389.

116 John Chrysostom, *Homilies on St. John: Chapter 3:5*, homily 25, 2, in Schaff, *Nicene and Post-Nicene Fathers*, 1st series, 14:89. John Chrysostom's course of eighty-eight homilies on the Gospel of St. John were composed around 391. In them he strongly defends the regenerational necessity of baptism and concurs with all that had been faithfully handed down since the apostles.

Church. God took the rib when Adam was in a deep sleep, and in the same way Christ gave us the blood and the water after his own death."[117]

Jerome (342–420)[118]

"All iniquities, we are told, are forgiven us at our baptism, and when once we have received God's mercy we need not afterwards dread from Him the severity of a judge. The apostle says, 'And such were some of you: but ye are washed, but ye are sanctified, but ye are justified in the name of the Lord Jesus, and by the Spirit of our God.' All sins then are forgiven; it is an honest and faithful saying. . . . What the true effect of baptism is, and what is the real grace conveyed by water hallowed in Christ, I will presently tell you."[119]

Let me now fulfill the promise I made a little while ago and with all the skill of a rhetorician sing the praises of water and of baptism [here he goes through a number of Old Testament examples of baptism]. . . . The Savior himself does not preach the kingdom of heaven until by His baptismal immersion He has cleansed the Jordan. Water is the matter of His first miracle. . . . To Nicodemus He

117 John Chrysostom, *Catecheses* 3, 13–19, in *The Office of Readings* (Boston, Mass.: Daughters of St. Paul, 1983), 479–80. Clearly Jesus' words in John 3:5, explaining the means of new birth, are understood universally by the early Church as the water of baptism. Water baptism, the sacrament of faith, brings about the forgiveness of sins and the new birth. The correlation between Adam and Christ, both "dying" to have a bride taken from their sides, is glorious. The sacraments were effectual as the oaths of God's covenant with his new covenant people, the Church.

118 Jerome was a renowned biblical scholar who studied in Rome, where he was baptized. After traveling to Gaul (modern France), he went to Palestine. After being convicted in a dream of preferring pagan literature to religious, he became a hermit and lived in the desert for five years and, while there, learned Hebrew. He was ordained a priest in Antioch and then spent time in Constantinople and Rome. The last years of his life were spent in Bethlehem, where he devoted his life to study and running a monastery. Jerome's writings display a scholarship unsurpassed in the early Church. He is especially celebrated for his translation of the Bible (the Vulgate) from the original languages into Latin, which was the language of the Roman world. (See Cross and Livingston, *Oxford Dictionary of the Christian Church*, 731.)

119 Jerome, *Letter* 69, 4–5, in Schaff, *Nicene and Post-Nicene Fathers*, 1st series, 6:144.

secretly says:—'Except a man be born of water and of the Spirit, he cannot enter into the Kingdom of God.' As His earthly course began with water, so it ended with it. His side is pierced by the spear, and blood and water flow forth, twin emblems of baptism and of martyrdom. After His resurrection also, when sending His apostles to the Gentiles, He commands them to baptize these in the mystery of the Trinity. . . . And it is to the grace of baptism that the prophecy of Micah refers: 'He will turn again, he will have compassion on us: he will subdue our iniquities, and will cast all our sins into the depths of the sea'. . . . Time would fail me were I to try to lay before you in order all the passages in the Holy Scriptures which relate to the efficacy of baptism or to explain the mysterious doctrine of that second birth."[120]

Augustine of Hippo (354–430)[121]

"A gouty doctor of the same city, when he had given his name for baptism, and had been prohibited the day before his baptism from being baptized that year, by black wooly-haired boys who appeared to him in his dreams, and whom he understood to be devils, and when, though they trod on his feet, and inflicted the acutest pain he had ever yet experienced, he refused to obey them, but overcame them,

120 Ibid., 6, 7, pp. 145–46.

121 Augustine of Hippo is one of the more impressive and influential Christians in the history of the Church. He was born in Tagaste, Numidia (Algeria). His father, Patricius, was a pagan (later converted to Christianity), but his mother, Monica, was a devout Christian. As a young man, Augustine led a wild and pagan life and lived with his mistress for fifteen years. He spent nine years in a heretical group called the Manichaeans. When they failed to provide answers to his many questions, he left for Rome and then Milan, where his mother's prayers for his salvation were eventually answered. In Milan he come in contact with Ambrose, the bishop of Milan (mentioned earlier in this work). "Having taken the decision to give up teaching and to forgo marriage, he retired toward the end of October . . . in order to prepare for baptism. He returned to Milan at the beginning of March, enrolled himself among the catechumens, followed the catechetical instruction of Ambrose and . . . was baptized by him at the Easter Vigil during the night of April 24–25, 387. [He said] 'And there fled from us all the anxiety of our past life' " (*Conf.* 9, 6, 14, in Quasten, *Patrology*, 4:348–49). He was ordained a priest in 391 and consecrated as a bishop in 395. Many, many books have been written on Augustine, and his own writings take up massive volumes.

and would not defer being washed in the laver of regeneration, was relieved in the very act of baptism, not only of the extraordinary pain he was tortured with, but also of the disease itself, so that, though he lived a long time afterwards, he never suffered from gout.

"And earlier in the same city of Carthage lived Innocentia, a very devout woman of the highest rank in the state. She had cancer in one of her breasts, a disease which, as physicians say, is incurable. Ordinarily . . . they amputate . . . though death is inevitable even if somewhat delayed, they abandon all remedies. . . . On the approach of Easter, she was instructed in a dream to wait for the first woman that came out from the baptistery after being baptized, and to ask her to make the sign of Christ [the cross] upon her sore. She did so, and was immediately cured."[122]

"Who is so impious as to wish to exclude infants from the kingdom of heaven by forbidding them to be baptized and born again in Christ?"[123]

"This [infant baptism] the Church always had, always held; this she received from the faith of our ancestors; this she perseveringly guards even to the end."[124] " 'Now ye are clean through the word which I have spoken unto you.' Why does He not say, Ye are clean through the baptism wherewith ye have been washed, but 'through the word which I have spoken unto you,' save only that in the water also it is the word that cleanseth? Take away the word, and the water is neither more or less than water. The word is added to the element [of water], and there results the Sacrament. . . . And whence has the water so great an efficacy, as in touching the body to cleanse the soul, save by the operation of the word; and that not because it is uttered,

---

122 Augustine, *City of God*, bk. 22, chap. 8, in Schaff, *Nicene and Post-Nicene Fathers*, 1st series, 2:486–87. This section in *The City of God* is a treasure-trove of miracle accounts passed on by Augustine to prove the mighty hand of God demonstrating his power, especially regarding the reality of the sacrament of baptism.

123 Augustine, *On Original Sin* 2, 20, in Schaff, *Nicene and Post-Nicene Fathers*, 1st series, 5:244.

124 Augustine, *Serm.* 11, *De Verb Apost.*, in *The Catholic Encyclopedia*, 2:270. Not only did the first Christians universally accept and teach infant baptism, but they considered it a great evil to withhold baptism from the infant, much the same as if the Jews were to refuse circumcision to their young.

but because it is believed? . . . 'This is the word of faith which we preach,' whereby baptism, doubtless, is also consecrated, in order to its possession of the power to cleanse."[125]

"Our Lord Jesus Christ showed the way, as you have heard, brethren, lest any man, arrogating to himself that he has abundance of some particular grace, should disdain to be baptized with the baptism of the Lord. For whatever the catechumen's proficiency, he still carries the load of his iniquity: it is not forgiven him until he shall have come to baptism. Just as the people of Israel were not rid of the Egyptians until they had come to the Red Sea, so no man is rid of the pressure of sins until he has come to the font of baptism."[126]

Baptism as Taught in Current Church Teaching

Catechism of the Council of Trent (1566)

"Besides a wish to be baptized, in order to obtain the grace of the Sacrament, faith is also necessary. Our Lord and Savior has said: 'He that believes and is baptized shall be saved.' "[127]

"With regard to the definition of Baptism although many can be given from the sacred writers, nevertheless that which may be gathered from the words of our Lord recorded in John, and of the Apostle to the Ephesians, appears the most appropriate and suitable. 'Unless,' says our Lord, 'a man be born again of water and the Holy Spirit, he cannot enter into the kingdom of God' [Jn 3:5]; and, speaking of the Church, the Apostle says, 'cleansing it by the laver of water in the word of life' [Eph 5:26]. Thus it follows that Baptism may be

125 Augustine, *On the Gospel of St. John*, tractate 80, 3, in Schaff, *Nicene and Post-Nicene Fathers*, 1st series, 7:344–45. The water needs the word of faith; when joined to the word of faith, the water becomes effective through the Spirit (Eph 5:26).

126 Ibid., tractate 13, 7, p. 89. The last Church Father we will look at in this study, Augustine summarizes quite nicely what the Church has taught from the beginning, what all orthodox Christians have embraced since the apostles, and what the Catholic Church teaches today.

127 *The Catechism of the Council of Trent* (Rockford, Ill.: Tan Books, 1982), 181; originally published by decree of Pope Pius V in 1566. Faith is required in conjunction with baptism; not *either* faith *or* baptism, rather it is *both* faith *and* baptism. The teaching of the apostles stands strong and rings clear in the Catholic Church of the sixteenth century.

rightly and accurately defined: The Sacrament of regeneration by water in the word. By nature we are born from Adam children of wrath, but by Baptism we are regenerated in Christ, children of mercy. For He gave power to men 'to be made the sons of God, to them that believe in his name, who are born, not of blood, nor of the will of the flesh, nor of the will of man, but of God' [Jn 1:12–13]."[128]

"In Baptism not only is sin forgiven, but with it all the punishment due to sin is mercifully remitted by God. . . . By virtue of the Sacrament we are not only delivered from what are justly deemed the greatest of all evils, but are also enriched with invaluable goods and blessings. Our souls are replenished with divine grace, by which we are rendered just and children of God and are made heirs to eternal salvation."[129]

"This law extends not only to adults but also to infants and children, and that the church has received this from apostolic tradition, is confirmed by the unanimous teaching and authority of the Fathers. Besides, it is not to be supposed that Christ the Lord would have withheld the Sacrament and grace of Baptism from children, of whom He said: 'Suffer the little children, and forbid them not to come to me; for the kingdom of heaven is for such;' whom also He embraced, upon whom He imposed hands, to whom He gave His blessing.

"Moreover, when we read that an entire family was baptized by Paul, it is sufficiently obvious that the children of the family must also have been cleansed in the saving font. Circumcision, too, which was a figure of Baptism, affords a strong argument in proof of this practice."[130]

---

128 Ibid., 163. Just as Jesus and the apostles defined baptism in the New Testament, and the Fathers closely echoed their doctrine, so the Catholic Church has always held fast to the divine revelation passed on by the apostles.

129 Ibid., 185, 187–88. These selections are all taken from the chapter on baptism, which is thirty-seven pages long and reflects with great fidelity what we have already discovered in the Scriptures and the Fathers. They give no comfort to those who strip baptism of its sacramental powers.

130 Ibid., 177. The Council of Trent reaffirms and confirms the ancient practice of infant baptism and pronounces an anathema on those who deny this sacramental grace to children and infants. (See *The Canons and Councils of Trent*, fifth session, 4.)

Second Vatican Council (1962–1965)
"This holy Council first of all turns its attention to the Catholic faithful. Basing itself on scripture and tradition, it teaches that the Church, a pilgrim now on earth, is necessary for salvation: the one Christ is mediator and the way of salvation; he is present to us in his body which is the Church. He himself explicitly asserted the necessity of faith and baptism (cf. Mk 16:16; Jn 3:5), and thereby affirmed at the same time the necessity of the Church which men enter through baptism as through a door. Hence they could not be saved who, knowing that the Catholic Church was founded as necessary by God through Christ, would refuse to enter it, or to remain in it."[131]

"Accordingly, just as Christ was sent by the Father so also he sent the apostles, filled with the Holy Spirit. This he did so that they might preach the Gospel to every creature and proclaim that the Son of God by his death and resurrection had freed us from the power of Satan and from death, and brought us into the Kingdom of his Father. But he also willed that the work of salvation which they preached should be set in train through the sacrifice and sacraments, around which the entire liturgical life revolves. Thus by baptism men are grafted into the Paschal mystery of Christ; they die with him, are buried with him, and rise with him. They receive the spirit of adoption as sons 'in which we cry, Abba, Father' (Rom 8:15)."[132]

Catechism of the Catholic Church (1994)[133]
"The different effects of Baptism. . . . Immersion in water symbolizes not only death and purification, but also regeneration and renewal. Thus, the two principal effects are purification from sins and new birth in the Holy Spirit."[134]

---

131 *Vatican Council II*, ed. Austin Flannery, O.P., vol. 1, new rev. ed. (Collegeville, Minn.: Liturgical Press, 1992), *Lumen gentium*, no. 14, pp. 365–66.

132 Ibid., *Sacrosanctum concilium*, no. 6, p. 4.

133 This is the first major catechism in four hundred years. It was released in English in June 1994. It is a wonderfully lucid book, easy to read, completely orthodox, carefully preserving and explaining the teaching of Scripture and the tradition of the Church as deposited by the apostles and expounded by the Fathers.

134 CCC 1262.

"The Lord himself affirms that Baptism is necessary for salvation. . . . The Church does not know of any means other than Baptism that assures entry into eternal beatitude; this is why she takes care not to neglect the mission she has received from the Lord to see that all who can be baptized are 'reborn of water and the Spirit.' *God has bound salvation to the sacrament of Baptism, but he himself is not bound by his sacraments.*"[135]

"Born with a fallen human nature and tainted by original sin, children also have need of the new birth in Baptism to be freed from the power of darkness and brought into the realm of the freedom of the children of God, to which all men are called. The sheer gratuitousness of the grace of salvation is particularly manifest in infant Baptism. The Church and the parents would deny a child the priceless grace of becoming a child of God were they not to confer Baptism shortly after birth."[136]

Conclusion: A Few Comments and Observations

Now that we have come this far through Holy Scripture, the apostolic tradition of the first centuries, and the *current* teaching of the Church, we should make a few concluding remarks. The book of Ecclesiastes says that a cord of three strands is not easily broken (Qo 4:12). If a rope has but one strand, it snaps as soon as stress is applied, but a rope with three strands is very strong. Our study here has drawn from the Old Testament, the New Testament, and the tradition of the apostles preserved in the early Church. The overwhelming witness of the collected scriptural passages eliminates objections to the regenerative necessity of baptism. Remember, one verse cannot override and negate another verse. They all must be applied to the final and full interpretation. Add to that the witness of the early Church and the current teaching of the Church, and you have a very strong cord of three strands. Any individual verse may be circumvented and dismissed, and Protestants often consider our Fathers in the faith to be irrelevant (even though they defined the Trinity and the deity of

135 CCC 1257. These few selections are only a slight reflection of the rich truths discussed and explained in the *Catechism*, which reflects the Scriptures and the tradition as developed in the whole history of the Church.

136 CCC 1250.

Christ and collected the canon of Scripture). But, taken as a whole, the witness of the Scriptures and the Church is insurmountable.

Disregarding non-Christian objections to baptism, we will look at the main stumbling blocks experienced by Evangelical and Fundamentalist Protestants. The first objection to arise is simply this: *The Bible teaches we are justified by faith [alone] and not by works or deeds of the law; it is faith that saves us, not baptism.* My response is simple and threefold.

First, we are not in a position to argue with the Lord Jesus' clear teachings or the teachings of his apostles in the New Testament. The intent of the Scriptures is clear, especially when we see how the apostles' contemporaries, with the words of Peter and Paul still fresh in their minds and preserved unaltered in the churches, understood the doctrine and practice of baptism.[137] Those who had followed close on their heels, within the apostolic tradition, given by Christ himself,[138] faithfully preserved and passed on the truth of Christ and the Church.

We have ample evidence in the preceding pages to dispel any doubts or ambiguities concerning the customs and instructions of the apostles and the ancient Church regarding baptism. One has to be quite bold to turn his back on the clear evidence of the Scriptures and sixteen hundred years of unswerving consistency to follow reactionary innovations— new theological recipes. Those who say the Protestant views are *not* new inventions: I challenge you to produce your evidence! The Catholic Church has biblical exegesis and history on her side. Those who say the Catholic Church teaches a different baptism: Produce your evidence! Who understands better the fullness of the apostolic preaching of Peter and Paul: those of us two thousand years removed, or those who still had the apostles' teaching ringing in their ears and their practices fresh before their eyes?

Second, I would ask: Why do we have to accept false dichotomies? Why do we acknowledge only one side of the coin and reject the other? Why did I, as an Evangelical, so readily espouse the *either/or* mentality that runs deeply through Protestant theology? Why did I feel it

---

137 Ignatius of Antioch, the *Didache*, Barnabas, Hermas, Clement, etc.

138 Mt 28:19–20; Jn 16:4, 12–13; Acts 1:2–3; 2 Th 2:15; 3:6; Acts 20:35; 1 Cor 15:3–11, etc.

necessary to pronounce it is "*Either* baptism *or* faith? *Either* baptism *or* the Spirit?" Is it not obvious that the Lord himself did not think this way? He simply said, "Unless a man is born of water *and* the Spirit, he cannot enter the kingdom of heaven" (Jn 3:5). These two components, as we have seen, flow together as a clear and undivided stream from Genesis 1:1, through Moses and the prophets, through the teachings of Christ and the Twelve, through the early centuries to the Council of Trent, Vatican I, and Vatican II. The stream has continued to flow clear and pure into our own century, with fidelity and constancy within the Catholic Church! Who dreamed up this *either/or* dichotomy, anyway?

Martin Luther added a little word to the New Testament that had a far-reaching impact—altering the thought processes of many Christians. It was the word *alone.*[139] This little word added a big idea. This idea, that two things cannot work together, started a snowball rolling that cut everything in two pieces. It set up false dichotomies. You were forced to choose one side or the other. You couldn't believe both, or you weren't a real Bible-Christian. It changed everything, and those who embraced this new way of thinking, myself included, were impoverished, as even the Reformers themselves soon understood.

Are we saved by faith alone *or* by baptism? Do we look to Scripture alone *or* the sacred tradition? Is baptism an effective sacrament *or* a symbol? Is Christ our only intercessor *or* do we ask others to pray

---

139 In Romans 3:28, where Paul writes, "For we hold that a man is justified by faith apart from works of law," Luther added the little word "alone" after the word "faith." Paul was not saying that we are saved by faith *alone*; he was saying we are saved by faith and not as a result of our own unaided efforts or by practicing all the ceremonies of the Jewish Law. Where is grace if we are saved by faith alone? Is faith a "work" we do— the *act* of believing (cf. Jn 6:28–29)? It is clear from the New Testament that we are not freed from the moral law of God subsequent to salvation. In fact, the first time the word *faith* is used by Paul in Romans, this is what is said: "to bring about the obedience of faith" (Rom 1:5). Guess how the word *faith* is used the last time in Romans, framing the book? You guessed it, "obedience of faith." This is not faith alone but obedience also. Obedience in what way? Obedience brought about by faith, working itself out in love. There is only one place in Scripture where we read of "faith alone." It is located in James 2:24: "You see that a man is justified by works and not by faith alone."

for us? Notice all the *either/or*'s, the mistaken and harmful divisions. Catholics see these as *both/and*'s. Did Jesus divide baptism from the Holy Spirit? No, he said water *and* Spirit. Does Paul say *either* Scripture *or* tradition? No, he said Scripture *and* tradition (2 Th 2:15). We need to consider seriously our approach to truth.

Third, why is it that some deny Christ the use of his own creation? Why do we deny God the freedom to use sacraments?[140] The Protestant idea is that the Old Covenant involved "visible things": like the blood of lambs, altars, incense, washings, circumcision, tabernacles, manna, and so on, but the New Covenant consists only of *invisible* things, seen by faith alone. There are no "real things," only symbolic language about spiritual things. However, this approach is belied by the fact that the New Covenant started out with gynecology and obstetrics, mangers and shepherds; it involved a real wooden cross and painful nails. There are tombs, bread and wine, touching real nail holes, washing dirty feet, bodily resurrections, withering fig trees, flames of fire, special days, "favorable years," and so on.

In between his birth and death, there were other "material things" involved to impart or facilitate spiritual life: Jesus took spittle and clay to heal a man's eyes (Jn 9:6)—why not faith alone? Jesus laid his hands on children to bless them (Mk 10:16); he breathed on the apostles to impart the Holy Spirit (Jn 20:22); he brought coins from a fish's mouth (Mt 17:27), fed thousands with five loaves and two fish (Jn 6:9–13), turned water into wine (Jn 2:2–12); he said that the loaf was his "body" (Mt 26:26); he revealed himself to men "through the breaking of the bread" (Lk 24:30–31); he also put his finger in a man's ears and spit and touched his tongue (Mk 7:33). What a strange way to start a New Covenant that won't involve *things*. Is it unbiblical, considering these scriptural passages, to think God would use sacraments, or physical matter, to impart his grace?

What about the strange situation in Ephesus, where handkerchiefs

140 "The word 'sacrament' means pledge, or mystery. It does not occur in the Bible, any more than do words like Trinity, substitution, prelapsarian, or inerrancy. Christian vocabulary is full of words that have come into use as the Christian mind has gone to work on what it finds in the Scripture" (Thomas Howard, *Evangelical Is Not Enough* [San Francisco: Ignatius Press, 1984], 105). A sacrament is an outward sign or symbol that brings about what it signifies. It is one of God's means of imparting grace to his Church.

were carried away from Paul's body and used to heal and expel demons? What about Peter's shadow?[141] And why in this new "thingless" era do we still have to eat bread and drink wine, and get wet for baptism? Why the need for the laying on of hands for spiritual gifts, ordination, and healing? And what's this in James about using oil to anoint people for healing and the forgiveness of sins?[142] This really sounds "Old Covenant" to me. And wasn't the new dispensation started by real tongues of fire dancing on real people's heads? Why is there an altar in heaven? And what about the golden bowls, burning coals, and incense in heaven? Can't the Creator still use his own creation? Can he use water to cleanse a soul if he so desires? Can he use clay to anoint a man's eyes, instead of just "speaking the word"? Can he really transform bread and wine into his body and blood? Wasn't he the one who turned water into wine and fed five thousand men with five loaves and two fishes? Can he use his oil to seal or anoint? Why is he denied the use of the things he has made for sacraments that can really impart grace, not merely symbolize it? Has this perhaps been extrapolated from the little word *only* again, the little word that was added?

God uses matter. He even created Adam from the dust of the ground and Eve from Adam's rib. He blew life into matter and created a being. He now creates in us his new life by his Spirit, through the agency of matter, in the form of water. It is not contrary to God's character or track record to do such a thing; in fact, the Incarnation of Christ—God taking on flesh—shows he is not adverse to using matter, physical things, to bring about spiritual ends. God became man through the Incarnation, and the sacraments are only an extension of the incarnational theology. God can use matter; he can use

---

141 Acts 19:11–12: "And God was performing extraordinary miracles by the hands of Paul, so that handkerchiefs or aprons were even carried from his body to the sick, and the diseases left them and the evil spirits went out."

Acts 5:15–16: "They even carried the sick out into the streets, and laid them on cots and pallets, so that when Peter came by, at least his shadow might fall on any one of them . . . and they were all being healed."

142 James 5:14–15: "Is anyone among you sick? Let him call for the elders of the church, and let them pray over him, anointing him with oil in the name of the Lord, and the prayer offered in faith will restore the one who is sick, and the Lord will raise him up, and if he has committed sins, they will be forgiven him."

sacraments to impart grace to his people.

I will close this section with a quotation explaining the Roman Catholic Church's teaching on salvation. It does not smack of humanism, as the Fundamentalist accusations would imply—as I once charged; rather it reflects the fullness of Scripture and the teachings of the Twelve. Referring to 1 Corinthians 6:11, the Catholic Church proclaims, "The followers of Christ, called by God not in virtue of their works but by his design and grace, and justified in the Lord Jesus, have been made sons of God in baptism, the sacrament of faith, and partakers of the divine nature, and so are truly sanctified. They must therefore hold on to and perfect in their lives that sanctification which they have received from God" (*Lumen gentium*, no. 40).

As a Protestant, I carefully studied the works of Harry A. Ironside, a stalwart Fundamentalist preacher and author. In his booklet *Baptism*, Ironside writes, "The query as to whether baptism brings its subject into the Kingdom of Heaven, the House of God, or the Body of Christ, has not really been touched. Here I need only to say that I do not believe it brings one into any of the three."[143] Now I see beyond the narrow customs of my childhood faith. I see and believe with the saints of the past that the Church is necessary and is entered through baptism as through a door. I am grateful to those who helped us see our way home, and I am grateful to the Father, the Son, and the Holy Spirit for leading us to the ark (that was so long hidden in a shroud of misinformation and fog), the Body of Christ, the "one, holy, catholic, and apostolic Church."

---

143 Harry A. Ironside, *Baptism*, 3d ed. (Neptune, N.J.: Loiseaux Bros., 1930), 4.

PART THREE

THE EUCHARIST IN THE SCRIPTURES AND IN THE ANCIENT CHURCH

Introduction

The doctrine of the Eucharist: the Real Presence of Christ and the sacrificial nature of the Mass are major stumbling stones for Evangelicals. Just as Judas Iscariot apparently stumbled at the Real Presence and parted ways with Christ at that point,[1] so the Evangelical leaves the historical teaching of Christ and the Church on this point. Did Jesus leave it up to each individual to decide for himself what the bread and wine were all about? Were there a multitude of different interpretations of our Lord's words "This is my Body" among the apostles and among the Fathers of the primitive Church? The answer is a resounding No! In this section we will investigate the Scriptures, the Fathers of the Church, the opposition, and the current Church teaching.

The following quotations and passages come from the Bible, the apostolic period, and the documents of the early Church. The pas-

---

1 The context of John 6:60–71 links Judas' betrayal with his disbelief in the Eucharist: "Jesus knew from the first who those were that did not believe, and who it was that would betray him. . . . Jesus answered them, 'Did I not choose you, the twelve, and one of you is a devil?' He spoke of Judas the son of Simon Iscariot, for he, one of the twelve, was to betray him." As Karl Keating writes, "There were many of his disciples who said, when they heard it, 'This is strange talk, who can be expected to listen to it?' (Jn 6:61). These were his *disciples*, people who already were used to his remarkable ways. . . . But he knew some did not believe, including the one who was to betray him. (It is here, in the rejection of the Eucharist, that Judas fell away.)" (Karl Keating, *Catholicism and Fundamentalism* [San Francisco: Ignatius Press, 1988], 234.) We also have the other Gospels that record Satan entering Judas at the Last Supper, the institution of the Eucharist.

sages are only a small sampling, gleaned from the most ancient sources and arranged chronologically to follow the flow of history. They were written by our forefathers, true heroes of the faith, and show the impressive continuity of doctrine concerning the Blessed Eucharist in the Catholic Church, both historically and geographically.

The initial reaction of some may be to think we are being very selective in our citations and using only those that support the Real Presence of Christ in the bread and wine. This is not true. The Church down through the ages has spoken with one voice. These penetrating passages reflect the ubiquitous doctrine of orthodox Christianity, and they speak here for themselves.

As we proceed with this overview of history, we will allow the Scriptures and the unobtrusive voice of the past to speak again in our century. In many quarters, over the last few centuries, their voices have been drowned out by the din of opposition and dissent. Revolutionary ideas, like a voracious flood, have attempted to wash away the foundations and the clear historical precedents of the Holy Spirit's work in the primitive Church.

History has a clear and distinct voice, but it does not force itself upon us uninvited. History is prudent and waits quietly to be discovered. Conversely, the ingenious inventions of later centuries are often loud, bursting upon our ears and minds, our lives and hearts, demanding our immediate attention and loyalties. The riches of history fall quietly aside as the prattling innovators blare their trumpets and loudly parade their followers through new streets, trampling the knowledge of the ages under their cumulative feet.

Here we will allow the voices of the past to speak again—for themselves. And what the reader will find is that the utterances of the past still resound with one voice, with clarity and force. Studying those who have gone before us, following in the footsteps of the Lord Jesus and his apostles, leads one to lose interest in much of the clamor of modern notions. We find the latter poorly devised, if not disingenuous. This is what John Henry Newman found when, as a Protestant clergyman, he studied the primitive Church. He concluded: "To be deep in history is to cease to be a Protestant."[2] As the

---

2 John Henry Newman, *Conscience, Consensus, and the Development of Doctrine* (New York: Doubleday, 1992), 50.

Protestant churches continue to ignore history and to fragment and lose the fervor and common ground of their past reform efforts, many Evangelicals and Fundamentalists are looking to the past to hear what the Fathers have to say today. They are beginning to listen to the unintrusive voice of the ancient Church, and they are finding it is quite different from what they thought. Reading the writings of these first soldiers of the faith allows us to tap into the very heartbeat of the apostolic teaching and tradition of the primitive Church. We will be asking the important question: Was the Church of the apostles and the Fathers essentially Catholic or Protestant? What I discovered surprised me. It is really a matter of empirical evidence; study is necessary, and we have done much of the work so that the reader can decide for himself. The short bibliography at the end of the book will aid further reading.

The Eucharist as Taught in Scripture

Genesis 14 (event took place *c.* 2150 b.c.–*c.* 1800 b.c.)

"And Melchizedek king of Salem brought out bread and wine; he was priest of God Most High. And he blessed him and said, 'Blessed be Abram by God Most High, maker of heaven and earth; and blessed be God Most High, who has delivered your enemies into your hand!' And Abram gave him a tenth of everything."[3]

---

3 Gen 14:18–20. Melchizedek is mentioned twice in the Old Testament and nine times in Hebrews, where the writer demonstrates that Christ, not from the priestly tribe of Levi, obtained a priesthood superior to that of Aaron and the Levites, according to the order of Melchizedek. We are the rich recipients of his Priesthood, partaking in the salvation it bestows. But, what about the bread and wine? How was this priestly meal understood by the early Church? Cyprian of Carthage (d. 258) wrote, "In the priest Melchizedek we see prefigured the sacrament of the sacrifice of the Lord, according to what divine Scripture testifies, 'And Melchizedek, king of Salem, brought forth bread and wine.' . . . For who is more a priest of the most high God than our Lord Jesus Christ, who offered a sacrifice to God the Father, and offered that very same thing which Melchizedek had offered, that is, bread and wine, to wit, His body and blood? . . . In Genesis therefore, that the benediction . . . might be duly celebrated, the figure of Christ's sacrifice precedes as ordained in bread and wine; which thing the Lord, completing and fulfilling, offered bread and the cup mixed with wine, and so He who is the fullness of truth fulfilled the truth of the image prefigured" (*Epistle to Caecilius on the Sacrament of the Cup of the Lord* [written in 253], sec. 4, in Alexander Roberts and James

Psalm 110
"The Lord says to my lord: 'Sit at my right hand, till I make your enemies your footstool.' . . . The Lord has sworn and will not change his mind, 'You are a priest for ever after the order of Melchizedek.' "[4]

Book of Exodus (*c.* fourteenth to *c.* thirteenth century b.c.)
"Your lamb shall be without blemish, a male a year old. . . . Then they shall take some of the blood, and put it on the two doorposts and the lintel of the houses in which they eat them. They shall eat the flesh that night. . . . And you shall let none of it remain until the morning. . . . In this manner you shall eat it: your loins girded, your sandals on your feet, and your staff in your hand; and you shall eat it in haste. It is the Lord's passover."[5]

Donaldson, eds., *The Ante-Nicene Fathers*, arr. A. Cleveland Coxe [Grand Rapids, Mich.: Eerdmans, 1985], 5:359). The Catholic Church "sees in the gesture of the king priest Melchizedek, who 'brought out bread and wine,' a prefiguring of her own offering [in the Eucharist]" (CCC 1333).

4 Ps 110:1–4; Heb 7:17. Jesus is the priest after the pattern of Melchizedek, a priesthood forever. He it is who brings the sacrifice of his own flesh and blood. He it is who brings us the gift of bread and wine. Around the year 202, Clement of Alexandria wrote in his *Stromata* 25, in Roberts and Donaldson, *Ante-Nicene Fathers*, 2:439, that "As Moses says, Melchizedek king of Salem, priest of the most high God, who gave bread and wine, furnishing consecrated food for a type of the Eucharist." Referring to Jesus in Psalm 110, St. Augustine says, "For you seek a sacrifice among the Jews; you have none after the order of Aaron. You seek it after the order of Melchizedek; you find it not among them, but through the whole world it is celebrated in the Church [the Eucharist]. 'From the rising of the sun to the setting thereof the name of the Lord is praised' " (*On the Psalms* 107, 8, in Philip Schaff, ed., *The Nicene and Post-Nicene Fathers*, 1st series [Grand Rapids, Mich.: Eerdmans, 1983], 8:535).

5 Ex 12:5, 7–8, 10–11. The Passover took place at one point in time but was never to be a one-time event. It was to be repeated in the spring of every year. It was to remind the Jews of the great deliverance through sacrifice and blood. It was to be a sacrifice of remembrance. In the Deuteronomic account (Dt 16), the sacrifice is no longer to be performed in private homes but "at the place which the Lord will choose, to make his name dwell there" [i.e., the Temple]. The Israelites were always to celebrate the Passover in the "present tense" to make it a present event. In both passages the eating of the Passover lamb was linked with eating of the unleavened bread. Jesus was recognized by

Book of Exodus (event took place *c.* 1450 b.c.)
"Then the Lord said to Moses, 'Behold, I will rain bread from heaven for you; and the people shall go out and gather a day's portion every day, that I may prove them, whether they will walk in my law or not. . . . ' And when the dew had gone up, there was on the face of the wilderness a fine, flake-like thing, fine as hoarfrost on the ground. When the people of Israel saw it, they said to one another, 'What is it?' For they did not know what it was. And Moses said to them, 'It is the bread which the Lord has given you to eat. . . . ' And the people of Israel ate the manna forty years, till they came to a habitable land; they ate the manna, till they came to the border of the land of Canaan."[6]

The Prophet Micah (Old Testament prophet who lived between 740 and 695 b.c.)
"But you, O Bethlehem [City of Bread] Ephrathah, who are little to be among the clans of Judah, from you shall come forth for me one

---

John the Baptist when John declared, "Behold, the Lamb of God, who takes away the sin of the world!" (Jn 1:29). Jesus announced that he gave his flesh for the life of the world. Each year at the Passover the lamb had to be eaten and no flesh could remain until morning. The word *eat* is emphasized in Exodus 12 (used twelve times). Notice that the sacrifice and offering, the lamb, had to be completely consumed for the Passover to be correctly reenacted, just as the flesh of Jesus is to be eaten in the celebration of the Eucharist. It was at the Passover dinner in Jerusalem, before his death, that Jesus converted the Passover meal into the sacrament of the Eucharist.

6 Ex 16:4, 14–15, 35. The manna prefigured the "Bread of Life" that came down from heaven. John records the words of Jesus, "I am the bread of life. Your fathers ate the manna in the wilderness, and they died. This is the bread which comes down from heaven, that a man may eat of it and not die. I am the living bread which came down from heaven; if any one eats of this bread, he will live forever; and the bread which I shall give for the life of the world is my flesh" (Jn 6:48–51). Paul also makes the correlation between the manna and the Eucharist (1 Cor 10:1–4), referring to the Eucharist as "spiritual food." At the Last Supper it is recorded that "he took bread, and when he had given thanks he broke it and gave it to them, saying, 'This is my body which is given for you. Do this in remembrance of me' " (Lk 22:19). The early Church understood the Eucharist to be the fulfillment of the promised manna, the Bread from heaven, the Body of Christ. The bread and wine, by the power of the Holy Spirit, were changed into the Body and Blood of Jesus—our "spiritual food."

who is to be ruler in Israel, whose origin is from of old, from ancient days. Therefore he shall give them up until the time when she who is in travail has brought forth; then the rest of his brethren shall return to the people of Israel. And he shall stand and feed his flock in the strength of the Lord, in the majesty of the name of the Lord his God. And they shall dwell secure, for now he shall be great to the ends of the earth."[7]

The Prophet Malachi (Old Testament prophet; written *c.* 433–425 b.c.)
"My name will be great among the nations [Gentiles], from the rising to the setting of the sun. In every place incense and pure offerings will be brought to my name, because my name will be great among the nations, says the Lord Almighty."[8]

7 Micah 5:2–4. Is it a coincidence that the Lord Jesus, the Bread of Life, the Manna come down heaven, was born in the "City of Bread"? Was it a coincidence that the Lamb of God was born in a shepherd's cave and laid in a manger and that the first to be notified of the Lamb's birth were "shepherds out in the field, keeping watch over their flock by night"? Nothing surrounding his birth was a coincidence; nothing in God's salvation history is accidental or unplanned. Some say the Gospel is no longer shrouded in symbolism. This is true; the Gospel is revealed and made clear by the use of symbolism.

8 Malachi 1:11 (New International Version [Grand Rapids, Mich.: Zondervan, 1984]). The apostolic Fathers and the whole early Church understood this passage to refer to the Eucharist. Protestant Old Testament scholar Joyce Baldwin sums up the verse by noting: (1) God's name will be honored among the nations (Gentiles), and they will come to know God; (2) this worldwide worship would not be dependent on Levitical sacrifices offered in Jerusalem; and (3) "is offered" refers to the imminent future, in which the pure offering will transcend all previous offerings. Baldwin makes the important point that "the adjective 'pure' . . . is not used elsewhere to describe offerings. . . . At their best the levitical sacrifices were never described in these terms" (*Haggai, Zechariah, Malachi*, vol. 24 in the *Tyndale Old Testament Commentaries* [Downers Grove, Ill.: InterVarsity Press; 1972], 229–30). Malachi's language is distinctly sacrificial and is clearly explaining a unique offering, not found elsewhere in the Old Testament. This sacrifice, offered worldwide, is superior to the Jewish Levitical sacrifices and could never conceivably be equated with pagan sacrifices, no matter how sincere the latter may be. The sacrifice (singular) will be offered worldwide (multiple sacrifices) and will supersede and be superior to all prior sacrifices. The unique sacrifice is fulfilled in the singular, once-and-for-all sacrifice of Christ, whereas the best explanation for the multiple sacrifices "from the rising to the setting of the sun" is the celebration of the Eucharist, as was understood by all those who sat at the apostles' feet.

The Gospel of John (*c.* 90–*c.* 100)[9]

"Now the Passover, the feast of the Jews, was at hand. . . . Jesus said, 'Make the people sit down.' Now there was much grass in the place; so the men sat down, in number about five thousand. Jesus then took the loaves, and when he had given thanks,[10] he distributed them to those who were seated. . . . And when they had eaten their fill, he told his disciples, 'Gather up the fragments left over. . . .' When the people saw the sign which he had done, they said, 'This is indeed the prophet who is to come into the world.' "[11]

This leads us to see the Church, the covenant opened to all nations, Jew and Gentile, as the setting for this "pure offering" that will be offered in "every place." That this reference to the Eucharist was taught in the Church can be seen as early as the *Didache* (*c.* 60). The sacrifice is a singular "pure sacrifice," yet it is "in every place": the Catholic Mass answers to this perfectly. St. Augustine says, "What do you answer to that: Open your eyes at last, then, any time, and see, from the rising of the sun to its setting, the Sacrifice of Christians is offered, not in one place only, as was established with you Jews, but everywhere; and not to just any god at all, but to Him who foretold it, the God of Israel. . . . Not in one place, as was prescribed for you in the earthly Jerusalem, but in every place, even in Jerusalem herself. Not according to the order of Aaron, but according to the order of Melchizedek" (William A. Jurgens, *The Faith of the Early Fathers*, 3 vols. [Collegeville, Minn.: Liturgical Press, 1970–1979], 3:168).

9 The Apostle John was a young man when he was a disciple of Jesus. We know from historical sources that after leaving Jerusalem he lived in Ephesus until the time of Emperor Trajan (reigned 98 to 117).

10 The word for "thanks" in Greek is εὐχαριστέω, from which we get the word "Eucharist." John deliberately repeats this verb in verse 23, where it should be regarded as a distinct allusion to the eucharistic intent of the passage. This conclusion is especially justified inasmuch as we know that the Gospel was written at the end of the first century, at a time when the Lord's Supper was already technically referred to as the Eucharist, as can be demonstrated by the letters of St. Ignatius of Antioch, a disciple of the Apostle John (e.g., *Philadelphians* 4, *Smyrnaeans* 7–8). Oscar Cullman writes, "The long speech which Jesus makes in John's Gospel . . . has, since ancient times, been considered by most exegetes a discourse on the Eucharist. . . . Here the author makes Jesus himself draw the line from the miracle of the feeding with material bread to the miracle of the Sacrament" (*Early Christian Worship*, trans. A. Stewart Todd and James B. Torrance [Philadelphia: Westminster Press, 1953], 93).

11 Jn 6:4, 10–14. This is the only miracle performed by Jesus during his earth-

"Jesus answered them, . . . 'I am the living bread which came down from heaven; if any one eats of this bread, he will live for ever; and the bread which I shall give for the life of the world is my flesh.' The Jews then disputed among themselves, saying, 'How can this man give us his flesh to eat?' So Jesus said to them, 'Truly, truly, I say to you, unless you eat the flesh of the Son of man and drink his blood, you have no life in you; he who eats my flesh and drinks my blood has eternal life,[12] and I will raise him up at the last day. For my flesh is food indeed, and my blood is drink indeed.' . . . After this many of his disciples drew back and no longer went about with him. Jesus said to

---

ly ministry that is recorded in all four Gospels, demonstrating the miracle's significance. Jesus is setting the stage for the discourse on the "Bread of Life" that has "come down from heaven." It is with the multiplication of the loaves that Jesus demonstrates his ability to provide bread for all, by preparing a table in the wilderness. We will soon see that Jesus explains that the bread he now offers, in the Eucharist, is his flesh, which is "food indeed" and which will be provided by his Church to all men, in all places, for all time. The eucharistic undertones included even in the Synoptic Gospels suggest that the early Christians associated the multiplication of loaves with the Eucharist at a very early date. Philip Schaff writes, "Here the deepest mystery of Christianity is embodied ever anew, and the story of the cross reproduced before us. Here the miraculous feeding of the five thousand is spiritually perpetuated. . . . Here Christ . . . gives his own body and blood, sacrificed for us, . . . as spiritual food, as the true bread from heaven" (*History of the Church* [Grand Rapids, Mich.: Eerdmans, 1980], 1:473).

In this narrative, John gives us a beautiful picture of the Church: "all the people" numbering five thousand men (excluding women and children) representing the universal Church, gathered in "small groups" of fifty to one hundred, representing the local churches, all being fed by Christ, the Great High Priest, who provides the "bread" to all the people through the hands of his priests, the apostles. Later he explains that the bread is his flesh, which must be eaten, just as the meat of the Passover Lamb had to be eaten.

12 How would the first recipients of John's Gospel perceive these words—remembering that the Gospel of John was written between 90 and 100? According to George Beasley-Murray, arguably the most prestigious Baptist exegete in print, "It is not necessary to interpret the statement exclusively in terms of the body and blood of the Lord's Supper. Nevertheless, it is evident that neither the Evangelist nor the Christian readers could have written or read the saying without conscious reference to the Eucharist; to say the least, they would have acknowledged it as supremely fulfilled in the worship event" (George Beasley-Murray, *John*, vol. 36 of *Word Biblical Commentary* [Waco, Tex.: Word Books, 1987], 95).

the twelve, 'Do you also wish to go away?' Simon Peter answered him, 'Lord, to whom shall we go? You have the words of eternal life.'"[13]

13 Jn 6:43, 51–55, 66–68. In this discourse it seems as if Jesus is being overly difficult and desires to scare off his disciples unnecessarily. He speaks extremely hard words to them, seemingly asking them to be cannibals, and, as a result, most of them turn away in disgust and leave him. The word translated "eat" in this passage is not a dignified word used to describe fine dining, but is the Greek word for "gnaw" and "munch" and could be translated "masticating the flesh" (see Raymond Brown, *The Gospel according to John I–XII* [New York: Doubleday, 1966], 283). "This offense," according to Cullman, "belongs now to the Sacrament just as the [offense of the] human body belongs to the [divine] Logos" (Cullman, *Early Christian Worship*, 100). This is the only recorded case of disciples turning away from Christ over doctrinal issues. Why didn't Jesus stop the departing disciples as they scattered in revulsion over the hillsides? He could have easily shouted out to them, "Wait, don't you understand that I was speaking symbolically? Come back, I was only speaking figuratively." He didn't do this, and many of his disciples left him. But the Twelve remained: they realized that his words were the words of eternal life.

This passage has been understood, from the first days of the Church, as an explanation anticipating the Eucharist. St. Basil the Great wrote in his epistle *To the Patrician Lady Coesaria concerning Communion*, "It is good and beneficial to communicate every day, and to partake of the holy body and blood of Christ. For he distinctly says, 'He that eats my flesh and drinks my blood has eternal life' " (Philip Schaff, ed., *Nicene and Post-Nicene Fathers*, 2d series [Grand Rapids, Mich.: Eerdmans, 1983], 8:179). According to Raymond Brown, "There are two impressive indications that the Eucharist is in mind. The first indication is the stress on eating (feeding on) Jesus' flesh and drinking His blood. This cannot possibly be a metaphor for accepting his revelation. . . . Thus, if Jesus' words in vs. 53 are to have a favorable meaning, they must refer to the Eucharist. They simply reproduce the words we hear in the Synoptic account of the institution of the Eucharist: 'Take, *eat*; this is *my body*; . . . *drink* . . . this is *my blood*.' The second indication of the Eucharist is the formula found in vs. 51 [when] . . . John speaks of 'flesh' while the Synoptic accounts of the Last Supper speak of 'body.' However, there is no Hebrew or Aramaic word for 'body,' as we understand the term; and many scholars maintain that at the Last Supper what Jesus actually said was the Aramaic equivalent of 'This is My flesh' " (*The Gospel according to John I–XII*, 284–85). It should be remembered that John wrote this Gospel between 90 and 100, when, early documents make clear, the Eucharist was being celebrated as the literal Flesh and Blood of Christ in the Catholic Church across the Roman Empire. Couldn't John have made an explanation to clarify these words (as he was wont to do, e.g., Jn 1:42; 21:19)? He could have told his readers that this was all symbolism and did not mean what the first generation Christians *thought* it meant. John wrote a sacramental Gospel and knew exactly what he

"Jesus answered them, 'Did I not choose you, the twelve, and one of you is a devil?' He spoke of Judas the son of Simon Iscariot, for he, one of the twelve, was to betray him."[14]

The Gospel of Mark (written in last half of first century)[15]
"And as they were eating, he took bread, and blessed, and broke it, and gave it to them, and said, 'Take; this is my body.'[16] And he took

---

was writing, and why.

14 Jn 6:70–71. The context of a passage is always important for its interpretation. While reading the Bible, one should ask questions such as: "Why did the author place this anecdote in this location instead of somewhere else?" or "What conclusion did the author expect us to draw by placing this incident here?" In our current passages, it seems contextually significant that John mentions Judas' betrayal at this point in his narrative. Where else in the Gospels do we find this event mentioned? In each of the Gospels the mention of Satan entering Judas is in the context of the Last Supper. Each account begins by noting that it was the Passover and ends with Satan entering Judas—so it is with John 6. *John frames his Eucharistic discourse in chapter 6 so that the reader will see the clear parallel with the Synoptic accounts of the Lord's Supper.* This anecdote about Judas seems to be out of place unless understood within the eucharistic framework of the whole chapter.

15 "The earliest statement about the origin of this Gospel [of Mark] is that given by Papias (preserved in Eusebius' *The History of the Church* 3, 39): 'Mark, who was the interpreter of Peter, wrote down accurately all that he remembered, whether of sayings or doings of Christ, but not in order. For he was neither a hearer nor a companion of the Lord; but afterwards, as I have said, he accompanied Peter, who adapted his instruction as necessity required, not as though he were making a compilation of the Lord's oracles. So then Mark made no mistake when he wrote down thus some things as he remembered them; for he concentrated on this alone—not to omit anything that he had heard, nor to include any false statement among them.

"Papias' information (*c.* a.d. 140) is amplified a generation or so later in Irenaeus. Irenaeus (*Against Heresies* 3, 1, 1), after referring to Mark as having been written 'when Peter and Paul were preaching the gospel in Rome and founding the church there,' adds that 'after their departure Mark, Peter's disciple, has himself delivered to us in writing the substance of Peter's preaching.' Both of these authorities therefore suggest a date shortly after Peter's death, though later Fathers claim, perhaps tendentiously, that it was written in Peter's lifetime" ("Mark, the Gospel", in J. D. Douglas, ed., *New Bible Dictionary* [Wheaton, Ill.: Tyndale House, 1982]).

16 It is interesting to note that the Greek word for body (σ□μα) has a definite article, making the statement appear stronger in Greek than can be expressed

a cup, and when he had given thanks he gave it to them, and they all drank of it. And he said to them, 'This is my blood of the covenant,[17] which is poured out for many.' "[18]

The Gospel of Luke (written in last half of first century)[19]
"And when the hour came, he sat at table, and the apostles with him. And he said to them, 'I have earnestly desired to eat this passover with you before I suffer; for I tell you I shall not eat it until it is fulfilled in the kingdom of God.' And he took a cup, and when he had given thanks he said, 'Take this, and divide it among yourselves; for I tell you that from now on I shall not drink of the fruit of the vine until the kingdom of God comes.' And he took bread, and when he had given thanks he broke it and gave it to them, saying, 'This is my body which is given for you. Do this in remembrance of me.' And likewise the cup after supper, saying, 'This cup which is poured out

---

in English. It is literally "This is the body of mine." It is a declaration that *this* (the bread) is *the body* of mine. Jesus would have spoken these words in Aramaic, the language used by Jesus and his disciples. Some scholars think that the original words of Jesus in this declaration were "This is my flesh," since there was no word in Aramaic for "body." This would tie in quite impressively with John 6, when Jesus says, "You must eat my flesh and drink my blood."

17 It appears Jesus intentionally used terminology taken from Exodus 24:8: "Behold the blood of the covenant which the Lord has made with you in accordance with all these words."

18 Mk 14:22–24. It is here that the Lord Jesus fulfilled his promise in John 6, "This is my body . . . this is my blood." What words could be plainer? He and his apostles were eating the Passover meal, eating the sacrificial lamb, the prefigured body of Christ, and now, sitting at the same table, he holds up a loaf of bread and says, "This is my body. . . ."

19 St. Luke the Evangelist is the author of the Gospel of Luke and the Acts of the Apostles. In both cases he gathered information from those who had known the Lord, in order to compile a historical account of the life of Jesus Christ. In the prologue to his Gospel, Luke writes, "Inasmuch as many have undertaken to compile a narrative of the things which have been accomplished among us, just as they were delivered to us by those who from the beginning were eyewitnesses and ministers of the word, it seemed good to me also, having followed all things closely for some time past, to write an orderly account for you, most excellent Theophilus, that you may know the truth concerning the things of which you have been informed" (Lk 1:1–4). Luke was a physician and a loyal companion of St. Paul. He is said to have died at eighty-four years of age, after writing his Gospel in Greece.

for you is the new covenant in my blood' "[20]

The Gospel of Luke

"That very day two of them were going to a village named Emmaus. . . . While they were talking and discussing together, Jesus himself drew near and went with them. But their eyes were kept from recognizing him. And he said to them, 'What is this conversation which you are holding with each other as you walk?' . . . And he said to them, 'O foolish men, and slow of heart to believe all that the prophets have spoken! Was it not necessary that the Christ should suffer these things and enter into his glory?' And beginning with Moses and all the prophets, he interpreted to them in all the scriptures the things concerning himself. So they drew near to the village to which they were going. He appeared to be going further, but they constrained him, saying, 'Stay with us, for it is toward evening and the day is now far spent.' So he went in to stay with them. When he was at table with them, he took the bread and blessed, and broke it, and gave it to them. And their eyes were opened and they recognized him and he vanished out of their sight. They said to each other, 'Did not our hearts burn within us while he talked to us on the road, while he opened to us the scriptures?' And they rose that same hour and returned to Jerusalem. . . . Then they told [the apostles] what had happened on the road, and

20 Paul and Luke add the element of "remembrance" (*anamnesis*), which is not included here or in the other Gospels. There is an indication of a liturgical development even within the New Testament period (see Cheslyn Jones et al., eds., *The Study of Liturgy*, rev. ed. [New York: Oxford Univ. Press, 1992], 204). The word "remembrance" is a sacrificial term and is used in the Greek Septuagint (the Septuagint was the Greek Old Testament widely read in Jesus' time). "In Lev. 24:7 it [*anamnesis*] stands for *'azkarah*, which was a memorial offering. . . . This particular *'azkarah* was evidently intended to be a perpetual reminder of the covenant" (Colin Brown, ed., *Dictionary of New Testament Theology* [Grand Rapids, Mich.: Zondervan, 1979], 3:239). *Anamnesis* is used in Numbers 10:10, where it is again regarding sacrifice, which would undoubtably bring to mind a sacrificial context for those who heard the words spoken at the Last Supper. That *anamnesis* was used of Old Testament sacrifices would not have missed Jesus' attention at such a crucial sacrificial meal. It would appear he was drawing attention to the sacrificial nature of the Eucharist that he was instituting during the Passover, a point that Paul seemed to understand well, as evidenced by First Corinthians.

how he was known to them in the breaking of the bread."[21]

The Letter to the Hebrews 9 (written in the last half of first century)[22]
"But when Christ appeared as a high priest of the good things that have come, then through the greater and more perfect tent he entered once for all into the Holy Place, taking not the blood of goats and calves but his own blood, thus securing an eternal redemption. . . . How much more shall the blood of Christ, who through the eternal Spirit offered himself without blemish to God, purify your

---

21 Lk 24:13–17, 25–33, 35. What a strange way for these travelers to describe how and when they recognized Jesus. After his Resurrection, Jesus was explaining the Scriptures to them as they walked along the road together. "And beginning with Moses and all the prophets, he interpreted to them in all the Scriptures the things concerning himself." This had to be one of the best expository sermons of all time—preached by Jesus himself. However, even with Jesus himself expounding the Scriptures, the disciples did not comprehend or grasp who he was. *But*, in the taking, breaking, blessing, and giving of the bread, "their eyes were opened and they recognized him." What a peculiar passage. They did not describe their "revelation" of Jesus as a result of "biblical preaching," but rather, "he was known to them in the breaking of the bread" (Lk 24:35). Luke recalls here the exact words Jesus used a few chapters earlier when he instituted the Eucharist (took, blessed, broke, and gave). The only times in the New Testament where these words are used in this manner occur when the writer is referring to the Eucharist—and here in Luke 24. Was Luke intending to make a point, a correlation by concluding his Gospel with this historical anecdote? Raymond Brown writes, "Luke's insistence that the disciples recognized Jesus in the breaking of the bread is often taken as Eucharistic teaching meant to instruct the community that they too could find the risen Jesus in their eucharistic breaking of the bread" (Raymond Brown, *The Gospel according to John XIII–XXI* [New York: Doubleday, 1966], 2:1100).

22 There have always been disagreements about the authorship of the Letter to the Hebrews. As early as the early fourth century we read in Eusebius, *History of the Church from Christ to Constantine*, trans. G. A. Williamson (Harmondsworth, Middlesex, England: Penguin Books, 1965), "Paul had communicated with the Hebrews by writing to them in their native tongue; and some say that the evangelist Luke, others that this same Clement translated the original text. The second suggestion is the more convincing, in view of the similarity of phraseology shown throughout by the Epistle of Clement and the Epistle of the Hebrews" (3, 38, 2). It is pretty well concluded that Paul was the source of the material, if not the author, and then someone may have translated it for him or for a wider audience.

conscience from dead works to serve the living God."[23]

The Revelation of John or The Apocalypse (written in the second half of the first century)

"And all that dwell upon the earth shall worship him [the beast], whose names are not written in the book of life of the Lamb slain from the foundation of the world."[24]

"And between the throne and the four living creatures and among the elders, I saw a Lamb standing, as though it had been slain."[25]

---

23 Heb 9:11–14. We see in this passage that Christ, the Lamb of God foretold in the Old Testament, has been slain once and for all. The priests of the Old Covenant were commanded to slay a lamb yearly for their own sins and the sins of the people. In the Passover celebration, the flesh of the lamb had to be physically eaten. Christ is the "Lamb of God, who takes away the sin of the world" (Jn 1:29).

24 Rev 13:8 (King James Version). We know that in space and time Christ was sacrificed for sins once and for all. But, according to many translations, commentators, and Greek scholars, from God's eternal perspective Christ was "the Lamb slain from the foundation of the world." How could this event be "from the foundation of the world" when elsewhere the Scriptures inform us that Christ was crucified *c.* 30 under Pontius Pilate? It is not *either/or*. This is a window into eternity and reveals the eternal aspect of Christ's sacrifice: in *time* it took place once; in *eternity*, where there is no time, it is an eternal event, eternally present in the eyes of God.

25 Rev 5:6. The word "slain" graphically recalls the sacrifices of the Old Covenant, where the sacrificial lambs were stretched out on the altar and their throats were slit with a knife, allowing the blood to flow over the altar. As the curtain of heaven is drawn back for us to glimpse the heavenly liturgy, we discover a golden altar in heaven before the throne of God. "And another angel came and stood at the altar, having a golden censer; and there was given unto him much incense, that he should offer it with the prayers of all saints upon the golden altar which was before the throne" (Rev 8:3; see also Is 6:1–7). The passage assumes that the Lamb "as though slain" is standing on the altar (as in the famous painting by Jan van Eyck entitled *The Adoration of the Lamb*). Protestant commentator Leon Morris writes, "When John speaks of the Lamb 'as it had been slain' there can be no doubt but that he is thinking in terms of sacrifice. But he does not think of the Lamb as 'slain.' The Lamb is 'as though slain,' for He is very much alive. The Greek perfect tense here signifies that the Lamb was not only slain at a point in time, but that the efficacy of His death is still present in all its power" (*The Revelation of St. John*, vol. 20 of the *Tyndale New Testament Commentary* series [Grand Rapids, Mich.: Eerdmans, 1980], 96–97).

Paul's Letter to the Romans (written *c.* 58)
"To be a minister of Christ Jesus to the Gentiles in the priestly service of the gospel of God, so that the offering of the Gentiles may be acceptable, sanctified by the Holy Spirit."[26]

The sacrifice of Christ was accomplished once *in time*, but in eternity it is seen as an eternal event, outside of time. Christ's sacrifice is eternally present before God and is re-presented to his people in the Eucharist. In the Old Testament, the lamb had to be eaten after it was slain; in the New Testament we have to eat the Flesh and drink the Blood of Christ in the same way. This is done in the Mass, where those of the New Covenant partake of the Flesh of the Lamb, the Paschal sacrifice. Christ is not crucified again on the altar, but his sacrifice is re-presented so that we can partake of the Body of the Lord (1 Cor 10:16). The eternal sacrifice is again placed before us, eternity slicing down into time, so that we might share in it by eating the eternal Lamb, by the grace and mercy of God.

26 Rom 15:16. The question arises: Why doesn't the New Testament refer to the leaders of the early Church as priests until the second century? A lengthy passage from *This Rock Magazine* (P.O. Box 17490, San Diego, CA 92177 [April 1995]) is in order here. The presbyters are not referred to as priests "for the same reason it [the term 'priest'] isn't applied more often to Jesus, the New Testament high priest—because most of these priests, like Jesus, were not from the tribe of Levi. In Jewish circles, the idea of a priest not being from Levi was absurd. Everyone knew God had given the priesthood to Aaron and his descendants (Ex 28:1; cf. Nb 16–17). Most Christian presbyter-priests were not from Levi, much less the Aaronic line, and it would have posed apologetic difficulties for Christians in Jewish communities to refer to their ministers as 'priests.' An ordinary, first-century Jew would snort at that idea, saying, 'Oh, yeah. Your ministers are priests. They aren't even Levites!' The early Christians faced the same problem when it came to the fact that Jesus is the New Testament high priest. Jesus was from the tribe of Judah, not Levi. A first-century Jew would scoff at that idea, too. . . . Thus there is only one book—Hebrews— which directly refers to Jesus as a priest and only one book— Romans—which directly refers to his ministers as priests. Other books of the New Testament show Jesus and the presbyters doing jobs only priests can do, but the term *hiereus* [priest] is not used for them. When Jesus' priesthood is directly stated, the author must go to great pains to justify the idea to Jews. Non-Christian Jews were arguing that Christianity could not possibly be true because Jesus could not be the high priest of the New Covenant. He was from the wrong tribe: He was not a Levite. To reclaim his Hebrew Christian readers, who were in danger of going back to Judaism, the author of Hebrews had to show that this fact did not matter. That is the basic function of [Hebrews] chapter 7. . . . Once the Church ceased to be

Letter to the Hebrews 13
"We have an altar from which those who serve the tent have no right to eat."[27]

---

mostly Jewish, this was no longer an apologetic problem. Gentiles did not have the idea that priests had to be from the tribe of Levi, so they could convert without this being an issue. Thus, after the Church became mostly Gentile, the priesthood of Christ and his ministers became more prominent" (43). See also *The First Letter of Clement to the Corinthians*, chaps. 40–44, and Cyprian, epistle 63, 14.

27 Heb 13:10. An altar is a place for offerings and sacrifices. What altar does the Church possess? Paul compares three different altars (tables) in 1 Corinthians 10; he also acknowledges an altar in the church. We also know that there is an altar before the throne of God in heaven (Is 6:6; Rev 6:9; 8:3, 5; 9:13; 11:1; 14:18; 16:7). Hebrews speaks of an altar that excludes the Jewish ceremonies and is unique to the Church. It opposes and is superior to both the tables (altars) of the Jews and the tables (altars) of the pagans.

The Cross of Christ is the new altar upon which the sacrificial Lamb of God is slain once and for all for the sins of the world. Again, Protestants habitually set up an *either/or* methodology with the Cross and the Eucharist. But, are the Cross and the Eucharist separated by an impenetrable barrier? Is it *either* the Cross *or* the Eucharist? No, in the Eucharist we "participate" in the Body and Blood of Christ. This altar of the Church is first and foremost the Cross of Christ, as is being argued by the author of Hebrews, but at the eucharistic celebration the Cross is reenacted and represented with the eucharistic sacrifice. At the altar of the Church, we are able to partake of the eternal sacrifice, the Body and Blood of Christ, which the Jewish priests were unable to do, being forbidden to eat of the sacrifices slain in the great Day of Atonement. It is at the altar of the Church, at the celebration of the Eucharist, that the Cross of Christ is remembered, and where the sacrifice of Christ is re-presented, where the believer eats the sacrificial Victim who is still presented before the Father as a "lamb slain" (Rev 5:6).

Protestant commentator John Bengel (1687–1752) writes, "An altar—The Cross of Christ, on which his body was sacrificed. Of which—They are partakers also of this altar who eat its sacrifice: comp. 1 Cor 10:18. To eat—The meat, Christ's flesh given for us. An antithesis to ceremonial meats. It is eaten especially in the Sacred Supper, where are set forth his body given for us, and his blood shed for us, in that single sacrifice of the cross" (*Bengel's New Testament Commentary*, trans. Charlton T. Lewis and Marvin R. Vincent [Grand Rapids, Mich.: Kregel, 1981], 2:688).

According to Rev. Leighton Pullan in *Early Christian Doctrine* (London: Rivington, 1909), "The theory that the word 'altar' in the latter passage has reference to the Lord's Supper is supported by the use of the word in a pas-

The Acts of the Apostles (written in the last half of the first century; events took place *c.* 30)

"So those who received his word were baptized, and there were added that day about three thousands souls. And they devoted themselves to the apostles' teaching and [the] fellowship, to the breaking of bread and the prayers."[28]

---

sage in Ignatius" (78). The passage from Ignatius of Antioch reads: "Take ye heed, then, to have but one Eucharist. For there is one flesh of our Lord Jesus Christ, and one cup to [show forth] the unity of His blood; one altar; as there is one bishop, along with the presbytery and deacons, my fellow-servants: that so, whatsoever ye do, ye may do it according to [the will of] God" (*Epistle to the Philadelphians* 4, in Roberts and Donaldson, *Ante-Nicene Fathers*, 1:81). Should one want to interpret the "altar" figuratively in this passage, then it would seem that bishops And deacons, the Body and Blood would also have to be interpreted figuratively. The early Church understood the Eucharist to be the new sacrifice of Malachi 1:11 and the "table of the Lord" as the altar upon which the new sacrifice is offered. (See also J. N. D. Kelly, *Early Christian Doctrines* [San Francisco: Harper & Row, 1978], 196.)

28 Acts 2:41–42. Even though many translations don't bring this out, one should notice the definite article in front of each of these four categories: *the* fellowship, *the* breaking of bread, *the* apostles' teaching, *the* prayers. In the Greek language, nouns with *no* articles (anarthrous construction) describe the quality of the noun; whereas nouns *with* articles (articular construction) point to or identify a specific object.

Therefore, this should *not* be read: "a general breaking of bread and general prayers" but rather "*the* breaking of bread and *the* prayers". This makes a tremendous difference in the meaning of the verse and gives a more accurate description of the worship and liturgy of the primitive Church. These phrases undoubtedly refer to the Eucharist, and the prayers were liturgical prayers, used in the liturgy of worship. We have ancient samples of the early Church's liturgical prayers and the format used for celebrating the Eucharist (see Justin Martyr and the *Didache*). For the first decade or so, the Eucharist was part of a common meal, but Paul recognizes a distinct development (probably in response to abuses) in this Letter to the Corinthians. By the first century the Eucharist was a liturgical celebration, containing the Liturgy of the Word, prayers and *the* prayers, and the celebration of the Eucharist and giving. This was performed every Sunday, as is made clear in St. Justin's writings, which we will study shortly.

First Letter of Paul to the Corinthians 11 (written *c.* 57)
"For I received from the Lord what I also delivered to you,[29] that the Lord Jesus on the night when he was betrayed took bread, and when he had given thanks, he broke it, and said, 'This is my body which is for you. Do this in remembrance[30] of me.' In the same way also the

29 The terms "received" and "delivered" are technical terms used for the transmittal of apostolic tradition (see also 1 Cor 15:3). The Corinthians did not learn of the Lord's Supper by reading the New Testament. They learned of it from the tradition delivered or passed down by Paul in oral teaching and hands-on example (1 Cor 11:2; 2 Th 2:15, 3:6), and he in turn received it directly from God, or most likely from the original twelve apostles. The letters of the New Testament were not to replace the tradition taught by the apostles, the living Word of God delivered in person (1 Th 2:13). The epistles of Paul were not sent as a comprehensive "Church manual" with instructions for the Lord's Supper, for the Corinthians had been instructed in proper procedures by Paul himself, in person. The epistles were intended to correct abuses and flaws in the practice of the Corinthians. The faith had been handed down orally, by the personal instruction of the apostles to the saints (Jude 3), that is, the Church. Epistles were sent later to encourage and exhort the churches in what they already knew through tradition (1 Cor 4:17; 2 Pet 3:1–2).

30 According to Thomas Howard, in *Evangelical Is Not Enough* (San Francisco: Ignatius Press, 1984), the English word "remembrance" does not bring out the full meaning of the Greek word *anamnesis*, which Christ used when instituting the Eucharist. "The word suggests a remembering that is also a making present" (106). Gerhard Kittel, *Theological Dictionary of the New Testament*, ed. and trans. Geoffrey W. Bromily (Grand Rapids, Mich.: Eerdmans, 1983), speaks of "re-presentation" and "the making present by the later community of the Lord who instituted the Supper" (1:348–49). "This 're-calling' means that something 'past' becomes 'present,' something which, here and now, affects us vitally and profoundly. In other words, the Eucharist is the making present of the true Paschal Lamb who is the Christ. . . . Thus from the earliest days, the Christian Church has understood the Eucharist as the 're-calling' of Christ's sacrifice, with its present redeeming power. All the early liturgies make it plain that in the worship of the Eucharist the Church is experiencing the power of the present Savior" (Olive Wyon, *The Altar Fire* [London: SCM Press, 1956], 35–36). Protestant writer Max Thurian wrote, "This memorial is not a simple subjective act of recollection, it is a liturgical action . . . which makes the Lord present . . . which recalls as a memorial before the Father the unique sacrifice of the Son, and this makes Him present in His memorial" (*The Eucharistic Memorial*, II, *The New Testament, Ecumenical Studies in Worship* as quoted in Colin Brown, ed., *Dictionary of New Testament Theology* [Grand Rapids, Mich.: Zondervan, 1979], 3:244).

cup, after supper, saying, 'This cup is the new covenant in my blood.[31] Do this, as often as you drink it, in remembrance of me.' For as often as you eat this bread and drink this cup, you proclaim the Lord's death until he comes. Whoever, therefore, eats the bread or drinks the cup of the Lord in an unworthy manner will be guilty of profaning the body and blood of the Lord."[32]

Paul in his First Letter to the Corinthians 10

"I want you to know, brethren, that our fathers were all under the cloud, and all passed through the sea, and all were baptized into Moses in the cloud and in the sea, and all ate the same supernatural food and all drank the same supernatural drink.[33] For they drank from the

31 This wording clearly draws upon Old Testament sacrificial language, Exodus 24:8 in particular: "And Moses took the blood and threw it upon the people, and said, 'Behold the blood of the covenant which the Lord has made with you in accordance with all these words.' " Jesus refers us to real blood, not a symbolic wine that represents blood. Jesus, referring back to the words of the blood covenant of Moses, says, "This is my blood of the covenant" as he hands the chalice to his disciples commanding them to drink his blood, which he had already explained to them in the discourse of John 6.

32 1 Cor 11:23–27. Most scholars agree that 1 Corinthians was probably written prior to the Gospel accounts, thus being the first *written* record of the Eucharist as instituted by Jesus Christ. The teaching on the Eucharist was either given directly to Paul by Christ, or he learned it through the apostolic tradition of the Lord's disciples. He then passed it on to his converts.

Being guilty of someone's "body and blood" was to be guilty of murder. How could one be guilty of murder if the body (bread) was only a symbol? The Real Presence of Christ's Body is necessary for an offense to be committed against it. How could one be guilty of the Body and Blood of Christ by simply eating a little bread and drinking a little wine? "No one is guilty of homicide if he merely does violence to the picture or statue of a man without touching the man in person. St. Paul's words are meaningless without the dogma of the Real Presence" (Leslie Rumble and Charles M. Carty, *Eucharist Quizzes to a Street Preacher* [Rockford, Ill.: Tan Books, 1976], 7 8).

33 Why does Paul refer to the elements of the Eucharist as "spiritual food"? He could have called them "symbolic food," or "food that represents Christ," but instead he refers to the elements as *spiritual*, implying the supernatural, sacramental aspect of the Lord's Supper. Gordon Fee concedes that there is a spiritual element but then sidesteps the issue when he writes, "The usage . . . suggests that it points to a 'spiritual reality' beyond that which meets the eye. But it is doubtful whether he is trying to say something about the sacramental character of the food, or that in some way it conveyed the Spirit"

supernatural Rock which followed them, and the Rock was Christ."[34] "I speak as to sensible men; judge for yourselves what I say. The cup of blessing which we bless, is it not a participation in the blood of

---

(*The First Epistle to the Corinthians*, in the *New International Commentary on the New Testament* [Grand Rapids, Mich.: Eerdmans, 1987], 447). It is not exegetical study of Scripture that forces Evangelical and Fundamentalist commentators to expunge the supernatural element of the sacraments, it is rather their antisacramental tradition inherited from Fundamentalist Protestantism. When 1 Corinthians 10 is read together with the sixth chapter of John, allowing "Scripture to interpret Scripture," it is clear that more is going on than a simple eating of regular food to remember a past event. This is "spiritual food," and it is a miracle of God, just as the manna was not a natural food, but a miracle of God. Who at this point believes in the literal interpretation of the Bible, the Fundamentalist or the Catholic?

34 1 Cor 10:1–4. Paul draws from Old Testament typology, in the exodus from Egypt, and in the historical events discovers, prefigured, the Christian sacraments of baptism and the Eucharist. He vividly expresses Christian sacramental terminology in describing the exodus. The fact that he immediately moves the discussion to an exhortation of the Eucharistic celebration ("The cup of blessing which we bless, is it not a participation in the blood of Christ? The bread which we break, is it not a participation in the body of Christ?") demonstrates that verses 1–4 are sacramental pictures (typology) relating to the two great sacraments of the Church: baptism and the Eucharist. Baptism has been dealt with in the previous section, but suffice it to say here that we see both the "water and the Spirit" that bring new birth in the cloud (the Spirit, Ex 13:21) and the water (the sea). Again, Paul does not present an *either/or* view of salvation but a *both/and* perspective.

The food and drink that preserved the lives of the Israelites represent the bread and wine (Body and Blood) of the New Covenant. Of the "spiritual food", Protestant reformer John Calvin writes, "Paul now mentions the other sacrament, which corresponds to the most Holy Supper of the Lord" (T. H. L. Parker, *Calvin's New Testament Commentaries* [Grand Rapids, Mich.: Eerdmans, 1980], 9:202). The manna (referred to as spiritual "meat" or "food") corresponds to the bread of the Eucharist, which Jesus refers to as "my flesh" (Jn 6:31ff.). The spiritual drink corresponds to the Blood of Christ, which is especially clear when Paul writes, "And all ate the same supernatural food and all drank the same supernatural drink. For they drank from the supernatural Rock which followed them, and the Rock was Christ" (1 Cor 10:3–4). In John 6, Jesus referred to his Blood as true drink. Paul refers to both elements of the Eucharist as the "spiritual food" God provides for his people, which perfectly corresponds to the Flesh and Blood of Jesus, which Jesus promised and commanded in John 6 and instituted at the Last Supper.

Christ? The bread which we break, is it not a participation[35] in the body of Christ? Because there is one bread, we who are many are one body, for we all partake of the one bread.[36] Consider the people of Israel; are not those who eat the sacrifices partners in the altar? . . . I imply that what pagans sacrifice they offer to demons and not to God. I do not want you to be partners with demons. You cannot drink of the cup of the Lord and the cup of demons. You cannot partake of the table of the Lord and the table of demons."[37]

---

35 What does the word "participation" mean? Is this just symbolic language? No, it means a real participation. St. Augustine places these words on Jesus' lips to describe what happens at the Eucharist: "You will not change me into you as happens with bodily food; rather, you will be changed into me" (*Confessions* 7, 10, 16, in Jurgens, *Faith of the Early Fathers*, 3:57). Even Gerhard Kittel, in the *Theological Dictionary of the New Testament*, 3:798, says, "κοινωνια denotes participation, fellowship, esp. with a close bond. It expresses a two-sided relationship. It means participation, impartation, fellowship."

St. John Chrysostom says, "For what is the bread? The Body of Christ. And what do they become who partake of it? The Body of Christ: not many bodies, but one body" (*Hom. on 1 Cor.* 24, in Schaff, *Nicene and Post-Nicene Fathers*, 1st series, 12:140). We are not just participating in a symbolic gesture, but, as Paul clearly says, we are actually participating in the Body and Blood of Christ.

36 There is no more striking example of the unity of the Body of Christ than that of the bread and wine. Bread is made of many individual grains that are gathered together and ground into flour before being baked into one integrated loaf. Individual grapes are gathered and crushed together to form wine. As the elements of the grains form a loaf, so all of us who eat of the one loaf, the Body of Christ, are formed into one body. We become his Body in a real way as we all partake of, or eat, his Flesh and drink his Blood. The Eucharist is the pinnacle and source of unity, as the *Catechism of the Catholic Church* so clearly states: "The Eucharist is our daily bread. The power belonging to this divine food makes it a bond of union. Its effect is then understood as unity, so that, gathered into his Body and made members of him, we may become what we receive" (CCC 2837, quoting from St. Augustine's *Sermon* 57, 7).

37 1 Cor 10:15–18, 20–21. "The sacramental status of the bread and wine is not only presupposed but is made the basis of the argument. . . .The *pneumatikos* [spiritual] food and drink now reappear more closely defined as the body and blood of Christ: although the ultimate basis of this definition will be given later (1 Cor 11:23–26), Paul can assume it as common ground shared with his audience, strong enough to support the further argument. . . . What the New Testament writings presuppose . . . is of greater importance than

The Eucharist as Taught by the Fathers

The Didache, or *The Teaching of the Apostles* (written prior to some of the New Testament documents)[38] "Assemble on the Lord's Day, and break bread and offer the Eucharist; but first make confession of your faults, so that your sacrifice may be a pure one. Anyone who has a difference with his fellow is not to take part with you until they

---

what they actually describe" (Jones, *The Study of Liturgy*, 189, 191).

St. Paul is comparing three categories of sacrifices offered on altars (tables): that of the Jews (v. 18), that of the pagans (vv. 19–21; offered to idols), and that of the Christians, the Eucharist. By his comparisons, Paul confirms the sacrificial nature of the Christian Eucharist. The "table of the Lord" is a common technical term in the Old Testament referring to the altar of sacrifice (Lev 24:6–7; Ezek 41:22; 44:15; Mal 1:7, 12); the correlation would have immediately been made by the readers. The "table of the Lord" in the Church, referred to by Paul, and drawing from Old Testament terminology and practice, is now the altar for the new sacrifice referred to by Malachi (Mal 1:11). Notice that the "table of the Lord" is mentioned twice in the first chapter of Malachi, before and after God's promise of a future, worldwide sacrifice offered by the Gentiles. The "table of the Lord," or sacrificial altar, will be the place of this offering, which corresponds to the Eucharist offered on the "table of the Lord" in 1 Corinthians 10:21. The parallels are striking and unmistakable: Malachi twice frames the "pure sacrifice" of the Gentiles with the sacrificial "table of the Lord." Paul then uses this same terminology to explain the new sacrifice offered on the "table of the Lord" in the Church. The sacrifice of the Eucharist on the "table of the Lord" is contrasted with the other well-known sacrifices offered on tables or altars. Paul, the brightest student of the brightest Jewish teacher, Gamaliel, is not using this Old Testament terminology lightly—he is a scholar. He knows his readers understand the significance of his sacrificial terminology relating to the Eucharist. Is there any question that Paul, the brilliant teacher of the Torah, understood the Eucharist in sacrificial terms, offered on the "table of the Lord" as a fulfillment of Malachi 1:11? "The parallelism that Paul draws between Jewish and pagan participation in their sacrifices through eating the meat of the victims and Christian fellowship with Christ through the Eucharist shows that he considers the eating of the Eucharist a sacrificial repast and implies that the Eucharist itself is a sacrifice" (Raymond E. Brown, Joseph A. Fitzmyer, and Roland E. Murphy, eds., *Jerome Biblical Commentary* [Englewood Cliffs, N.J.: Prentice-Hall, 1968], 269).

38 The *Didache* is an invaluable document that scholars have dated early in the second half of the first century. This would place it earlier than St. John's writings and contemporary with the later writings of Paul. This document gives us a substantial window into the workings of the Christian communities during the New Testament era.

have been reconciled, so as to avoid any profanation of your sacrifice. For this is the offering of which the Lord has said, 'Everywhere and always bring me a sacrifice that is undefiled, for I am a great king, says the Lord, and my name is the wonder of nations' [Malachi 1:11]."[39]

Ignatius of Antioch (*c.* 35–107)[40]

"Make certain, therefore, that you all observe one common Eucharist; for there is but one Body of our Lord Jesus Christ, and but one cup of union with His Blood, and one single altar of sacrifice—even as also there is but one bishop, with his clergy and my own fellow-servitors the deacons. This will insure that all your doings are in full accord with the will of God."[41] "But look at those men who have

---

39 The *Didache*, or *The Teachings of the Twelve Apostles*, sec. 14, "On Sunday Worship", in *Early Christian Writings*, trans. Maxwell Staniforth [Harmondsworth, Middlesex, England: Penguin Books, 1968], 197). This text was widely used as early as the first century. Section 9 presents detailed liturgical instructions for celebrating the Eucharist, entitled "Of the Eucharist." We know, with confirmation from the *Didache*, that the Eucharist was referred to as a *sacrifice* based on the prophecy of Malachi 1:11, which the *Didache* actually quotes. As we will discover, Malachi's prophecy was used throughout the primitive Church to describe the Eucharist—even during the lifetime of apostles. The apostolic Fathers interpreted Malachi as a description of the pinnacle of worship within the Catholic Church.

The *Didache* contains a complete eucharistic liturgy, word for word, that clearly shows the liturgy of the Church in the first century. It starts out, "At the Eucharist, offer the eucharistic prayer in this way. Begin with the chalice . . . then over the broken Bread . . ." (*Didache* 9, 10, in *Early Christian Writings*, 194). Interestingly enough, St. Athanasius says of the *Didache*, "Appointed by the Fathers to be read by those who newly join us, and who wish for instruction in the word of godliness . . . that which is called the 'Teaching of the Apostles' [the *Didache*]" (Schaff, *Nicene and Post-Nicene Fathers*, 2d series, 4:552). The *Didache*, with its instruction on the Eucharist and the Eucharistic prayers, was still required reading by catechumens and neophytes (those newly received into the Church) well into the fourth century.

40 Ignatius was an old man when he wrote his epistles in 106 and is therefore a witness of the first century rather than the second.

41 Ignatius of Antioch, *Epistle to the Philadelphians* 4 (written *c.* 106), in *Early Christian Writings*, 94. Notice the four key words that continually crop up: body, blood, altar, and sacrifice. J. N. D. Kelly comments on this last quotation, "Ignatius' reference to the 'one altar, just as there is one bishop,' reveals that he too thought in sacrificial terms" (*Early Christian Doctrines*, 196).

those perverted notions about the grace of Jesus Christ which has come down to us, and see how contrary to the mind of God they are. . . . They even abstain from the Eucharist and the public [liturgical] prayer, because they will not admit that the Eucharist is the self-same body of our Savior Jesus Christ, which [flesh] suffered for our sins, and which the Father in His goodness raised up again. Consequently, since they reject God's gifts, they are doomed in their disputatiousness. They should have done better to learn charity, if they were ever to know any resurrection. . . . Abjure all factions, for they are the beginning of evils."[42]

"Obey your bishop and clergy with undivided minds. . . . Share in one common breaking of bread—the medicine of immortality, and the sovereign remedy by which we escape death and live in Jesus Christ for evermore."[43]

Pliny the Younger (62–*c.* 114)[44]

42 Ignatius of Antioch, *Epistle to the Smyrnaeans* 6, 7 (written *c.* 106), in *Early Christian Writings*, 102–3. There is no question that Ignatius considered the Eucharist to be the Real Presence of Christ, the self-same flesh that was crucified and raised again. This was no innovation; he was writing nothing new to the believers across Asia, only confirming what they already knew and practiced. He expounded the common doctrine of the whole Church, and no one treated his letters as radical or out of line with the universal apostolic teaching. Historian Warren Carroll tells us that at the time of his martyrdom Ignatius was "at least thirty years a bishop, probably trained by the Apostle John, and was apparently at this time the most venerated living member of the whole Church" (*The Founding of Christendom* [Front Royal, Va.: Christendom Press, 1993], 1:455).

43 Ignatius of Antioch, *Epistle to the Ephesians* 20 (written *c.* 106), in *Early Christian Writings*, 66. This is the church over which St. John had presided only a few years earlier. These are incredible and powerful words, with no ambiguity. Do we find a record of anyone chastising Ignatius for any deviation from *faith alone* or for his "overly enthusiastic exaggerations"? No, in fact he is utterly respected and carefully emulated by all contemporary and later Christians. Representing apostolic Christianity, he was a mouthpiece for orthodox Christian teaching and practice as laid down by Jesus and the apostles.

44 Pliny the Younger was the governor of Bithynia, which was under Roman Emperor Trajan (who reigned from 98 to 117). Bithynia was located in Asia Minor, just north of Galatia. This was an area that had attracted the attention of Paul (Acts 16:7), who was forbidden by the "Spirit of Jesus" to go there. It is possible that Peter had already preached the gospel in Bithynia and estab-

"In the examination of Christians I have never taken part; therefore I do not know what crime is usually punished or investigated or to what extent. So I have no little uncertainty whether there is any distinction of age, or whether the weaker offenders fare in no respect otherwise than the stronger; whether pardon is granted on repentance. . . . Meanwhile I have taken this course with those who were accused before me as Christians: I have asked them whether they were Christians. Those who confessed I asked a second and a third time, threatening punishment. Those who persisted I ordered led away to execution. . . . They had been accustomed to assemble on a fixed day before daylight and sing by turns [i.e., antiphonally] a hymn to Christ as a god; and that they bound themselves with an oath [*sacramentum*], not for any crime, but to commit neither theft, nor robbery, nor adultery, not to break their word and not to deny a deposit when demanded; after these things were done, it was their custom to depart and meet together again to take food, but ordinary and harmless food."[45]

---

lished the churches in that region (1 Pet 1:1; also see Eusebius, *History of the Church* 3, 1, 1). By the year 111, there was a well-established church in Bithynia, even extending to rural areas, which had excited much local opposition. One reason for the outcry against Christians was the drastic drop in the sale of meat for pagan sacrifices (Pliny, *Ep.* 10, 96). Many Christians suffered under the persecution; they kept their vows of loyalty to Christ and his Church and were willing to die rather than deny the Lord Jesus.

45 *Epistulae* 10, 96 (written *c.* 112), as quoted by Joseph Cullen Ayer in *A Source Book for Ancient Church History* (New York: Charles Scribner's Sons, 1948), 20–21. In Pliny's epistle we have an unimpeachable source of information about the state of the early Church and her mode of worship. The New Testament frequently uses the word *mystery* (μυστήριον), which was translated into Latin as "sacrament" (*sacramentum*). Though some have seen this as referring to baptism, it seems more probable that Pliny, without knowing the details of the liturgy, was referring to the Eucharist. It is common knowledge that the early Church met before sunrise for worship and kept the eucharistic liturgy strictly secret, not even revealing the sacrament to prospective converts. The word *sacramentum* was probably used at a very early date by the Christians who spoke Latin to denote all the most sacred and secret elements of religion. "In the letter written about the Christians by Pliny to the Emperor Trajan in 112, the word '*sacramentum*' is used in a manner which suggests that the Christians, though not Pliny himself, already applied it to the Eucharist. By the year 200 a.d. its use was quite established. . . . Thus Tertullian speaks of 'the Sacrament of Baptism and of the Eucharist.' As St. Paul had spoken of the revealed secrets of God as 'mysteries,' and called the

Justin Martyr (*c.* 100–*c.* 165)[46]

"And on the day called Sunday, all who live in the cities or in the country gather together to one place and the memoirs of the apostles or the writings of the prophets are read, as long as time permits; then, when the reader has ceased, the president [priest] verbally instructs, and exhorts to the imitation of these good things. Then we all rise together and pray, and, as we before said, when our prayer is ended bread and wine are brought, and the president in like manner offers prayers and thanksgivings, according to his ability, and the people assent, saying Amen; and there is a distribution to each and a participation of that over which thanks have been given [Eucharist elements] and to those who are absent a portion is sent by the deacons."[47]

"And this food is called among us Εὐχαριστία [the Eucharist], of which no one is allowed to partake but the man who believes that the things which we teach are true, and who has been washed with the washing that is for the remission of sins, and unto regeneration, and who is so living as Christ has enjoined. For not as common bread and common drink do we receive these; but in like manner as Jesus Christ our Savior, having been made flesh by the Word of God, had both flesh and blood for our salvation, so likewise have we been taught that

---

apostles 'stewards of God's mysteries,' the Fathers of the Church continued his practice" (Pullan, *Early Christian Doctrines*, 72). The fact that Pliny refers to the Eucharist in his letter is substantiated by Tertullian's reference to the Eucharist as a "*sacramentum*." (See *On the Soldier's Crown* 3.)

46 Justin Martyr wrote convincingly to the Roman authorities attempting to persuade them of the truth and reasonableness of the Christian faith. Rumors spread widely that Christians were atheists, ate human flesh, and practiced gross immorality. The intent of the *Apologies* (defenses) was to remove all suspicions against the loyalty and morality of the Christians and thus to gain tolerance from the rulers. It was often in the face of great personal risk and bodily harm that these men defended the faith, as was proved with Justin, who was beheaded for his outspoken witness.

47 Justin Martyr, *First Apology* 1, 67, in Roberts and Donaldson, *Ante-Nicene Fathers*, 1:186. Notice the resemblance to the liturgy of the Catholic Church today. The Eucharist is celebrated every Sunday, it is prayed over by the presider, the people join in with "Amen," the Eucharist is distributed and even taken to those who are absent. We also see the two-part liturgy of the Word and of the Eucharist. Notice the word "participation," which corresponds to Paul's usage in his First Letter to the Corinthians.

the food which is blessed by the prayer of His word, and from which our blood and flesh by transmutation are nourished, is the flesh and blood of that Jesus who was made flesh."[48] "Hence God speaks by the mouth of Malachi, one of the twelve [prophets], as I said before, about the sacrifices at that time presented by you [Jews]: 'I have no pleasure in you,' says the Lord, 'and I will not accept your sacrifices at your hands; for, from the rising of the sun to the going down of the same, My name has been glorified among the Gentiles, and in every

48 Ibid., 1, 62, in Roberts and Donaldson, *Ante-Nicene Fathers*, 1:185. Several things should be noted from this passage. First, the bread is no longer common bread but has *become* the Body of Christ. Second, the change in the bread takes place when the "presider" prays with "his word"—Jesus' words of consecration—which he then recites, over the offering of bread and wine. Third, this is something he had been taught at his conversion and is the consistent liturgy and practice of all the churches.

The mysteries of the Church were practiced in secret. No one outside the group of baptized Christians could see or partake of the Eucharist. Pagans and Jews misunderstood what the Eucharist was, thinking it was an act of cannibalism and debauchery. When asked for an explanation of the Christian sacrifice, Christians were sworn to absolute secrecy. According to C. Lattery, "The answer could not be given without betraying secret doctrines to the Jew. But [Justin's] Apology had made the whole [event] public, in popular and simple language. For the esoteric teaching of the Christians had got abroad, and it was rumored that in their secret reunions they slew a human child, and fed on human flesh. Could the report have arisen because the Christians used realistic language in their liturgy with a merely symbolical meaning? If so, it would have been easy to refute the report by stating that mere bread and wine with water were taken in common as a sign of fellowship; nay, the heathen might well have been invited to come and see what was done. But it appears that the Christians never took this line. On the contrary, they made their mysteries more mysterious and private than ever; they hid them from the eyes of all but the instructed and baptized, and refused to publish any explanations. St. Justin's Apology offers us the one exception to the rule of secrecy. But the hope of getting the excellent Emperor Pius to change the laws against Christians had no result, and the attempt seems never to have been repeated. Consequently St. Justin's candid exposition is of unique interest.

"He describes the secret meetings of Christians, he implies that only believers who have been baptized can be present, and declares that they are taught that what they eat is the Body and the Blood of Jesus Christ. It is obvious that if he could possibly have said that it was ordinary bread and wine, he must have seized the opportunity of proclaiming the fact. The truth obliges him to say it is not" (C. Lattey, S.J., *Catholic Faith in the Holy Eucharist* [Cambridge, England: W. Heffer & Sons, 1923], 24–25).

place incense is offered to My name, and a pure offering: for My Name is great among the Gentiles says the Lord, but you profane it.' [So] He then speaks to those Gentiles, namely us, who in every place offer sacrifices to Him, i.e., the bread of the Eucharist, and also the cup of the Eucharist, affirming both that we glorify His Name and you profane it."[49]

"Accordingly, God, anticipating all the sacrifices which we offer through this name, and which Jesus the Christ enjoined us to offer, i.e., in the Eucharist of the bread and the cup, and which are presented by Christians in all places throughout the world, bears witness that they are wellpleasing to Him . . . saying, ' . . . from the rising of the sun to its setting my name is glorified among the Gentiles [Malachi 1:11].' "[50]

"Is there any other matter, my friends, in which we are blamed? . . . Are our lives and customs also slandered by you? And I ask this: have you also believed concerning us, that we eat men, and that after

49 Justin Martyr, *Dialogue with Trypho the Jew*, chap. 41 (written *c.* 135), in Roberts and Donaldson, *Ante-Nicene Fathers*, 1:215. Justin explains that the Eucharist is a sacrifice and that it had been prophesied hundreds of years earlier by Malachi. This was the universal teaching of the primitive Church. Protestant scholar J. N. D. Kelly writes, "Justin speaks of 'all the sacrifices in this name which Jesus appointed to be performed, viz. in the Eucharist of the bread and the cup, and which are celebrated in every place by Christians.' Not only here but elsewhere too, he identifies 'the bread of the Eucharist, and the cup likewise of the Eucharist,' with the sacrifice foretold by Malachi. . . . It was natural for early Christians to think of the Eucharist as a sacrifice. The fulfillment of prophecy demanded a solemn Christian offering, and the rite itself was wrapped in the sacrificial atmosphere with which our Lord invested the Last Supper. The words of institution, 'Do this,' must have been charged with sacrificial overtones for second century ears. . . . The bread and wine, moreover, are offered 'for a memorial of the passion,' a phrase which in view of his identification of them with the Lord's body and blood implies much more than an act of purely spiritual recollection. Altogether it would seem that, while his language is not fully explicit, Justin is feeling his way to the conception of the Eucharist as the offering of the Savior's passion" (Kelly, *Early Christian Doctrine*, 196–97).

50 Justin Martyr, *Dialogue with Trypho the Jew*, chap. 117, in Roberts and Donaldson, *Ante-Nicene Fathers*, 1:257. Justin is very explicit that the Eucharist is the pure sacrifice which God through the true Messiah has substituted for those of the Jewish Temple. He explains that it is the universal teaching of the early Church.

the feast, having extinguished the lights, we engage in promiscuous concubinage?"[51]

Irenaeus (c. 130–*c.* 200)[52]

"When, therefore, the mingled cup and the manufactured bread receives the Word of God, and the Eucharist of the blood and the body of Christ is made, from which things the substance of our flesh is increased and supported, how can they affirm that the flesh is incapable of receiving the gift of God, which is life eternal, which [flesh] is nourished from the body and blood of the Lord, and is a member of Him? . . . A spirit has not bones nor flesh; but [Paul refers to] that dispensation [by which the Lord became] an actual man, consisting of flesh, and nerves, and bones—that [flesh] which is nourished by the cup which is His blood, and receives increase from the bread which is His body. And just as a cutting from the vine planted in the ground fructifies in its season, or as a corn of wheat falling into the earth and becoming decomposed, rises with manifold increase by the Spirit of God, who contains all things, and then, through the wisdom of God, serves for the use of men, and having received the Word of God, becomes the Eucharist, which is the body and blood of Christ; so also our bodies, being nourished by it, and deposited in the earth, and suffering decomposition there, shall rise at their appointed time, the Word of God granting them resurrection to the glory of God, even the Father, who freely gives to this mortal immortality, and to this corruptible incorruption."[53]

---

51 Ibid., chap. 10, p. 129. The obvious reference to the Eucharist is unavoidable and confirms the early Christian view of the Real Presence. We learn from Robert Wilken, "Not so long after Pliny [a.d. 112], Christians were accused of clandestine rites involving promiscuous intercourse and ritual meals in which human flesh was eaten. . . . By the late second century such charges had become widespread" (*The Christians as the Romans Saw Them* [New Haven: Yale Univ. Press, 1984], 17).

52 Irenaeus of Lyons wrote his magnificent treatise against the Gnostic heresies *c.* 180. He studied their philosophies in great detail and decimated them with orthodox teaching and proofs written with great strength and clarity. His eloquent writing against Gnosticism is a wonderful source of information on the doctrine, life, and practice of the early Church.

53 Irenaeus, *Against Heresies* 5, 2, 3, in Roberts and Donaldson, *Ante-Nicene Fathers*, 1:528. Irenaeus teaches that "the idea of the passion pervades this

"He took the created thing, bread, and gave thanks, and said: 'This is my body.' And the cup likewise, which is part of that creation to which we belong, He confessed to be His blood, and taught the new oblation [offering] of the new covenant, which the Church, receiving from the apostles, offers to God throughout all the world, . . . concerning which Malachi . . . spoke beforehand: 'I have no pleasure in you, saith the Lord Omnipotent, and I will not accept sacrifice at your hands. For from the rising of the sun, unto the going down, My name is glorified among the Gentiles, and in every place incense is offered to My name, and a pure sacrifice' . . . indicating in the plainest manner by these words, that the former people [the Jews] shall indeed cease to make offerings to God, but that in every place sacrifice shall be offered to him, and that a pure one; and his name is glorified among the Gentiles."[54]

"The oblation [sacrifice] of the Church, therefore, which the Lord gave instructions to be offered throughout all the world, is accounted with God a pure sacrifice, and is acceptable to Him. . . . And the class of oblations in general has not been set aside. . . . There are sacrifices here [among the Christians]. . . . Sacrifices there are, too, in the Church: but the species alone has been changed. . . . Inasmuch,

---

approach too, for Irenaeus identifies the gifts with Christ's body and blood and describes them, in language reminiscent of the Lord's words at the Last Supper, as 'the oblation of the new covenant.' This leads us to consider the significance attached to the elements themselves in this period. From the *Didache* we gather that the bread and wine are 'holy'; they are spiritual food and drink communicating immortal life" (Kelly, *Early Christian Doctrines*, 197).

Eminent Church historian Jaroslav Pelikan comments on the effect received by the participant. He says, "Another prominent theme of Eucharistic doctrine was the belief that participation in the Lord's Supper would prepare the communicant for immortality. . . . Irenaeus explicitly drew a parallel between these two transformations when he declared that the bodies that had received the Eucharist were no longer corruptible, just as the bread that had received the consecration was no longer common" (*The Emergence of the Catholic Tradition 100–600* [Chicago: Univ. of Chicago Press, 1971], 169).

54 Irenaeus, *Against Heresies* 4, 17, 5, in Roberts and Donaldson, *Ante- Nicene Fathers*, 1:484. Notice that he, like the others, has explained the Eucharist in terms of the sacrifices mentioned by the last Old Testament prophet, Malachi. This application of Malachi's prophecy to the Eucharist is one of the most consistent and widely written acknowledgments of the primitive Church.

then, as the Church offers with single-mindedness, her gift is justly reckoned a pure sacrifice with God."[55]

Clement of Alexandria (*c.* 150–*c.* 215)[56]
"Accordingly, as wine is blended with water, so is the Spirit with man. And the one, the mixture of wine and water, nourishes to faith; while the other, the Spirit, conducts to immortality. And the mixture of both—of the drink and of the Word—is called Eucharist, renowned and glorious grace; and they who by faith partake of it are sanctified both in body and soul."[57]

"The Scripture manifestly applying the terms bread and water to nothing else but to those heresies, which employ bread and water in the oblation, not according to the canon of the Church. For there are those who celebrate the Eucharist with mere water."[58]

55 Ibid., 4, 18, 1–4, in Roberts and Donaldson, *Ante-Nicene Fathers*, 1:484–85. Jaroslav Pelikan states, "It does seem 'express and clear' that no orthodox father of the second or third century of whom we have record either declared the presence of the body and blood of Christ in the Eucharist to be no more than symbolic. . . . Within the limits of those extremes was the doctrine of the real presence. . . . The adoration of Christ in the Eucharist through the words and actions of the liturgy seems to have presupposed that this was a special presence, neither distinct from nor merely illustrative of his presence in the church. . . . The theologians did not have adequate concepts within which to formulate a doctrine of the real presence that evidently was already believed by the church. . . . The real presence believed by the church and affirmed by its liturgy was closely tied to the idea of the Eucharist as a sacrifice" (*Emergence of the Catholic Tradition*, 167–68).

56 Eusebius comments on Clement: "In Book I he [Clement] shows that he himself was almost an immediate successor of the apostles. . . . In his work *The Easter Festival* he declares that his friends insisted on his transmitting to later generations in writing the oral traditions that had come down to him from the earliest authorities of the Church" (6, 13, p. 191). In the same passage we find a letter to Origen from a man named Alexander in which Clement is mentioned: "For we have found true fathers in those blessed ones who trod the road before us, with whom we shall soon be reunited—Pantaenus, my truly blessed friend, and holy Clement, my friend and helper, and others like them" (Eusebius, *History of the Church* 6, 14, p. 193).

57 Clement of Alexandria, *Paedagogus* 2, 2, in Roberts and Donaldson, *Ante-Nicene Fathers*, 2:242.

58 Clement of Alexandria, *Stromata* 1, 19, 96, in Roberts and Donaldson, *Ante-Nicene Fathers*, 2:322. Clement's wording presupposes that he is acquainted

"Melchizedek, king of Salem, priest of the most high God, who gave bread and wine, furnishing consecrated food for a type of the Eucharist."[59]

Tertullian (*c.* 160–*c.* 225)[60]
"We take also, in congregations before daybreak, and from the hand of none but the presidents, the sacrament of the Eucharist, which the Lord both commanded to be eaten at meal-times, and enjoined to be taken by all alike. . . .We feel pained should any wine or bread, even though our own, be cast [fall] upon the ground. At every forward step and movement, at every going in and out, when we put on our clothes and shoes, when we bathe, when we sit at table, when we light the lamps, on couch, on seat, in all the ordinary actions of daily life, we trace upon the forehead the sign [of the cross]."[61]

---

with an "oblation" (sacrifice), is concerned with the precise physical elements used in the Eucharist, and is familiar with the "canon of the Church," which speaks of the laws and customs of the Church (singular) known to all. He is also aware at this early date that the celebration of the Eucharist is not just an empty symbol open to many interpretations and different manners of celebration. It had to be celebrated in complete subjection to the canons of the Church.

59 Ibid., 4, 25, in Roberts and Donaldson, *Ante-Nicene Fathers*, 2:439—further confirmation that the early Church saw the offering of Melchizedek as a prefiguring of the Eucharist. Thus, in this setting Clement recognizes the Eucharist as a sacrifice and as a holy food for believers.

60 Tertullian was from Africa and one of the more influential theologians of the second century. Later in his life he joined the rigorous group called the Montanists. His writings fall into three periods: Catholic orthodoxy from 197 to 206, semi-Montanist from 206 to 212, and Montanist from 213 to 220.

61 Tertullian, *The Chaplet* or *On the Soldier's Crown* 3, 4 (written *c.* 204), in Roberts and Donaldson, *Ante-Nicene Fathers*, 3:94–95. Reverence for the Blessed Sacrament is shown by the pain experienced if any should fall to the ground, a reverence that is still shown today in the Catholic Church—eucharistic ministers are taught the careful recovery procedures necessary should any particle of the elements fall to the ground. If mere food and drink of common sort were at issue, why would Christians express such reverence? Tertullian believes so much in the Real Presence in the Eucharist that he chides the Marcionite heretics (who denied the corporal body of Christ but still continued in the eucharistic service). If there had not been a real body on the Cross, there could not be any real Body in the Eucharist!

Origen (*c.* 185–*c.* 254)[62]

"We give thanks to the Creator of all, and, along with thanksgiving [Eucharist] and prayer for the blessings we have received, we also eat the bread presented to us; and this bread becomes by prayer a sacred body, which sanctifies those who sincerely partake of it."[63]

"You who are wont to assist in the Divine Mysteries, know how, when you receive the body of the Lord you take reverent care, lest any particle of it should fall to the ground and a portion of the consecrated gift escape you. You consider it a crime—and rightly so—if any particle thereof fall down through negligence."[64]

Eusebius (*c.* 260–*c.* 340)[65]

"I will tell you of one instance that occurred here. Among our num-

---

62 Origen was a celebrated Christian writer, teacher, and theologian. He is known for his many doctrinal writings and multiple volumes of biblical commentaries. He was a student of Clement of Alexandria. Origen taught in Alexandria for about twenty-eight years, instructing not only Christians but pagans as well. Origen may well have been the most accomplished biblical scholar of the early Church.

63 Origen, *Contra Celsum* 8, 33 (written *c.* 248), in Quasten, *Patrology*, 2:85. Again the teaching of Jesus is brought into play: the bread is the Sacred Body, and those who eat of it are sanctified; in other words, they become what they eat.

64 Origen, *Homilies on Exodus* 13, 3 (written after 244), in Quasten, *Patrology*, 2:86. Origen makes the definite correlation between what was bread and what is now the "body of the Lord."

65 Out of all the books I have read in my life, Eusebius' *History of the Church* will always rank among my personal top five. Eusebius, considered the "Father of Church History," preserved for later generations the invaluable record of the first centuries. Much of what we know today would have been lost had it not been for him. He wrote the history of the early Church from the time of the Jews, through the life of Christ and the apostles, and into the fourth century. The content of the book is astonishing. It gives us insight, as Christians, into who we are, who our early brothers and sisters were, and how we fit in the whole flow of the Holy Spirit's work in history. It gives us a family tree and examples of faith that elicit tears and joy. Eusebius was the bishop of Caesarea. During persecutions he spent many months in prison. He personally witnessed many Christians tortured mercilessly, and he gives an eyewitness account of their sufferings and courage. His *History of the Church* was completed in 303, with the last chapters added as the events occurred up to 325. All Christians would profit from reading Eusebius' account.

ber was an old believer named Serapion, whose conduct for most of his life had been beyond reproach, but who had lapsed when trial came [denied Christ under torture]. Again and again he pleaded, but no one listened—he had sacrificed [to Roman gods]. He fell sick and for three days on end remained speechless and unconscious, but on the fourth day he was a little better, and called his grandson to his bedside. . . . 'You go yourself and bring one of the presbyters [priests].' But it was night time, and he was unwell and unable to come. I had, however, given instructions that those departing this life, if they desired it, and especially if they happened to have pleaded before, should be absolved, so they could depart in sure hope; so he gave a portion of the Eucharist to the little boy, telling him to soak it and let it fall drop by drop into the old man's mouth.

"The boy returned with it to the house, but before he could enter, Serapion rallied again and said: 'Is that you, child? The presbyter could not come, but you must do as he told you, and let me depart.' The boy soaked it, and poured it into the mouth of the old man, who after swallowing a little immediately died. Was he not plainly preserved and kept alive until he was released and, his sin blotted out, could be honored for his many good deeds?"[66]

Athanasius (*c.* 296–373)[67]

"You shall see the Levites bringing loaves and a cup of wine, and placing them on the table. So long as the prayers of supplication and entreaties have not been made, there is only bread and wine. But after the great and wonderful prayers have been completed, then the bread is become the Body, and the wine the Blood, of our Lord Jesus Christ. *And again:* Let us approach the celebration of the mysteries. The bread and wine, so long as the prayers and supplications have not

66 Eusebius, *History of the Church* 6, 44, p. 218. Eusebius is quoting from a letter written by Dionysius (d. *c.* 264) to Fabius. Fabius was "inclined a little toward the schism" of Novatius, and Dionysius was encouraging him toward repentance. This story was his example of the need for, and the effectiveness of, repentance and the Eucharist. This letter was written *c.* 250 and shows the early Church's reverence for the Holy Eucharist.

67 Athanasius' unbending character and unswervingly orthodox theology was the main reason the correct doctrine of the deity of Christ finally prevailed in the East. We owe an eternal debt of gratitude to Athanasius for standing against all odds to defend orthodox Christianity.

taken place, remain simply what they are. But after the great prayers and holy supplications have been sent forth, the Word comes down into the bread and wine—and thus is His Body confected."[68]

Council of Nicaea (325)
"Neither canon nor custom has handed down that they who have not authority to offer, should give the body of Christ to those who do offer."[69]

"Concerning those who are departing (this life), the old and canonical law shall be observed now also, that if any one is departing, he must not be deprived of the viaticum [Holy Communion as provision for the journey] of the Lord; but if, after having been given over, and having partaken of the oblation, he be again numbered amongst the living, let him be amongst those who communicate in prayer only. But generally, and as regards every one who is departing, and who asks to partake of the Eucharist, let the bishop, after examination, communicate to him of the oblation."[70]

Basil the Great (*c.* 330–379)[71]

68 Athanasius, *To the Newly Baptized*, in Jurgens, *Faith of the Early Fathers*, 1:345–46. The bishop of Alexandria and premier defender of the deity of Christ and the Holy Trinity sits down to write a sermon for those newly baptized into the Church. What is of primary importance for these new Christians to know and understand? He teaches them about the central mysteries and doctrines of the faith, including the Eucharist. The Eucharist is central to Christian worship and a means by which God imparts his grace. There can be no mistaking Athanasius' doctrine of the Eucharist as he expounds the Scriptures to these newest members of the Catholic Church.

69 Council of Nicaea, canon 18, in Berington and Kirk, *Faith of Catholics*, 2:235.

70 Ibid., canon 13, in Berington and Kirk, *Faith of Catholics*, 2:235. The Council of Nicaea reaffirmed ancient customs, passed down from the earliest Fathers, regarding the Holy Sacrament of Communion. The council continued to affirm the deity of Christ, as well the Real Presence of Christ in the Eucharist.

71 Basil the Great, Father and Doctor of the Church, was born of wealthy parents in Caesarea Mazaca (modern Kayseri, Turkey) and educated in Athens and Constantinople. He visited a number of Christian hermits in the deserts of Egypt and Syria and decided to give up his career in order to become a hermit himself by the river Iris in Neo Caesarea. He was noted for

"It is good and beneficial to communicate every day, and to partake of the holy body and blood of Christ. For He distinctly says, 'He that eateth my flesh and drinketh my blood hath eternal life [Jn 6:54].' And who doubts that to share frequently in life, is the same thing as to have manifold life. I, indeed, communicate four times a week, on the Lord's day, on Wednesday, on Friday, and on the Sabbath, and on the other days if there is a commemoration of any Saint. It is needless to point out that for anyone in times of persecution to be compelled to take the communion in his own hand without the presence of a priest or minister is not a serious offence, as long custom sanctions this practice from the facts themselves. All the solitaries in the desert, where there is no priest, take the communion themselves, keeping communion at home. And at Alexandria and in Egypt, each one of the laity, for the most part, keeps the communion, at his own house, and participates in it when he likes. For when once the priest has completed the offering, and given it, the recipient, participating in it each time as entire, is bound to believe that he properly takes and receives it from the giver. And even in the church, when the priest gives the portion, the recipient takes it with complete power over it, and so lifts it to his lips with his own hand. It has the same validity whether one portion or several portions are received from the priest at the same time."[72]

Cyril of Jerusalem (*c.* 315–386)[73]

---

his brilliant mind and holiness of life and was therefore called upon by the bishop of Caesarea to defend Christian doctrine against the heretical attacks of the Arians. In 370, he was elected bishop of Caesarea, an office he nobly fulfilled until his death on January 1, 379. Basil, his brother St. Gregory of Nyssa, and his friend St. Gregory Nazianzen are known collectively as the Cappadocian Fathers. Basil's grandmother Macrina; his parents, Basil and Emmelia; his sister Macrina, and his younger brothers Gregory and Peter of Sebaste are all venerated as saints.

72 Basil the Great, *Epistle 93: To the Patrician Lady Coesaria concerning Communion*, in Schaff, *Nicene and Post-Nicene Fathers*, 2d series, 8:179. This is one of the more remarkable documents regarding the Eucharist and the history of the Holy Communion. It is a short letter, written in 372, and is very enlightening as to the practice of the ancient Church.

73 Cyril, bishop of Jerusalem, spent sixteen of his thirty-five years as bishop in exile. He was a staunch defender of the Nicene Creed and the orthodox

"Since then He Himself has declared and said of the bread, 'This is My Body,' who shall dare to doubt any longer? And since He has affirmed and said, 'This is My blood,' who shall ever hesitate, saying, that it is not His blood? . . .He once turned water into wine, at Cana of Galilee, at His own will, and shall not we believe Him when He changes wine into blood? . . . Therefore with fullest assurance let us partake as of the Body and Blood of Christ: for in the figure of bread is given to thee His Body, and in the figure of wine His Blood; that thou by partaking of the Body and Blood of Christ mayest become of one body and one blood with Him. For thus we shall become Christ-bearers because His Body and Blood are diffused through our members; thus it is that, according to St. Peter (2 Pet 1:4) 'we become partakers of divine nature'. . . . Contemplate therefore the bread and wine not as bare elements, for they are, according to the Lord's declaration, the Body and Blood of Christ; for though sense suggests this to thee, let faith establish thee. Judge not the matter from taste, but from faith be fully assured without misgiving, that thou hast been vouchsafed the Body and Blood of Christ. . . . That what seems bread is not bread, though bread by taste, but the Body of Christ; and that what seems wine is not wine, though the taste will have it so, but the Blood of Christ."[74]

"Upon the completion of the spiritual Sacrifice, the bloodless worship, over the propitiatory victim we call upon God. . . . We all pray and offer this Sacrifice for all who are in need."[75]

---

teaching of Christ against the Arian heresy.

74 Cyril of Jerusalem, *Mystagogical Catecheses* 22:1–3, 6, 9, in Quasten, *Patrology*, 3:375. This passage is based upon Cyril's reading of 1 Corinthians 11:23–25. He also refers in this document to the Eucharist as "a spiritual sacrifice, a bloodless service, a propitiatory sacrifice, offered by the way of intercession for all who are in need of help, even for the departed. It is nothing less than Christ slain as a victim for our sins, that is offered in this oblation" (ibid., 3:376).

75 Ibid., 23:8, in Jurgens, *Faith of the Early Fathers*, 1:363. Cyril's *Catechetical Lectures* are made up of twenty-four lectures for new catechumens. The first eighteen were prebaptismal discourses delivered to catechumens during Lent, and the last five (*Mystagogical Catecheses*) were delivered to the neophytes (newly converted and baptized) after their baptism. The lectures were delivered *c.* 350. In order to get a perspective of time and history, it should be recalled that the documents that make up the New Testament had not yet been col-

Gregory of Nyssa (*c.* 335–*c.* 395)[76]
"Rightly then, do we believe that the bread consecrated by the word of God has been made over into the Body of God the Word . . . who pitched His tent in the Flesh. From the same cause, therefore, by which the bread that was made over into the Body is made to change into divine strength, a similar result now takes place. As in the former case, in which the grace of the Word made holy that body the substance of which is from bread, and in a certain manner is itself bread, so in this case too, the bread, as the Apostle says, 'is consecrated by God's word and by prayer'. . . . He spreads Himself to every believer by means of that Flesh, the substance of which is from wine and bread, blending Himself with the bodies of believers, so that by this union with the Immortal, man, too, may become a participant in incorruption. These things He bestows through the power of the blessing which transforms the nature of the visible things to that [of the Immortal]."[77]

Ambrose of Milan (*c.* 339–397)[78]
"So, lest any one should say this, we will take great pains to prove that the sacraments of the Church are both more ancient than those of the synagogue, and more excellent than the manna. [The former

---

lected and canonized when Cyril wrote these lectures to train the catechumens.

76 Gregory of Nyssa was overshadowed by his famous brother Basil, whom he considered, along with his sister Macrina, "his teacher." Under the direction of Basil, he briefly held the position of reader in church but chose to teach rhetoric instead. Gregory Nazianzen urged him to return to serving the Church.

77 Gregory of Nyssa, *The Great Catechism* 37 (written *c.* 383), in Jurgens, *Faith of the Early Fathers* 2:49. This catechism covers the chief doctrines of the Church, including the Trinity, the redemption of man through the Incarnation of the Logos, and the personal acceptance by faith of redeeming grace through baptism and the Eucharist.

78 Ambrose of Milan, one of the celebrated Fathers of the Church and one of the four early Doctors of the Church (along with Gregory the Great, Augustine, and Jerome), was born in Trier (in what is now Germany) and educated in Rome. Ordained the bishop of Milan in 374, he defended the churches of Milan against the introduction of Arian doctrines.

he proves from Melchizedek, and then he continues:] . . .We have proved the sacraments of the Church to be the more ancient, now recognize that they are superior. [He proves this point from the manna, and then he continues:] . . . All those who ate that food died in the wilderness, but that food which you receive, that living Bread which came down from heaven, furnishes the substance of eternal life; and whosoever shall eat of this Bread shall never die, and it is the Body of Christ. . . . Perhaps you will say, 'I see something else, how is it that you assert that I receive the Body of Christ?' And this is the point which remains for us to prove. And what evidence shall we make use of? Let us prove that this is not what nature made, but what the blessing consecrated, and the power of blessing is greater than that of nature, because by blessing nature itself is changed. . . . Shall not the word of Christ, which was able to make out of nothing that which was not, be able to change things which already are into what they were not? For it is not less to give a new nature to things than to change them."[79]

"For even if Christ is not now seen as the one who offers the sacrifice, nevertheless it is He Himself that is offered in sacrifice here on earth when the Body of Christ is offered. Indeed, to offer Himself He is made visible in us [the priests], He whose word makes holy the sacrifice that is offered."[80]

Gregory Nazianzen (*c.* 329–389)[81]

---

79 Ambrose of Milan, *The Mysteries*, chaps. 8–9 (written *c.* 390), in Schaff, *Nicene and Post-Nicene Fathers*, 2d series, 10:323–24.

80 Ambrose of Milan, *Commentaries on Twelve of David's Psalms* 38, 25, in Jurgens, *Faith of the Early Fathers*, 2:150. These commentaries were completed September 6, 393.

81 Gregory Nazianzen was best of friends with Basil the Great even though their personalities were at opposite ends of the spectrum. Basil was fiery and somewhat arrogant, whereas Gregory was precise and logical but also a mild and gentle soul. Basil died without ever seeing the defeat of Arianism, but Gregory was more fortunate. The Church in Constantinople invited Gregory to be their bishop, and he assumed the position. We find that when he arrived, "there was a mere handful of Catholics left in that bulwark of Arianism. Gregory set up a small place of worship named *Anastasia* ("resurrection") in a private house. He set out to preach the true doctrine of Christ and the Trinity, to see the truth "resurrected" from the grave of heresy. He was

"Cease not to pray and plead for me when you draw down the Word by your word, when in an unbloody cutting you cut the Body and Blood of the Lord, using your voice as a sword."[82]

John Chrysostom (*c.* 347–407)[83]

"This is that Body which was blood-stained, which was pierced by a lance, and from which gushed forth those saving fountains, one of blood and the other of water, for all the world. . . . This is the Body which He gave us, both to hold in reserve and to eat."[84]

"When you see the Lord immolated (sacrificed) and lying on the altar, and the priest bent over the sacrifice praying, and all the people empurpled by that precious blood, can you think that you are still among men and on earth? Or are you not lifted up to heaven?"[85]

"What then? do not we offer every day? We offer indeed, but making a remembrance of His death, and this [remembrance] is one and not many. How is it one, and not many? Inasmuch as that [sacrifice]

---

so brilliant in his knowledge of theology and Scripture and so eloquent that he soon earned the titles "the Theologian" and "Defender of the Godhead of the Word." "In the short space of less than two years and in the face of the fiercest opposition from the Arian populace, he restored the ascendancy of Catholicism" (John Laux, *Church History* [Rockford, Ill.: Tan Books, 1989], 122).

82 Gregory Nazianzen, *Letter to Amphilochius, Bishop of Iconium* (written *c.* 383), in Jurgens, *Faith of the Early Fathers*, 2:41. Gregory asks his friend and fellow bishop to pray for him at the moment of the consecration of the bread and wine. This is further evidence of the Fathers' belief in the Real Presence and the sacrificial nature of the Eucharist.

83 John Chrysostom has, in modern times, been called the "Doctor of the Eucharist," though the title is never mentioned in the early centuries. He is a powerful witness to the Real Presence of Christ in the Eucharist and its sacrificial character. His references to these qualities are clear, positive, and detailed. He provides an excellent summary of the teachings and beliefs of the early believers.

84 John Chrysostom, *Hom. on 1 Cor.* 24, 4, in Jurgens, *Faith of the Early Fathers*, 2:118.

85 John Chrysostom, *The Priesthood* 3, 5 (written *c.* 386), in Jurgens, *Faith of the Early Fathers*, 2:89. *The Priesthood* is the most celebrated of Chrysostom's works. It is a dialogue with his friend Basil and reiterates with great clarity and depth the priesthood of the New Covenant, the Real Presence of Christ, and the sacrificial nature of the Eucharist.

was once for all offered, [and] carried into the Holy of Holies. This is a figure of that [sacrifice] and this remembrance of that. For we always offer the same, not one sheep now and tomorrow another, but always the same thing: so that the sacrifice is one. And yet by this reasoning, since the offering is made in many places, are there many Christs? But Christ is one everywhere, being complete here and complete there also, one Body. As then while offered in many places, He is one body and not many bodies; so also [He is] one sacrifice. He is our High Priest, who offered the sacrifice that cleanses us. That we offer now also, which was then offered, which cannot be exhausted. This is done in remembrance of what was then done. For (saith He) 'do this in remembrance of Me' [Lk 22:19]. It is not another sacrifice, as the High Priest, but we offer always the same, or rather we perform a remembrance of a Sacrifice."[86]

"Believe that there takes place now the same banquet as that in which Christ sat at table, and that this banquet is in no way different from that. For it is not true that this banquet is prepared by a man while that was prepared by Himself."[87]

"Today as then, it is the Lord who works and offers all."[88]

"We assume the role of servants; it is He who blesses and transforms.[89]

It is not man who causes what is present to become the Body and Blood of Christ, but Christ Himself who was crucified for us. The priest is the representative when he pronounces those words, but the power and the grace are those of the Lord. 'This is my Body,' he

86 John Chrysostom, *Homilies on the Epistles to the Hebrews* 17, 6, in Schaff, *Nicene and Post-Nicene Fathers*, 1st series, 14:449. This is part of a series of thirty-four homilies given during his last years in Constantinople. He continues with the same themes that flowed from the apostles right into the unified Church spread throughout the known world. In Hebrews the writer is not speaking of the Mass but rather is comparing the superiority of Christ's once-for-all sacrifice with the inferior daily sacrifices for sin offered by the Jewish priests. Chrysostom demonstrates that the early Church did not see a contradiction between the sacrifice of Christ "in time" and the daily reenactment of and participation in that one sacrifice, which is ever present before God and the Church as an eternal event (Rev 5:6).

87 John Chrysostom, *Hom. 50 in Matth.* no. 3, in Quasten, *Patrology*, 3:481.

88 Ibid., *Hom. 27. in I Cor.* no. 4.

89 Ibid., *Hom. 82 in Matth.* 5.

says. This word changes the things that lie before us; and as that sentence 'increase and multiply,' once spoken, extends through all time and gives to our nature the power to reproduce itself; even so that the saying 'This is My Body,' once uttered, does at every table in the Churches, from that time to the present day, and even till Christ's coming make the sacrifice complete."[90]

Cyril of Alexandria (*c.* 376–444)[91]

"He states demonstratively: 'This is My Body,' and 'This is My Blood,' lest you might suppose the things that are seen are a figure. Rather, by some secret of the all-powerful God the things seen are transformed into the Body and Blood of Christ, truly offered in a sacrifice in which we, as participants, receive the life-giving and sanctifying power of Christ."[92]

Jerome (342–420)

"As regards the holy eucharist you may receive it at all times without qualm of conscience or disapproval from me. You may listen to the psalmist's words:—'O taste and see that the Lord is good;' you may sing as he does:—'my heart poureth forth a good word.' But do not mistake my meaning. You are not to fast on feast-days, neither are you to abstain on the week days in Pentecost. In such matters each province may follow its own inclinations, and the traditions which have

---

90 Ibid., *Hom. 2 de. prodit. Judae* no. 6. This is an interesting summary, an anthology of sorts, of the writings of John Chrysostom on the sacrifice of the Eucharist. The sacrificing priest is Christ himself, and the consecration takes place the moment the words of the institution are pronounced. He makes a very interesting observation: As the command to increase and multiply was given long ago and still operates effectively today, so the words "This is my Body" continue to provide Christ's Body to the Church down to this day.

91 Cyril of Alexandria aggressively disputed the heresies of Novatianism and Neoplatonism as well as debating the Jews and the Imperial prefect. His main battle was with the Nestorians (who claimed that Christ was actually two separate persons, one divine and one human, fused together). He worked hard to defend the truth of the deity and the humanity of Christ in one Person. He was a true champion of the faith, and we owe him a great debt of gratitude.

92 Cyril of Alexandria, *Commentary on Matthew 26:27*, in Jurgens, *Faith of the Early Fathers*, 3:220. Again we have a Church Father denouncing the idea that the Eucharist is merely a figure or symbol.

been handed down should be regarded as apostolic laws."[93]

Augustine of Hippo (354–430)[94]

"All catechumens are such [as was Nicodemus, who believed in Jesus but was not yet reborn, so that Jesus did not trust Himself to him]. They already believe in the name of Christ, but Jesus does not trust Himself to them. Listen, beloved brethren, and understand. If we should say to a catechumen: 'Do you believe in Christ,' he will answer, 'I do believe,' and he will sign himself. He already carries the cross of Christ on his forehead, and he is not ashamed of the cross of the Lord.—See, he believed in his name! Let us ask him: 'Do you eat of the flesh of the Son of Man and drink the blood of the Son of Man?' He does not know what we are talking about, because Jesus has not entrusted Himself to him."[95]

"He took flesh from the flesh of Mary. He walked here in the

---

93 Jerome, *Letter 71: To Licinius* 6 (written *c.* 397), in Schaff, *Nicene and Post-Nicene Fathers*, 2d series, 6:154. This private correspondence from Jerome while he was living in Bethlehem gives a good summary of his teaching on the Eucharist. The Lord's Supper was being taken daily, and the customs that had been handed down were to be obeyed as "apostolic laws." Even as late as the end of the fourth century it is the apostolic tradition passed down by the Church that is considered binding upon the individual and the Church as a whole. This tradition, the laws of the apostles, are contained in the Scriptures, the tradition, and the bishops of the Church. This is confirmed throughout the writings of Jerome.

94 St. Augustine, bishop of Hippo, was the greatest of the Latin Fathers and one of the eminent Western Doctors of the Church. John Calvin and Martin Luther, leaders of the Protestant Reformation, were both students of Augustine's works.

95 Augustine, *Homilies on John* 11, 3, in Jurgens, *Faith of the Early Fathers*, 3:117. The catechumens are those preparing for baptism and reception into the Church. They understand the Cross, but they do not yet understand the mysteries of the Eucharist. It is understood by faith, because we have good and sufficient reasons to trust the Scriptures, the apostles' teachings, and the retention of their tradition in history and in Scripture. This passage offers further confirmation of the strict secrecy of the eucharistic celebration in that even the catechumens are not yet fully instructed in the mysteries until after baptism and reception into the holy Church. Catechumens were allowed to participate in the first portion of the Mass, the Liturgy of the Word, but they were required to leave the celebration before the celebration of Holy Communion.

same flesh, and gave us the same flesh to be eaten unto salvation. But no one eats that flesh unless first he adores it. . . . We do sin by not adoring."[96]

"They are infants, but they become sharers in His table, that they may have life in themselves."[97]

"Christ is both the Priest, offering Himself, and Himself the Victim. He willed that the sacramental sign of this should be the daily sacrifice of the Church, who, since the Church is His body and He the Head, learns to offer herself through Him."[98] "For then [with Melchizedek] first appeared the sacrifice which is now offered to God by Christians in the whole wide world."[99]

---

96 Augustine, *Explanation of the Psalms* 98, 9, in Jurgens, *Faith of the Early Fathers*, 3:20.

97 Augustine, *Sermon* 174, 7; C. Lattey, ed., *Catholic Faith in the Holy Eucharist* (Cambridge, England, 1923), 70: The teaching that the Eucharist is profitable for infants "establishes that St. Augustine held that the real Body and Blood of Christ are present in the Eucharist. What life can they, being infants, have in themselves, unless our Lord's Body and Blood are substantially present in the Sacrament?"

98 Augustine, *City of God* 10, 20 (written between 413 and 426), in Jurgens, *Faith of the Early Fathers*, 3:99. This lengthy work was occasioned by the confusion and popular anti-Christian feeling that followed the sack of Rome by Alaric in 410. Augustine defended Christianity against the charge that it had caused the collapse of the Roman Empire. Rome had fallen, and many who had placed their hope in the physical, "Eternal City" had had their world dashed to pieces. Augustine affirmed that the City of God is not a physical city but the Church. "Augustine censures the pagans, who attributed the calamities of the world, and especially the recent sack of Rome by the Goths, to the Christian religion, and its prohibition of the worship of the gods. He speaks of the blessings and ills of life, which then, as always, happened to good and bad men alike" (introduction to *The City of God*, in Schaff, *Nicene and Post-Nicene Fathers*, 1st series, 2:1).

99 Ibid., chap. 22, p. 323. And so we end where we began, with St. Augustine demonstrating that the offering of Melchizedek, the priest of the Most High God in Genesis, is the prefiguring of the Eucharist we offer and celebrate today, "from the rising of the sun to its setting." The new priesthood and sacrifice are established in the Church. Here we see the priesthood of Melchizedek and the pure sacrifice of Malachi, the Bread come down from heaven, the Body and Blood of Christ—a sacrifice well pleasing to God.

The Eucharist in Current Church Teaching

A few short selections from recent Church documents will confirm beyond a doubt that the Catholic Church still holds faithfully to the teachings of the Scriptures and of the Fathers. These documents go into great detail defending the faith and the Eucharist—these are only representative passages.

Catechism of the Council of Trent (1566)

"As of all the sacred mysteries bequeathed to us by our Lord and Savior as most infallible instruments of divine grace, there is none comparable to the most holy Sacrament of the Eucharist; so, for no crime is there a heavier punishment to be feared from God than for the unholy or irreligious use by the faithful of that which is full of holiness, or rather which contains the very author and source of holiness (1 Cor 11:30)."[100]

"The Catholic Church firmly believes and professes that in this Sacrament the words of consecration accomplish three wondrous and admirable effects. The first, is that the true body of Christ the Lord, the same that was born of the Virgin, and is now seated at the right hand of the Father in heaven, is contained in the Sacrament. The second, however repugnant it may appear to the senses, is that none of the substance of the elements remains in the Sacrament. The third . . . . the substance of the bread and wine is so changed into the body and blood of our Lord that they altogether cease to be the substance of bread and wine."[101]

"This doctrine, handed down by the Catholic Church, concerning the truth of this Sacrifice, she received from the words of our Lord, when, on that last night, committing to His Apostles these same sacred mysteries, He said, 'Do this for a commemoration of me'; for then, as was defined by the holy Council, He ordained them priests, and commanded that they and their successors in the priestly office, should immolate and offer His body. . . . By the table of the Lord [1 Cor 10:21] can be understood nothing else than the altar on which Sacrifice was offered to the Lord. Should we look for figures and

100 *The Catechism of the Council of Trent* (Rockford, Ill.: Tan Books, 1982), 213. The original was issued by order of Pope Pius V in 1566.

101 Ibid., 228–29.

prophesies of this Sacrifice in the Old Testament, in the first place Malachy most clearly prophesied thereof in these words: 'From the rising of the sun even to the going down, my name is great among the Gentiles, and in every place there is sacrifice, and there is offered to my name a clean oblation; for my name is great among the Gentiles, saith the Lord of hosts.'"[102]

Second Vatican Council (1962–1965)
"At the Last Supper, on the night he was betrayed, our Savior instituted the eucharistic sacrifice of his Body and Blood. This he did in order to perpetuate the sacrifice of the Cross throughout the ages until he should come again, and so to entrust to his beloved Spouse, the Church, a memorial of his death and resurrection: a sacrament of love, a sign of unity, a bond of charity, a paschal banquet in which Christ is consumed, the mind is filled with grace, and a pledge of future glory is given to us."[103]

Catechism of the Catholic Church (1994)
"At the heart of the Eucharistic celebration are the bread and wine that, by the words of Christ and the invocation of the Holy Spirit, become Christ's Body and Blood. Faithful to the Lord's command the Church continues to do . . . . what he did on the eve of his Passion: 'He took bread. . . . ' 'He took the cup filled with wine. . . . ' The signs of bread and wine become, in a way surpassing understanding, the Body and Blood of Christ; they continue also to signify the goodness of creation. . . . The Church sees in the gesture of the king-priest Melchizedek, who 'brought out bread and wine,' a prefiguring of her own offering."[104]

"We carry out this command of the Lord by celebrating the *memorial of his sacrifice*. In so doing, we *offer to the Father* what he has himself given us: the gifts of his creation, bread and wine which, by the power of the Holy Spirit and by the words of Christ, have become the body and blood of Christ. Christ is thus really and mysteriously made *pres-*

---

102 Ibid., 257.

103 *Sacrosanctum concilium*, no. 47, in *Vatican Council II*, ed. Austin Flannery (Collegeville, Minn.: Liturgical Press, 1992), 16.

104 CCC 1333.

ent."[105]

"Because it is the memorial of Christ's Passover, the Eucharist is also a sacrifice. The sacrificial character of the Eucharist is manifested in the very words of institution: 'This is my body which is given for you' and 'This cup which is poured out for you is the New Covenant in my blood.' In the Eucharist Christ gives us the very body which he gave up for us on the cross, the very blood which he 'poured out for many for the forgiveness of sins.' "[106]

"By the consecration the transubstantiation of the bread and wine into the Body and Blood of Christ is brought about. Under the consecrated species of bread and wine Christ himself, living and glorious, is present in a true, real, and substantial manner: his Body and his Blood, with his soul and his divinity."[107]

Summary

When one looks at the New Testament, the apostles, their followers, and the first centuries of the early Church, one sees an extraordinary unity of doctrine and practice in the celebration of the Eucharist. We have as much witness from the past on this doctrine as we do on any other, and the unity of doctrine and practice is astounding—exactly what one would expect from the visible Church that Jesus promised to protect and accompany "to the close of the age."

Where does one go to find this blessed unity of doctrine and practice? Where does one go to celebrate the Eucharist as Peter and Paul celebrated it? Is it possible today to find continuity with the theology and practice of the Fathers? The answer is a resounding Yes! The Catholic Church has carefully preserved the deposit of faith and celebrates the Mass today as she did in the first centuries of the Church. The truths and traditions have been preserved through the centuries, and the Real Presence of Christ in the sacrifice of the Mass is still celebrated with joy, the focal point of worship in the Roman Catholic Church.

---

105 CCC 1357.

106 CCC 1365.

107 CCC 1413.

John Henry Cardinal Newman on the Eucharist

"I betake myself to one of our altars to receive the Blessed Eucharist; I have no doubt whatever on my mind about the Gift which that Sacrament contains; I confess to myself my belief, and I go through the steps on which it is assured to me. 'The Presence of Christ is here, for It follows upon Consecration; and Consecration is the prerogative of Priests; and Priests are made by Ordination; and Ordination comes in direct line from the Apostles. Whatever be our other misfortunes, every link in our chain is safe; we have the Apostolic Succession, we have a right form of consecration; therefore, we are blessed with the great Gift.'

"Here the question rises in me, 'Who told you about the Gift?' I answer, 'I have learned it from the Fathers: I believe the Real Presence because they bear witness to it. St. Ignatius calls it "the medicine of immortality": St. Irenaeus says that "our flesh becomes incorrupt, and partakes of life, and has the hope of the resurrection," as "being nourished from the Lord's Body and Blood"; that the Eucharist "is made up of two things, an earthly and an heavenly": perhaps Origen, and perhaps Magnes, after him, say that It is not a type of our Lord's Body, but His Body: and St. Cyprian uses language as fearful as can be spoken, of those who profane it. I cast my lot with them, I believe as they.' "[108]

The Real Presence: A Short History of the Resistance

Every teaching has some opponents. Sooner or later someone will always stand up and say "No!" for one reason or another. For the first fifteen centuries, the Church's teaching on the Eucharist was like an unrent garment. Who eventually opposed the universal teaching on the Real Presence of Christ in the Eucharist—when, and why?

Conclusion: A Few Comments and Observations

I could go on and on digging through the historical records. We have touched on only a few centuries of the Christian Church. This is a very small sampling of writings and quotes concerning the Eucharist. There is an overwhelming consistency throughout the periods of

---

108 John Henry Cardinal Newman, *An Essay on the Development of Christian Doctrine* (London: Longmans, Green & Co., 1955), 23.

the New Testament, the apostles, the disciples and followers of the apostles, and the Church through twenty centuries. Even many of the "Reformers" partially adhered to the convictions of the primitive Church, hesitating and fearful to stray too far.

Pascal's Wager Extended

Pascal once proposed a wager, which is recorded in his *Pensées.* He wrote, "You must wager. It is not optional. You are embarked. Which will you choose then? . . . You must of necessity choose . . . Let us weigh the gain and the loss in wagering that God is. Let us estimate these two chances. If you gain, you gain all; if you lose, you lose nothing. Wager, then, without hesitation that he is."[109] In other words, if you wager that God is, and live accordingly, you cannot lose either way. If God is, you win all, and if God is not, you lose nothing. The opposite is also true: If you wager that God is not, and in fact God is, you lose everything and gain nothing.

Do you see how this applies to the Eucharist? Again you must wager; it is not optional. You are forced to make a choice. If you wager that the Eucharist *is* the Body of Christ, you have everything to gain and nothing to lose. On the other hand, if you wager the Eucharist is nothing but a mere symbol, when in fact it is the gracious gift of God—the Body and Blood of his Son, "the medicine of immortality for the soul"—you have nothing to gain and everything, including possibly your soul, to lose. If the constant instruction of the Church is correct, this is a very serious matter and one that needs the immediate attention of all Christians. As for me and my house, we will side with the Fathers. It is a wager we cannot, and will not, lose.

It is a weighty and central issue that demands sober consideration by those who claim the name of Christ. Catholics must awaken and open their eyes with wonder, gratitude, and godly fear; Protestants must step back and see things with a more finely focused, more historical and biblical lens. We all need to listen to the Holy Spirit in his Church and in his Scriptures, remembering what Paul reminded Timothy, that the Church is "the pillar and bulwark of the truth" (1 Tim 3:15). Through all the many centuries God spoke with one voice

109 Blaise Pascal, *Pensées*, sec. 3, 233, in *The Great Books*, trans. W. F. Trotter (Chicago, Ill.: Encyclopedia Britannica, 1980), 33:214–15.

through his Church. Today the world hears many dissonant voices, and, as a result, many turn away, disillusioned by the cacophony of rival trumpets, each claiming to play the correct tune.

The Silence of the Church

We have looked into the past to discover what the earliest believers and the Fathers preserved from the apostles. We have heard what the past has to say to us today. However, it is important to consider the *silence* of the early Church as well as what she proclaimed. If the idea of sacrifice and Real Presence were an early invention and diversion from the apostles' proclamation, why do we hear nothing from those great writers and preachers of the truth who spoke out so quickly against other heresies and false teaching? When the deity of Christ was challenged, when the Trinity was attacked, when the visible, organic unity of the Church was questioned, what did the early Fathers do? They fought vociferously with tongue and pen. They left no stone unturned, no argument unused. Where is their diatribe against the Real Presence? Where are their invectives against the sacrificial nature of the Mass? Why did Athanasius, who was exiled into the desert five times for defending the deity of Christ, not cry out against the "heresy" of the Real Presence? In fact, he strongly advocated this doctrine. As an Evangelical anxious to disprove the Catholic Church's dogmas, I searched in vain for the Fathers who would come to my rescue, but I found none. The more I read, the more I realized that the early Church was Catholic and did not support my Evangelical conclusions. What the Church does *not* say and write is as significant as what she *does* say and write. Silence speaks as loudly as words. Those who have ears to hear, let them hear what the teachers and pastors, bishops and saints have *not* said as well as what they have said to the churches.

Who Has Better Insight?

We must ask ourselves: Who would understand the teachings of Christ and the apostles more accurately: those who knew them and the generations immediately following, or those living two thousand years later? Who would have a better grasp of the language, the tradition, the religious milieu, and the spiritual teachings and practices:

people today, many of whom have cut themselves off from the anchor of history, or those who suffered and died for the faith, with the "apostles' teaching still ringing in their ears"?

Protestant Traditions

Fundamentalists claim, and firmly believe, that they are people of the "Book," whereas Catholics are products of tradition. Yet, Protestants, too, are people not only of the "Book" but also of tradition in a definite and real way. As a Protestant, I contended that "I do not follow tradition, I am a follower of the Bible alone—I read and interpret it for myself and don't need any old tradition." But the truth is I was deeply immersed in a very definite tradition that could be traced back to "revivalist, tent-meeting Fundamentalism" of the last century, which grew from the root of the Anabaptist movement that had split off from Luther and Zwingli in the Reformation. But that's where the history stops.[110] The Reformation was not a recovery of what had been lost; rather, it was a radical departure from that which had always been.

Those of us who live in the twentieth century were not in the Up-

110 Baptist professor and historian James Edward McGoldrick writes, "Perhaps no other major body of professing Christians has had as much difficulty in discerning its historical roots as have the Baptists. A survey of conflicting opinions might lead a perceptive observer to conclude that Baptists suffer from an identity crisis. . . . Many Baptists object vehemently and argue that their history can be traced across the centuries to New Testament times. Some Baptists deny categorically that they are Protestants and that the history of their churches is related to the success of the Protestant Reformation of the sixteenth century. Those who reject the Protestant character and Reformation origins of the Baptists usually maintain a view of church history sometimes called 'Baptist Successionism' . . . enhanced enormously by a booklet entitled *The Trail of Blood*." The author, after acknowledging his initial advocacy of the "successionist" view, and referring to himself in the third person, goes on to say, "Extensive graduate study and independent investigation of church history has, however, convinced him that the view he once held so dear has not been, and cannot be, verified. On the contrary, surviving primary documents render the successionist view untenable. . . . Although free church groups in ancient and medieval times sometimes promoted doctrines and practices agreeable to modern Baptists, when judged by standards now acknowledged as baptistic, not one of them merits recognition as a Baptist church. Baptists arose in the seventeenth century in Holland and England. They are Protestants, heirs of the Reformers" (*Baptist Successionism: A Crucial Question in Baptist History* [Metuchen, N.J.: American Theological Library Assoc. and Scarecrow Press, 1994], 1–2).

per Room when Jesus and his apostles ate the Passover meal, which was transformed into the Lord's Supper by the Lamb of God himself. When Jesus taught his apostles to "Do this in remembrance of me," was he standing, still sitting, or kneeling? At whom was he looking, and what was the expression on his face? What details were discussed to which we were not privy? What details did he give them—what other questions did they ask? How did he teach them to carry out this rite in the future? What did they understand his words to mean? Was this to be simply a meal together or a sacred sacrifice? How did the apostles and their disciples who were eventually appointed bishops and deacons perceive the event; how were they trained to carry out this command? Why did the first generation always refer to the table as an "altar"? In fact, the Scriptures give us very little information. The richness of the sacrament and the celebration details were carried on in the tradition of the Church. The early Church, without the New Testament, learned to celebrate the Eucharist from the apostles and the Fathers themselves. It is incumbent upon us to listen to them today.

We must be connected to our roots, or we must be honest and forsake our claim to be the progeny of the first believers. We cannot claim to be followers of Jesus and his apostles if we condemn their students, the bishops, presbyters, and deacons, who carried out their commands and practices with detailed precision in the first centuries of the Church. Can we really think we are the true followers of Christ if we ignore his Church and follow our own private judgment based on the Bible alone? Is it logical to insist on our own interpretation of the New Testament and yet ignore, or even condemn as "paganized," those who formed the very canon of books Evangelicals and Catholics alike call the New Testament? How can we trust those bishops in their recognition and choice of inspired books if we reject their teaching on baptism and the Eucharist, not to mention the primacy of Rome and the visible unity of the Church?

How can we confidently recite the Nicene Creed where it touches on the deity of Christ and the Trinity and yet brush over the phrases "one, holy, catholic, and apostolic Church" and "baptism for the remission of sins"? My wife and I were members of an Evangelical church that actually changed the words of the Apostles' Creed from "catholic" to "Christian" in an attempt to avoid the obvious implications.

So ends our story. As Jewish converts to the Christian faith often refer to their experience as one of becoming "fulfilled Jews," Janet and I, in our conversion to the Catholic Church, have had the same experience: we are now fulfilled Christians. We are still Evangelicals in the best sense of the word, and we love and admire the fervor and zeal of our Evangelical brethren. Evangelicalism taught us to love the Lord, to learn the Scriptures, to believe in absolute truth, and to be bold about our faith. Evangelical Protestantism was a wonderful nursemaid, bringing us up to find eventually the fullness of the faith in the Catholic Church.

The depth of joy, peace, confidence, and emotion accompanying our conversion has been inexpressible. We find this to be a common experience for those around us who have also made the same amazing discovery and crossed the Tiber to the faith and Church of our Fathers. We have come into port, we have found the oasis, we are home. I will close with the words of my oldest daughter, Cindy, who turned eighteen years old while I was writing this book. "Dad," she said, "joining the Catholic Church was the best thing our family has ever done." Thank you, Lord Jesus, we are truly and humbly grateful.

A SHORT BIBLIOGRAPHY FOR INTERESTED READERS

Catechism of the Catholic Church. Rome: Libreria Editrice Vaticana, 1994. This catechism is the compendium of the teachings of the Church. This long-awaited historic document is a beautifully written and clearly stated synthesis of the Catholic Church's teaching on faith, doctrine, morals, prayer, and the sacraments.

Early Christian Writings. Trans. Maxwell Staniforth. Harmondsworth, Middlesex, England: Penguin Books, 1968. This book will open the doors of history and challenge the reader to compare his modern suppositions with those of the very first Christian writers, the men who personally knew, and were trained by, the apostles themselves. This book contains the *Didache*, the *Epistle of Clement*, *Epistles* of Ignatius, *Epistles* and *Martyrdom of Polycarp*, *Epistle to Diognetus*, and the *Epistle* of Barnabas.

The Navarre Bible. With commentary by the theology faculty of the University of Navarre. Dublin: Four Courts Press, 1990. Written in Greek and Latin, with the commentaries in English. These commentaries consist of a set of twelve volumes covering the entire New Testament and draw upon ancient and modern Catholic theologians and Church documents.

Chesterton, G. K. *Collected Works*, vol. 3. San Francisco: Ignatius Press, 1990. This volume contains the works *The Catholic Church and Conversion*, *The Thing: Why I Am a Catholic*, and others. A brilliant mind makes one proud to convert to the ancient Church.

Cross, F. L., and E. A. Livingston. *The Oxford Dictionary of the Christian Church*. New York: Oxford Univ. Press, 1989. An invaluable companion for readers of Church history. It was referred to constantly in this study.

Currie, David B. *Born Fundamentalist, Born Again Catholic*. San Francisco: Ignatius Press, 1996. Dave Currie details his background as a Fundamentalist Protestant and the process of his conversion to the Catholic Church. He covers the issues of Scripture, the Eucharist, authority, Mary, salvation, moral concerns, and many others.

Eusebius. *The History of the Church from Christ to Constantine*. Trans. G.

A. Williamson. Harmondsworth, Middlesex, England: Penguin Books, 1965. Written in a.d. 325. Eusebius is the first Church historian, and he clearly records our Christian history—our Catholic history—from the time of the Jews before Christ to Emperor Constantine in 324. Eusebius utilizes sources available at his time and draws back the curtain so we can glimpse the personalities and workings of the primitive Church. I will always consider this one of the more important books I have read.

Graham, Henry. *Where We Got Our Bible, Our Debt to the Catholic Church.* Rockford, Ill.: Tan Books, 1911, in its seventeenth printing. This book gives a realistic view of the Church and the Bible through the centuries and dispels all the myths of the "Catholic Church keeping the Bible from the people." It discusses the sources of our canon, of both the Old and New Testaments, the copying and preservation of the Bible through the centuries, the Protestant versions of the story, and the high reverence the Catholic Church has always accorded the Scriptures.

Hardon, John A. *The Catholic Catechism.* New York: Doubleday, 1981. This is a very extensive, easily read, and well-organized compilation of Church teaching.

Howard, Thomas. *Evangelical Is Not Enough.* San Francisco: Ignatius Press, 1984. An Evangelical writes about his search for reality in worship and faith. Howard discusses the worship of God in liturgy and sacrament and contrasts it with Protestant forms of worship. He also explores many commonly held assumptions and exposes the flaws of the Protestant tradition. Also, read his more recent book, *Lead, Kindly Light.* Steubenville, Ohio: Franciscan Univ. Press, 1994, which gives a detailed account of his journey from Protestant Fundamentalism to Anglicanism and finally to the Catholic Church.

Jurgens, William A.. *The Faith of the Early Fathers.* 3 vols. Collegeville, Minn.: Liturgical Press, 1970. This is an indispensable set, a compilation of original source materials treating theological and historical passages from the Christian writers of the first eight centuries of the Church. It is easy to use, with detailed indexes, and puts volumes of information at your fingertips.

Keating, Karl. *Catholicism and Fundamentalism.* San Francisco: Ignatius

Press, 1988. This is an excellent book dealing with all the major differences between Catholics and Protestants. It is a very valuable resource for dispelling misconceptions and getting to the bottom of a lot of the doctrinal issues. Well indexed and easy to read.

Madrid, Patrick. *Surprised by Truth.* San Diego, Calif.: Basilica Press, 1994. Eleven converts give the biblical and historical reasons for their becoming Catholics.

Newman, John Henry Cardinal. *An Essay on the Development of Christian Doctrine.* New York: Doubleday, 1992. Newman was a convert to the Church and wrote this seminal work on the development of Catholic doctrine and the need for the living Magisterium in the Church. This is an essential book for those who want to understand Catholic doctrine and the underlying principles and development.

Ott, Ludwig. *Fundamentals of Catholic Dogma.* Rockford, Ill.: Tan Books, 1960. Ott presents and defends the teachings of the Catholic Church in a methodical and systematic way, drawing on the wealth of Catholic history. Good index and user friendly.

Quasten, Johannes. *Patrology.* 4 vols. Westminster, Md.: Christian Classics, 1992. Patrology means the "study of the Fathers".. This is another indispensable set. It is an easily approachable compendium of historical, theological, and biblical passages, along with biographies of the early Church Fathers and discussions of their particular writings. This collection provides basic information that should be familiar to anyone seriously interested in his Christian and Catholic heritage.

Roberts, Alexander, and James Donaldson, eds. *The Ante-Nicene Fathers.* 10 vols. Arr. A. Cleveland Coxe. Grand Rapids, Mich.: Eerdmans, 1985.

Rumble, Leslie, and Charles M. Carty. *Radio Replies.* 3 vols. Rockford, Ill.: Tan Books, 1979. Contained in this book is every conceivable question a Protestant could ask a Catholic, with very lucid and perceptive responses. Rumble and Carty gleaned these questions and answers from their radio program.

Schaff, Philip, ed. *The Nicene and Post-Nicene Fathers.* 1st and 2d series. 28 vols. Grand Rapids, Mich.: Eerdmans, 1983. These volumes and those edited by Alexander Roberts and James Donaldson are comprised of the writings of the early Church through the first five centuries, from the apostolic Fathers through St. Augustine. Invaluable resource, though it is edited and annotated with an anti-Catholic perspective.

Schreck, Alan. *Catholic and Christian*. Ann Arbor, Mich.: Servant Books, 1984. A very simple, easy-to-read, and gentle explanation of the commonly misunderstood Catholic beliefs. It is recommended for all who want a basic understanding of the Catholic Church and her teachings.

INDEX